Backpacking with the Saints

Backpacking with the Saints

Wilderness Hiking as Spiritual Practice

BELDEN C. LANE

OXFORD
UNIVERSITY PRESS

OXFORD
UNIVERSITY PRESS

Oxford University Press is a department of the University of Oxford.
It furthers the University's objective of excellence in research, scholarship,
and education by publishing worldwide.

Oxford   New York
Auckland   Cape Town   Dar es Salaam   Hong Kong   Karachi
Kuala Lumpur   Madrid   Melbourne   Mexico City   Nairobi
New Delhi   Shanghai   Taipei   Toronto

With offices in
Argentina   Austria   Brazil   Chile   Czech Republic   France   Greece
Guatemala   Hungary   Italy   Japan   Poland   Portugal   Singapore
South Korea   Switzerland   Thailand   Turkey   Ukraine   Vietnam

Oxford is a registered trade mark of Oxford University Press
in the UK and certain other countries.

Published in the United States of America by
Oxford University Press
198 Madison Avenue, New York, NY 10016

© Oxford University Press 2015

Cataloging-in-Publication data is on file at the Library of Congress

9780199927814

1   3   5   7   9   8   6   4   2

Printed in the United States of America on acid-free paper

For my Dad, William Belden Curnow
Presumed to be lost on wilderness paths,
but not for a lack of love.

A man is never lost, he has only been mislaid.
—*Terry Russell,* On the Loose[1]

Stand still. The forest knows
where you are. You must let it find you.
—*David Wagoner, "Lost"*[2]

Wilderness is not a luxury, but a necessity of the human spirit.
—Ed Abbey, *Desert Solitaire*

There are some who can live without wild things, and some who cannot.
—Aldo Leopold, *A Sand County Almanac*

Simplicity in all things is the secret of the wilderness and one of its most valuable lessons. It is what we leave behind that is important.
—Sigurd Olson, *The Singing Wilderness*

In the first place you can't see *anything* from a car; you've got to get out of the goddamned contraption and walk, better yet crawl, on hands and knees, over the sandstone and through the thornbush and cactus. When traces of blood begin to mark your trail you'll see something, maybe. Probably not.
—Ed Abbey, *Desert Solitaire*

I wasn't out here to keep myself from having to say I am not afraid. I'd come, I realized, to stare that fear down, to stare everything down, really—all that I'd done to myself and all that had been done to me. I couldn't do that while tagging along with someone else.
—Cheryl Strayed, *Wild: From Lost to Found on the Pacific Crest Trail*

All truly great thoughts are conceived by walking.
—Friedrich Nietzsche

Not being lost is not a matter of getting back to where you started from; it is a decision not to be lost wherever you happen to find yourself. It's simply saying, "I'm not lost, I'm right here."
—Laurence Gonzales, *Deep Survival*

Some people, in order to discover God, read books. But there is a great book: the very appearance of created things. Look above you! Look below you! Note it; read it. God, who you want to discover, never wrote that book with ink; instead He set before your eyes the things that He had made. Can you ask for a louder voice than that?
—Augustine, *The City of God*

I don't think it is enough appreciated how much an outdoor book the Bible is. It is a hypaethral book, such as Thoreau talked about—a book open to the sky. It is best read and understood outdoors, and the farther outdoors the better.

—Wendell Berry, *Christianity and the Survival of Creation*

Solvitur ambulando (It is solved by walking)

—Medieval saying, attributed to St. Jerome

Contents

Permissions

Prologue

An intellectual is all the time showing off.
Lovers dissolve and become bewildered.
Intellectuals try not to drown,
while the whole purpose of love is drowning.

JELALUDDIN RUMI[3]

I GO OVER the checklist of things I carry into wilderness, spread out on the basement floor. Simplicity is what counts here. None of this is high-end gear—more Army surplus and Campmor than REI. There's a Kelty pack with internal frame, a WhisperLite stove, my water filter and matching Nalgene bottle. Next to the old Peak mummy bag (good down to 15°F) are the Maglite, waterproof match case, and a first-aid kit from the Wilderness Medicine Institute. The usual stuff. This time I've added the Rhodes Mountain topog map for Wolf Hollow . . . and a dog-eared copy of Cassian's *Conferences* (from the "Classics of Western Spirituality" series). Deciding what to carry—and what to leave behind—is always the first step.

That's why I'm ambivalent about a book with a title like *Backpacking with the Saints*. You don't plunge into wilderness with a "how-to-do-it" book in tow. You can't squeeze spiritual insight into your sack along with a Swiss Army knife. The wilderness doesn't open itself to books. Nor do the "saints" offer easy answers. So I'm wary of hauling a library along on a backcountry trip—even one of the spiritual classics.

Will Rogers, the wry humorist from the Oklahoma hill country, had little confidence in the power of books to teach what the land usually teaches better. "There are three kinds of men," he remarked. "The one that learns by reading. The few who learn by observation. The rest of them have to pee on the electric fence for themselves."[4] Some of us, men and women alike, have to learn the hard way, even though we carry a book along with us out of habit.

Women who write of their experience in wilderness say the same thing. Cheryl Strayed, in her recent book, *Wild*, recounts the mistakes she made on a three-month trip, hiking the Pacific Crest Trail alone. Anne LaBastille, wildlife ecologist and author of the *Woodswoman* series, writes of lessons learned living for years in the Adirondack Mountains of upstate New York. Gretel Ehrlich, struck by lightning while hiking in a thunderstorm on her Wyoming ranch, found healing in trekking the Greenland ice cap. Among the risks that Roshi Joan Halifax has taken in her life is a circumambulation (*perikerama*) of Mt. Kailas in Tibet. There she reached the top of the Dolma Pass at 18,600 feet, leaving the ashes of Tenzing Norgay, the first person to climb Mt. Everest. In 1955, Emma Gatewood was the first woman to hike the 2,168-mile Appalachian Trail—solo, at the age of sixty-seven. Initially thinking the trip would be "a nice lark," she drolly replied, "It wasn't."[5]

Like many of these women, my chief reason for hiking is to "walk off" an inordinate attachment to words. I'm there to let the mind empty itself, usually after a long period of overuse. I follow my body instead, as it focuses on the demands of the trail. The last thing I want is a prepackaged interpretation of somebody else's experience.

Taking a saint along on the trail, therefore, isn't an intellectual exercise. It's more like hiking with a Zen master, having someone to slap me upside the head as may be required. The words of the saint aren't meant to absorb me in thoughtful insight. More often than not they stop thought altogether. "Pay attention to what's going on around (and within) you . . . right now!" That's what they invariably insist. So I seldom spend much time poring over a book in the wilderness. I *graze*, like bighorn sheep making their way over a rocky crag. I ponder lines I've underlined in a previous reading. I let the words sink in. Poetry is usually the best choice. A single saying of the Desert Fathers and Mothers can be more than enough.

Sometimes the experience of the trip may evoke an altogether different author from the one I've carried with me. Kicking myself for making a big mistake on the trail, I may have to go home to reread Luther on forgiveness. Witnessing an ecological disaster that cries out for justice, I return to dig out my worn-out copy of *The Essential Gandhi*. Saints have a way of coming to mind even when they haven't been bought along on the trail. The reality to which they point doesn't need a text to bring it to life.

What makes this practice all the more necessary is that I'm a recovering scholar, a university professor overly dependent upon words, working his program. For too long I've been addicted to footnotes, a compulsive attachment to critical analysis, an ugly habit of reading and writing to impress others.[6] I've been trying for years, as an academic in recovery, to lure myself out of the university and into wilderness. I've been asking how the history of spirituality and a study of place (especially wild places) illumine the spiritual life.

I long to hear the saints speak with a stark clarity, six miles in from the trailhead. Their task is to call me up short. They leave me speechless before a mystery that's beyond my understanding, but not beyond my love. "Become a lover," urged Hāfez, the fourteenth-century Sufi mystic. "As long as you see yourself as learned and intellectual, you'll lodge with the idiots; moreover, if you can stop seeing yourself at all, you will be free."[7]

Candor is essential here. After thirty years of modest experience, I'm still a novice with respect to the skills of backpacking and wilderness wandering. I stand in amazement at Robert Kull's fortitude in spending a year alone on a deserted island off the coast of Patagonia. I'm in awe of Doug Peacock's reckless forays into the grizzly country of northern Montana. I marvel at Craig Childs' rambling through the Utah desert for weeks at a time, disappearing from civilization as we know it. Compared to them, I'm just another Ed Abbey wannabe, like a lot of Western storytellers after a couple of beers in the local tavern.

All I know is that solo backpacking is a practice that feeds me, even in moderately tame wilderness terrain. I don't have to face down grizzly bears or survive flashfloods in desert slot canyons to feel fully alive in backcountry. Facing down myself is enough. Flashfloods of imagined dangers are as scary for me as real ones. The interior landscape is the most dangerous territory I'm likely to explore. Yet to get there I have to keep venturing "further up and further in," as Aslan urged at the end of the Narnia tales.[8] The spiritual life, in my experience, is a matter of moving ever deeper into backcountry, both literally and figuratively.

I'm fascinated by the discipline of body and mind that wilderness backpacking requires. Being pushed to your limits you discover things about yourself (and God) that you wouldn't find in the safety and comfort of home. I'm not talking about a high-endurance, thrill-seeking embrace of risk. It's not macho prowess that attracts me to backpacking. I'm drawn by its attention to details: packing light, "going without," being alone, leaving no trace. My backpacking practice has no similarity to the "extreme sports" obsession of NCSM hikers in the High Sierras. These "Nothing Can Stop Me" enthusiasts draw a straight line on a U.S. Geological Survey map and follow wherever it leads across miles of wild terrain—up rock faces, down talus slopes, across alpine lakes. I have no particular interest in extreme sports or extreme spirituality. I don't consider the pillar saints of fifth-century Syria to be a model of spiritual formation, for example, despite their physical heroics in wilderness survival. They lived for years in solitude on a tiny platform thirty feet off the ground.[9]

My idea of going into wilderness isn't pushing the envelope in search of esoteric mystical experience. I might wish for that (in my wildest dreams), but it never happens. Instead, I sit by an Ozark stream in the unpretentious company of sycamores and hawks. My body's relationship to the ordinary and earthbound is what I find most compelling. Like a lot of people, my experience of wilderness *and* spirituality is embarrassingly simple and unexceptional.

In giving shape to this book, I've divided it into two sections. Part I includes two introductory chapters that survey the overarching themes of the work—the appeal of wilderness in the spiritual life and the dynamics of reading as it changes in a wilderness setting. The chapters in the second part of the book share my experiences on particular backpacking trips into the Missouri Ozarks and the four-corners region of the American Southwest. They explore spiritual practices illuminated by the discipline of wilderness wandering.

The reader who is ready to plunge straightaway into backcountry experience without the baggage of analysis might skip the first part of the book, preferring to come back to it at the end. That's certainly the order in which it was lived, as well as the pattern of all meaningful encounters. On the other hand, the reader who is more curious about historical interpretations of wilderness and the saints' practice of outdoor reading can turn to an appendix at the end of the book. It deals with some of the residual concerns of a scholar. (Old habits are hard to break.) Nonetheless, it's important to clarify what I mean by "wilderness spirituality" and why I find it helpful to read the saints in a wilderness context.

The book draws on the insights of saints and mystics from various religious traditions. These include an early Celtic saint, five Catholics, four Protestants, a Buddhist, a Hindu, and a Sufi Muslim. In addition, references to the Desert Fathers and Mothers in early Christianity are woven throughout the narratives, offering a unifying thread. The challenges that emerge in backcountry hiking are curiously akin to the monastic practice of those "roughing it" in the Egyptian desert of the fourth and fifth centuries.

The Desert Christians were firmly committed to a practice of silence and simplicity, to a reckless compassion and a fierce indifference to unimportant things. What I'm calling the "wilderness spirituality" of these early desert adventurers involves the following convictions:

- There are no easy routes to self-realization; it begins, ironically, with self-abandonment.
- The spiritual life thrives on the margins of society, in a solitude framed by community.

- Desire and relinquishment are a recurring pattern in wilderness experience.
- Failure and making mistakes don't hinder spiritual growth; they occasion it.
- The body, when disciplined, becomes an important teacher of spiritual insight.
- Wilderness breeds a lifestyle of resistance, cultural critique, and cantankerous honesty.
- A wider community of exchange becomes more apparent out in the wilds.

For years I've been trying to live my way into the truth these men and women taught. The most effective way I've found of doing so has been to shoulder a pack, setting out with a spiritual guide who's been that way before, following a slim trail into wilderness.

Yet launching out into the boondocks isn't necessary for the practice of what I'm calling "wilderness spirituality." You don't have to hike into backcountry (or plunge into the desert) to embrace a life lived on the edge. It means confronting whatever "wilderness" you happen to be facing in your life right now, whatever growth is imperative but also threatening in your experience. Sitting in the waiting room of Radiation Oncology, attending Twelve-Step meetings, working the desk at a homeless shelter—all these force you into a wilder terrain than anything found at the end of a dirt road. They all involve risk . . . all require a discipline. Wilderness takes a different shape for everyone.

What proves especially instructive to me in backpacking as a spiritual practice is how it surfaces the interior baggage I bring along on the trail. Entering the disarming silence of wilderness, neglected things rise to consciousness. Backpacking has as much to do with what I carry inside as with what goes into the pack. It connects me with woundedness as well as with wonder.

Carl Jung says we repeat the significant traumas and ecstasies of our lives through dreams, rituals, and symbolic actions—continually renegotiating an interior landscape. Backpacking, in this sense, becomes a form of ritual activity, helping me explore unmapped trails of the psyche. Wilderness takes me back to the solace and threat I've found in other places in my life. The stars I recognize, the red sumac bringing the color of fire to autumn fields, the sound of falling water near a campsite—this is the same wilderness where trails quickly disappear, where lightning strikes closer to the tent than I'd like, where a copperhead lies coiled on the other side of the rock I've just climbed. It all leads to the deep mystery that I am healed, says Rilke, by the beauty that so coolly disdains to destroy me. The God I meet in wilderness is as fiercely loving as he or she is wild.

Those who have helped in the writing of this book include the participants in Men's Rites of Passage conducted through Richard Rohr's Center for Action and Contemplation in Albuquerque, New Mexico. These are men I've encountered in wilderness areas all over the world—in the Sonoran desert of Arizona, the Australian bush, the Wicklow Mountains of Ireland, and the Highlands of Scotland. In their honesty and courage, they've chosen to live what I've tried to write. I'm also indebted to wilderness hikers, poets, and activists (they are often the same) who have taught me by their example. These include Douglas Christie, Bill Plotkin, Joanna Macy, David Abram, Terry Minchow-Proffit, Eric Miller, Pat Coy, Mike Bennett, Adrian Scott, Patrick Landewe, and Dan Baer. Marcus Borg, God bless him, believed in the book before it was even started. What I owe to Cynthia Read, my editor at Oxford University Press, is beyond words. Richard Rohr, O.F.M., and Joan Delaplane, O.P., have been my desert teachers. Kyle Schenkewitz and Robert Munshaw helped with research.

I give thanks, at last, for my wife Patricia, who understands how my need for solitude and wilderness enhances my love for her . . . and for a dog named Desert, an old German shepherd who loved the trail as much as the one with whom she hiked.

Backpacking with the Saints

PART ONE

The Power of Wilderness and the Reading of Dangerous Texts

"We are animal in our blood and in our skin," says Jay Griffiths, exulting in the wilderness from which we've all come and to which our souls are still bent. "We were not born for pavements and escalators, but for thunder and mud."[1]

Out of the crucible of the desert wilderness in fourth-century Egypt a new form of spiritual life emerged among early Christian monks. Men and women tested by its wild terrain and welcomed by its beauty learned to read the mysteries of faith from its sandy pages. Others were attracted to these Desert Fathers and Mothers, hungry for the power and simplicity they found in their lives. Over the centuries a wide network of desert communities developed. Having fallen in love with a God of fierce compassion, these crusty desert dwellers shaped their lives after the pattern of the wild.

The desert communities had very few books, but the ones they had, including the land itself, were held in high regard. The monks learned to read their scant texts, not as *consumers* (extracting what is useful, informative, or entertaining), but as *lovers* (wanting to lick, smell, and savor the words on the page, lingering over it). They read the book in the way you might study a fascinating and dangerous landscape, as if it were writing itself into your psyche.

I

The Allure of the Wild: Backpacking as Spiritual Practice

I only went out for a walk and finally concluded to stay out
till sundown, for going out, I found, was really going in.

JOHN MUIR[2]

The human body is not a closed or static object, but an
open, unfinished entity utterly entwined with the soils,
waters, and winds that move through it.

DAVID ABRAM[3]

FOR YEARS I'VE been making solo backpacking trips into the wilderness of the Missouri Ozarks. Leaving on a Friday afternoon, I'll invariably stuff a copy of one of the spiritual classics into my well-worn Kelty pack. I hike at times with John Ruysbroeck or Hildegard of Bingen, now and then with Rumi or Lao-tzu. Old mountains seem to invite the company of old teachers. Some of the oldest rock on the continent lies in the St. Francois Mountains of southeast Missouri. The creek beds are lined with Precambrian granite and pink rhyolite, rocks over a billion and a half years old. In terrain like this, the earth itself is an ancient teacher, illuminating in unexpected ways the text I bring with me.

These trips into backcountry are my way of occasionally retreating like a hermit into an isolated place, receiving spiritual direction from an old master. Without this regular discipline every few months, my life would move off center. Experience in backcountry feeds me like nothing else in my life. I'm fascinated by how the chosen site, the embrace of solitude, and the spiritual guide I happen to take along often have a way of coming together for me. I discover the holy in the smell of pine needles, the dread of gathering storm clouds, and the ache of shoulder muscles at the end of the day.

The purpose of this book is to show how wilderness backpacking can be a form of spiritual practice, what Bill Plotkin calls a "soulcraft" exercise.[4] Exposure to the harsh realities and fierce beauties of a world not aimed at my comfort has a way of cutting through the self-absorption of my life. The uncontrolled mystery of nature puts the ego in check and invites the soul back (in more than one way) to the ground of its being. It elicits the soul's deepest desire, enforces a rigorous discipline, and demands a life marked by activism and resistance. It reminds me, in short, that spiritual practice—far from being anything ethereal—is a highly tactile, embodied, and visceral affair.

Aravaipa Canyon: Entering the Body of Wilderness

Take Aravaipa Canyon, a stunning stretch of wilderness in southeastern Arizona—a place I've come to love. This is a remote land of red-rock side canyons, white-haired cholla cactus, and paloverde trees that can't get enough of the color green. Studded with prickly pear and mesquite brush, the twelve-mile-long canyon has been sacred to the Western Apache for centuries. It is a dazzling but wounded body of a place. Its deep ravines and tall saguaro cactuses possess a haunting beauty. This is a "land that stalks people," the old teachers say.[5] Its mystery is everywhere.

Yet its vulnerability is apparent, too. On the way to the canyon, you pass miles and miles of mine tailings along the San Carlos Mineral Strip. Years of lead, zinc, and copper mining have left the land naked and wounded. A site traditionally known as Big Sycamore Stands Alone, near the canyon's entrance, holds a still more painful memory: The Camp Grant Massacre of 1871 occurred here, leaving 125 Apache women, children, and elders slaughtered by local ranchers and vigilantes. Scars of hatred and misuse linger in the soil, despite the ravishing beauty of the place. It resonates with the loss of many things.[6]

Places like this are able to make momentary mystics of almost anyone. They evoke a powerful sense of presence, offering a point of entry into the deep interiority of things. G. K. Chesterton once observed that there are places that "seem to *happen* and not merely to exist."[7] Aravaipa Canyon is such a place. It doesn't stay fixed on any of the maps you draw. Going there is like walking into a dream you're just beginning to remember.

A few years ago, at a turning point in my life, I spent a day and night alone in the desert above Brandenburg Wash near Aravaipa Canyon Ranch. I was transitioning toward retirement at the time, moving away from my role as a scholar, loosening myself from the bookish and theological world of the academy. I was being introduced to my *body* as a teacher instead.

Walking alone into the desert that morning, carrying a gallon of water and a tarp, I hiked down a dry arroyo under the shadow of Flat Top Mountain near the canyon's western end. The colors and textures of rock were radiant in the morning sun. Suddenly the arroyo I was following made a sharp turn and the floor in front of me fell away, dropping a hundred feet straight down. If I hadn't caught myself I'd have walked right over the edge.

I sat down by the rim to catch my breath, imagining flash floods in the past having rushed through this ravine, careening over the edge. My body began to enter the place in a way my mind hadn't yet been able to do. I sensed that I had been hiking all morning *across* the surface of the desert's body and had now been abruptly plunged *inside* it, seeing it from within. I'd been winding through swirling corridors of living rock (in multiple shades of mauve, red, and pink), descending into the earth's breathing body. The memory of water, gouged into stone, was apparent everywhere. In purple-veined boulders I imagined the internal organs of a great sleeping beast. Rocks eroding in convoluted folds looked like the gray matter of a living brain, neural pathways racing under the surface. Sitting by the drop-off, I felt as if I'd walked into the belly of a stunningly beautiful creature, hardly moving but very much alive.

It was a fleeting experience of what Buddhists call non-separation, seeing everything with a sudden familiarity and intimacy—from the *inside*. I'd stumbled onto an exterior landscape that echoed my interior being. The painted rocks in the dry creek bed were the colors of *my* internal organs—heart, kidneys, lungs, torn ligaments, enlarged prostate. Pulsing red, dark blue, shining purple, vibrating with life—like an aching in the loins. The blowing wind was the susurrating sound of blood flowing. The side canyons were cavities within the earth's vital tissue, the innermost body of the Sonoran Desert. But I knew it also as *my* body.

Hildegard of Bingen might have said that I'd touched the body of God as well, running my hand across a startling vulnerability. Blood-stained rocks and strip-mining scars lingered in its flesh, but the vibrating life was unmistakable. Here was a God known in the sinew and flesh of bedrock and cactus, smitten by longing—a great desert cat prowling the edges of abandonment, lurking unseen in the shadows, hungry for love.

What made the experience even more vivid was the fact that a few weeks earlier I'd been at the Whitney Western Art Museum in Cody, Wyoming. There I had stood in amazement in front of Thomas Moran's huge painting of the "Grand Canyon of the Yellowstone." At the time I hadn't known why the lower, right-hand corner of the scene affected me so much, but I would recognize it later at Aravaipa Canyon. In the right foreground of Moran's painting the artist moves beyond the signature grandeur of Western rimrock and waterfalls to reveal a mass of exposed red rock. He lays open the earth's living body, allowing the viewer's intrusive eyes to gaze on its pulsing fragility. I stood there, staring at the bleeding form of a wounded animal, as if watching raw meat hanging in a butcher shop. I felt embarrassment at an intimacy violated, glimpsing something too personal to observe in another, as if I were gaping at a naked, strip-mined mountain in a desolate West Virginia landscape. I imagined the artist shouting through his work, "Look *deeper* than the frickin' scenery. All this is *alive!*"

At the edge of the cliff at Aravaipa I found myself *inside* Moran's painting, recognizing the earth's throbbing aliveness as deeply familiar. It was my body, too. Yet nothing in my culture or religious upbringing had prepared me for such an experience. I'd grown up accepting as perfectly normal the "intellectual apartheid" practiced by human beings in treating other forms of life as mere objects to be used. I hadn't read Jay Griffiths' beautifully outrageous book, *Wild*, with her reprimand of Descartes' arrogance, proclaiming humans the "masters and possessors of nature."[8] What we've gained in mastery, we've certainly lost in magic.

John Burroughs, by contrast, took an exquisite joy in the Catskill Mountains as "a sort of outlying part of himself." John Muir regarded the boulders of Yosemite in the same familiar way. He noticed on one of his forays into the wild that they "seemed talkative, and more lovable than ever. They are dear friends, and have warm blood gushing through their granite flesh; and I love them with a love intensified by long and close companionship."[9] This is the *body's* rich and feral knowing of the land. I experience it myself in those rare moments on the trail when I know that I *belong*, that the others there have been expecting me. I've come home in a deeply visceral way. I'm reminded again that loving is the truest way of "knowing" anything.

A Wilderness Way of Knowing: Thinking with the Body

One's body is the supreme teacher in backcountry hiking. Plodding an uphill trail, mile after mile, it's the body that leads, not the mind. When I yield to its prompting, it carries me into a slow, steady pace I can maintain for hours. It releases endorphins producing a profound sense of well-being, as well as increased levels of serotonin, a neurotransmitter that reduces stress.

I bring along the 100-million-year history of my reptilian brain, moving like the highly refined animal that evolution has produced. I read the landscape with the distant memory of the African savannas. The oldest part of my brain is ready for "fight or flight," pumping adrenaline into the bloodstream to protect me from saber-tooth tigers as may be necessary. The frontal lobes help me anticipate the consequences of choices I make along the trail. The physical movement of walking activates the subcortical region of the brain, including the limbic system with its sensitivity to emotional states. Clearly, something far deeper and older than culture goes with me into wilderness.

The body is an extremely reliable guide. It knows instinctively how to move over difficult terrain, when to stop for rest, how to breathe deeply and relax in crisis situations. Panic, by contrast, has its source in the mind (in the amygdala, to be precise). It forces me into action after I've failed to listen to the body's cues, its early warning system. The body is more naturally at home in wilderness, able to practice there the alive and alert presence in which it delights. Gary Snyder says wild terrain fosters a "state of complete awareness . . . That's why we need it."[10] It evokes an intuitive way of knowing—the way a newborn baby knows its mother's breast, the way a dancer anticipates her partner's practiced turn, the way a climber and the cliff he ascends share a reciprocity of touch. It is our most basic, animal-like, and impassioned way of knowing anything. What the mind hardly fathoms, the body already knows.

Sometimes the body slides so completely into the rhythm of the trail that the mind follows its lead, relaxing comfortably into an effortless pattern of "flow." Psychologists speak of this as a wondrous state of unforced, complete absorption in the activity at hand. It is what athletes speak of as being "in the zone," acting on instinct and training without having to exercise deliberate thought. In a moment of flow, the ego falls away. Time flies. The body's fatigue is experienced as a "high," opening the soul to an unexpected fluidity and immediacy of presence.[11]

This is something the mind can appreciate, but only the body knows. In wilderness hiking, one's body is the distinctive vehicle for experiencing mystery. It responds with inexplicable fear or delight to what the mind hardly recognizes. The power of shamanism in indigenous cultures around the world is rooted in this deep attunement of the body to the natural world. The shaman's gift doesn't depend on physical strength or prowess. She may even possess what others consider a physical "disability," a unique sensitivity making access to the spirit world easier. The body is her fundamental connection to a deeper knowledge.

The long-distance runners of the Tarahumara in Mexico, like the bushmen of the Kalahari in Botswana, have trained their bodies so well that they're able (over a period of days) to run down an antelope until it dies of exhaustion. Theirs is an intensely spiritual form of hunting that probes the depths of endurance for hunter and hunted alike. Religious experience not infrequently involves the body's being taken to its limits.[12] In many folk traditions, yielding to "bewilderment"—the submission of body and mind to the ultimate challenges of wilderness—is a cultivated spiritual condition.

The body, therefore, plays a major role in authentic soul work. Any radical separation of body and soul makes the spiritual life impossible, in fact. The Bible itself asserts the indissoluble relationship between the *adam* (the human) and the *adamah* (the grounded earth). In the Jewish Scriptures, the deepest realities of existence are always concrete, earth-related, and wild. One might best think of the soul, then, as the place where the body and the rest of the vibrant world converge. The German Romantic poet Novalis argued that the human soul isn't *inside* the body, hidden and encased, like a "seed." Rather, he said, "The seat of the soul is where the inner world and the outer world meet."[13] Soulfulness is our ability to discover a vital connection with the ordinary details of everyday experience—what we share along our outermost edges with others.

We are like trees, growing (and touching) at our periphery. The living core of a tree lies within an inch or so of its outer bark, where phloem and xylem tubes carry its life-blood up and down the trunk. The rest of the interior is deadwood, a ringed history of growth and struggle. We, too, most readily encounter the "other" at our physical extremities. Like trees, our perimeters are where body and soul become most vulnerable . . . and most connected to the rest of the world.

Whenever I plunge into wilderness, my body and the environment move in and out of each other in an intimate pattern of exchange. I wade through water and inhale air filled with the scent of honeysuckle. I'm wrapped in cobwebs and pierced by briars. I swallow gnats drawn to the sweat on my body and feel the rocks on the trail through my boots. Where I "end" and everything else "begins" isn't always clear. What seems to be "me" doesn't stop at the fixed boundary of my skin. I come back with the sun having deeply penetrated this presumably impassible barrier. Rain and cold, not to mention poison ivy, chiggers, and ticks, move across this "thin boundary of *me*" with complete abandon. My skin isn't a rigid line of demarcation, but a permeable membrane that opens me to continual interchange with others. My "personal identity" is stretched to include the aching beauty of an alpine meadow or the raucous cry of loons on the other end of the lake.

The addition of a saint seems to extend this encounter still further. The book of a wisdom elder becomes for me a silent yet tangible companion, assuming its own perilous adventure into wilderness. It moves, like me, into liminal space—risking rain and dirt, torn pages and loss. Reading in the wilds is a hazardous experience of reading *with* everything that is there. Far from being wholly cerebral, it connects my experience of the saint to the physical vulnerability of the text, the palpable reality of the surrounding terrain, and my own heightened sense of wilderness awareness . . . all of it riven with tactility and risk.

Ecologist and poet David Abram speaks of an "improvised duet" that goes on between one's body and "the fluid, breathing landscape it inhabits," molding one's experience of the text. The sounds of buzzing insects, the movement of squirrels and tree frogs, the breeze sweeping through the trees all suggest the origins of language. Human speech initially arose out of our mimicry of nature.[14] Thought patterns were influenced by our physical interaction with the terrain. Reading, therefore, especially in a wilderness setting, becomes a magical participation in the sounds and gestures of the natural world. It moves with the larger flow of an encircling landscape. The body is as important as the brain in this highly participatory process. That's why we need to think of the body in more fluid and communicative ways.

"For some people," says Barry Lopez, "what they are is not finished at the skin, but continues with the reach of the senses out into the land."[15] They find it difficult to maintain the illusion of the unmistakable difference between themselves and everything else. I remember reading Wendell Berry's poetry one summer morning, sitting at Togwotee Pass overlooking the expanse of the Grand Tetons to the west. The distinction between myself, the green paperback edition of his *Collected Poems*, and the adjacent Wyoming meadow filled with fireweed began to blur. In a singular moment of meeting, what I'd previously considered to be "me" had to be radically rethought.

When Martin Buber observed that "all real living is meeting," he was speaking a biological as well as spiritual truth. When John Muir spoke of "going out" as a way of "going in," he knew that his deepest entry into himself (and God) came through the sensory immediacy of the High Sierras. He *loved* the mountains. He experienced them as an extension of his own body, an extension of God's exuberant grace. When he climbed Cathedral Peak in the summer of 1869, he realized how closely bound he was to everything there. He became a wonder to himself, a window onto the universe, a wilderness in his own right, pointing to mystery.

Connecting with God in Wilderness

What I seek most in going into wilderness is not exercise or escape, but a physical and spiritual depth of intimacy. I'm moved by nature's power and beauty, but what sets me afire is the *longing* I sense there of everything else wanting to connect, the desire for an intimacy that is as alluring as it is frightening. I go to spend time alone with God . . . in a robust and full-bodied way. The two of us marvel at fresh deer tracks in the mud and black clouds looming over the ridge. We revel in the wildness and grieve over what isn't wild enough. We argue over the bloody business of insects devouring each other. We fall in love all over again. We connect.

Abraham Heschel said we usually fail to understand the divine, "not because we aren't able to extend our concepts far enough, but because we don't know how to begin close enough."[16] We think of the holy as "up" or "out" there, beyond the realm of campsites and chigger bites. Yet God is an intimate reality found at the very heart of the universe (and of ourselves). *This*, says Teilhard de Chardin, is the divine milieu. The highly sensory way of "knowing" that wilderness requires is the most natural and meaningful way I have of experiencing anything holy.

My own earliest experiences of God go back to the lakes and swamps I haunted as a kid growing up in central Florida. With other ten- to twelve-year-olds, I made bamboo rafts, built huts of palmetto fronds, and caught crayfish and water snakes in makeshift nets. We were fascinated by the dark and overgrown places that other people avoided. Cypress swamps filled us with the wonder and terror of huge herons suddenly taking to flight, rotting things lying under shallow water, dragonflies descended from a prehistoric world of dinosaurs. We came home scratched and muddy, smelling something awful, but we loved it . . . because of its edginess, its bizarre beauty, its welcoming of things that didn't fit anywhere else.

My awakening sense of mystery was heightened still further by the stories of Jesus I heard in the furnace room where the boy's Sunday School class met each week. It was the only space available to us, but it was perfect—hidden away, worldly and masculine, the one place in the church without any trappings of religion. We came to associate Jesus with wrenches on the workbench nearby, with the smell of fuel oil and a pilot light waiting to blow. I knew him to have Spanish moss in his hair and swamp muck between his toes. He was wild, he saw splendor in what others thought repulsive, and he loved (I was told) even me. These earthy images constitute my first experience of God. They fed a longing for what I couldn't put into words, but would always rediscover in wilderness places and hardware stores.

Intimacy with God is an astonishing experience of distance traversed. As in the beginning of any relationship, the space between you and the "other" seems insuperable. You can't imagine yourself having the nerve to talk to a girl that fascinating or a guy that full of life. You can't conceive of a forest that dark and threatening becoming a place by which you are loved. Yet it happens. What initially had put you off, because of admiration or fear, is overcome. You manage to arrange that first date and it's amazing. You keep wandering into the forest and you find it strangely healing. The greater the distance bridged, the greater your astonishment at the intimacy that results.

What bothered me about church, however, was its notion of a distant, angry, masculine God who could only be approached through a gentle, meek, effeminate Jesus. This didn't match what I'd experienced in the boys' class in the furnace room. I couldn't imagine loving or being loved by a God like that. Florida swampland, on the other hand, suggested images of a wild joy and welcoming presence that was comfortable with everything *outside* of the church. It fed a hunger in me for wholeness, for a love without bounds. I knew I was outgrowing my early church experience of God, even as I continued to memorize Bible verses and sit through Revival meetings. My God was too big to be confined—too ravishing, too rough-edged, too passionate in seeking relationship.

Only later would I learn—from the Christian mystics—that a love for God and for wilderness experience weren't incompatible at all. John of the Cross referred to God as "a remarkably deep and vast wilderness . . . an immense, unbounded desert, the more delightful, savorous, and loving, the deeper, vaster, and more solitary it is." Meister Eckhart spoke of the soul being thrown into the "boundless hinterland" of the divine, losing its identity there, yet discovering an utterly new life. For these mystics, being unhinged by the wild expanse of the Sierra Morena range in Spain or the towering furs of a Thuringian forest in Germany was an apt description of meeting the divine. "All wildness is finer than tameness," John Muir proclaimed. "In God's wildness lies the hope of the world."[17]

I found what I'd sought in Hildegard of Bingen's experience of the holy, as earthy as it was sublime. This twelfth-century German Benedictine received a vision of the universe as God's body. "I flame above the beauty of the fields," she heard God declare, "I shine in the waters; in the sun, the moon and the stars, I burn." She felt the "airy wind" thriving in all "its green power and its blossoming," mountain waters flowing "as if they were alive." She heard God thundering in it all: "I, the fiery power, lie hidden in these things and they blaze from me."[18] Hers was a God stretching a vast web of relationship, binding all things together as one. The greening power of the Spirit filled her with an exuberance that was contagious.

Still another medieval mystic, Mechthild of Magdeburg, pictured this God of majesty (her "true wilderness") as utterly smitten by love for souls like herself. Her God was undone in his aching desire to be reunited with everyone and everything from which he had been estranged. One night she imagined God saying to her, "Woman, I confess that I'm lovesick in my longing for you. I don't know if I can handle being God without you. I'm eternally wounded because of my love for your soul."

Besotted by this wondrous confession, Mechthild responds to God in turn, "Let me find the salve that will heal your wound, dear Love. I'll cut my heart in half and place you between the two pieces. I'll be your physician for all eternity."[19] In her vision, God consents to her being the healer of his injured heart, longing to multiply their personal exchange in God's relationship with every other creature as well. Mechthild knew that the love wounds of the divine, scored in the earth itself, remain unhealed until the universe is knit together in love. In this medieval saint, I discovered the earthy, sensuous, and intensely personal relationship with God that I had longed for as a child.

These mystics all insisted that knowing God is a matter of "tasting," "savoring," and "relishing." It isn't an intellectual apprehension of something *outside* their experience, but a full-bodied encounter—evoking images of desire, sensual delight, even sexual intimacy. God, in fact, is what gives vitality and meaning to the very notion of sensuality itself. Jonathan Edwards suggested that God is far more "sensuous"—more full of infinite delights, more prone to the endless expansion of relationships, more astonishingly *beautiful*—than anything we can imagine in the stunningly sensuous world around us. In effect, he said, if you think *this* world is sensual and beautiful, you haven't seen anything yet![20]

I finally came to recognize a love for wilderness and a longing for God as a perfectly natural combination. *Everything* in creation is hungry for relationship. All bodies yearn for connectedness with each other and with the Source of their energy and life. Indeed, one of the vital insights of the mystics (and of the new cosmology) is that everything is *already* linked by an underlying bond. Their prior connection is a "given" in the life of the universe. Ultimately, nothing is separate from anything else. The Hasidic master Yehudah Aryeh Leib argued that if there is no other god than the one true God, then all things *must* be joined in this one reality. We need to confess, then, that:

there is no being *other* than God. This is true even though it seems otherwise to most people. . . . *Everything that exists in the world, physical and spiritual, is God Himself.* . . . Because of this, every person can become attached to God wherever he is, through the holiness that exists in every single thing, even corporeal things. . . . This is the foundation of all the mystical formulations in the world.[21]

This bold and adventurous language—bordering on pantheism—echoes a theme that stretches throughout the history of Jewish, Christian, and Muslim mysticisms.[22] Nothing has "being" apart from its existence in God. The very "foundations of the deep" are grounded in Yahweh. God is that mystery in which we "live and move and have our being." Allah, the Merciful and Compassionate, is closer to us than our jugular vein.

What intrigues me in all of this is the crucial role the body plays in bridging the distance between ourselves and everything else. The body—this dazzling flesh we inhabit—is the necessary vehicle by which everything in creation connects. Our deepest spiritual relationships are inescapably material, substantial, and ecologically linked. The training of the body and the deepening of the soul are not, ultimately, separate realities. The monastic traditions have been reminding us of this for centuries.

The Desert Fathers exulted in the physically demanding wilderness beyond the Nile. They saw it as an ideal locale for practicing the discipline of the body they considered essential to the spiritual life. For them, the body was a "mentor of the soul." The physical challenges and harsh beauty of a desert landscape stripped them of nonessentials, drew them into silence, and assured them that they could be loved in the most uncaring of places. The *body* taught them this as it took them to the edge . . . the edge of themselves, the desert, and God.

John Climacus at Mt. Sinai found it astonishing that "the spiritual can be purified and refined by clay." "What is this mystery in me?" he asked, marveling at his body's ability to touch the heights as well as the depths of human experience.[23] When the body is brought under discipline, it becomes a grand teacher—in its sensitivities and in its frailties. Nowhere do we discover this better than in the wild places where our limits become most apparent.

I want to end this chapter by juxtaposing two parallel experiences of the wild. One is deeply religious and mystical, the other much more earthy and prophetic. Yet both are profoundly sensuous in the way they savor a uniquely transformative experience. The first is from William of St-Thierry, a twelfth-century French monk writing from his abbey in the heavily forested, vine-growing region of Champagne. The other is from Chellis Glendinning, a twentieth-century ecopsychologist living in the high desert country of northern New Mexico. They each struggle to convey an experience for which they lack adequate language.

William of St-Thierry sits in prayer, gazing out the cloister window onto the vineyards growing in the shadow of the Ardennes. I imagine a glass of wine on the table nearby, as he muses:

> Sometimes, Lord, while I am gaping toward you, eyes closed, you place something in me, in the mouth of the heart. . . . I certainly sense a flavor, so soft, so sweet, so comforting, that if it were left perfect in me, I would no longer go searching for anything else. But when I receive it, you do not let me figure out what it is. . . . Yet I hope to transfuse it through all the veins and marrow of my soul like some life-giving sap, so as to lose the flavor of all other affections, and no longer savor anything except it alone [*you* alone].[24]

Chellis Glendinning speaks, in turn, of the astonishment she encounters on a magical New Mexican evening:

> I had been eating a simple dinner of brown rice and greens on the roof when I felt something occur in my body, something like a door swinging open. Wide open. A golden sun was just setting behind the Jemez Mountains: bursts of orange and pink were shooting like streamers through the fading sky. To my surprise, I was sensing the full-bodied aliveness of every juniper and rock and hawk on the Earth. By the front door to my house I saw, really *saw*, the tall piñon that I ordinarily brushed by; its needles and cones were bursting with presence, its branches and trunk with consciousness. I had never before communicated directly with it, nor with any other wild being. I saw how foolish I had been. My recovery from western civilization was under way.[25]

Both of these experiences involve a deep sense of immediacy, an avid yearning for relationship, a quality of presence far more than the mind can grasp. Though written in very different idioms, they speak of analogous things. My goal in this book is to foster a conversation between those (like William) who hunger for a sensuous spirituality and those (like Chellis) who are fed by an earthy experience of the natural world. Hopefully, readers who can identify with only one of the two, finding the other suspicious, might begin to discern new ways of naming what they've already experienced.

But we need Beginner's Mind in doing this—a widening of our previous grasp of what *is*, a reorientation of language. "When we are stunned to the place beyond words, we're finally starting to get somewhere," says Anne Lamott.[26] I marvel at how wilderness cuts through my tired interpretations of reality, my expectations of what the universe ought to be like. In its hush of all that stirs within me, I discover new ways of articulating the world. I learn, with Jack Kerouac, that "Silence itself is the sound of diamonds [cutting] through anything."[27] He wrote this in 1956, during his sixty-three days as a fire lookout on Desolation Peak in the North Cascades. There his soul reveled in what his body needed most—the stillness and stark simplicity of wilderness. Getting to where we need to go often means finding a new language for where we've already been.

2

The Risk-Taking Character of Wilderness Reading

Books, not [the ones] which afford us a cowering enjoyment, but in which each thought is of unusual daring; such as an idle man cannot read, and a timid one would not be entertained by, which even make us dangerous to existing institutions—such call I good books.

HENRY DAVID THOREAU[1]

Books are made with razor-sharp paper that can easily cut you.

Dangers of Reading Books, Yourguidetolive.com, the Internet

SPIRITUAL READING CAN be dangerous. I'm not talking about the devotional pabulum you find in most religious bookstores, but the truly risky stuff—from Hāfez and Eckhart to Toni Morrison and Oscar Romero. This is especially true of the spiritual "classics," says theologian David Tracy. They confront us with the disturbing notion that "something else might be the case."[2] They haunt us with fundamental questions, overthrowing our previous ways of viewing the world.

Reading a potentially dangerous book in a landscape perceived to be dangerous can be doubly hazardous. The place heightens the vulnerability occasioned by the text. Challenging books lose their bite when they're read comfortably at home in a favorite armchair. Their riskiness increases, however, when read by firelight in a forest glade, ten miles from the nearest road.

The place where you encounter a book indelibly affects the way you receive it. Claus Westermann read the Psalms in a Russian prison camp, discovering patterns that changed his life as well as his approach to biblical scholarship. Eldridge Cleaver read Thomas Merton in Folsom Prison. Aleksandr

Solzhenitsyn read Dostoyevsky in a Soviet cancer ward. Karl Marx read the history of capitalism in the elegance of the British Museum. Potentially revolutionary changes occur when people read explosive texts in unsettling places.

The stories of the saints are filled with instances of this. Isaac of Nineveh's world was turned upside down as he read the Scriptures in the desert solitude of the Zagros Mountains in sixth-century Persia. He allegedly made himself blind through his constant pondering of the tear-stained pages. Near the end of his life, Francis of Assisi read the story of Christ's passion not simply from the pages of the Gospels, but from the huge, split rocks atop Mt. La Verna. He said these cracks had appeared on Good Friday when the stones on Calvary were also rent. He experienced their truth in the opening of wounds in his body through the gift of the stigmata. The mountainous terrain and his body's interaction with it became active participants in his reading of the text.[3]

The saints often gave themselves to outdoor (especially wilderness) reading at periods of transition in their lives. St. Jerome read his Greek New Testament outside a cave in the Syrian desert before beginning his work on the Vulgate. Prior to being made Bishop of Lindisfarne, St. Cuthbert read the Psalms each morning standing waist deep in the surf on Northumberland's rocky coast. Hildegard of Bingen started recording her visions at the age of forty-two, as she and her sisters—fresh from their work in the vineyards— read the Holy Office with dirt under their fingernails. St. Bernard delighted in the valley of the Aube outside his monastery at Clairvaux as he began preaching his eighty-six sermons on the Song of Songs. St. Seraphim studied the *Philokalia* each day in the dense forest of nineteenth-century Russia before undertaking his midlife ministry to pilgrims.

Encountering texts—even familiar ones—in out-of-the-way places at moments of significant change has an unnerving way of prompting new insight. The book assumes a fresh life in the offbeat, unpredictable place.

When I ponder the writings of a given saint in a wilderness setting, multiple things are going on at the same time. (1) There's the reading of the surrounding landscape, demanding my careful attention in hiking it alone. (2) There's the reading of the unexplored *interior* wilderness that I bring along with me, mirrored by all that is wild beyond the trail. (3) There's the life and thought of the saint I carry, formed out of the *ascesis* (or spiritual discipline) of his own venture into wilderness. (4) There's the book itself that I've sealed in a Ziploc bag, carrying a stubborn life of its own. (5) And finally, there's the reading of God's wild splendor in between the lines of all these other "texts." What is born in these sundry readings is a deeper apprehension of the truth I encounter. My sense of vulnerability and compassion are expanded as I share in a wider community of receptiveness.

The best way I can exemplify the process is to provide several examples of my own wilderness encounters with particular texts. I've included three vignettes in this chapter, offering a taste of how backpacking serves as a spiritual practice. They draw on the pattern of wilderness spirituality seen in the Desert Fathers and Mothers. The narratives are all taken from a single year of Ozark hiking, in places along the eastern edge of the Missouri Ozark bioregion. This is a rugged and beautiful landscape known for its spring-fed streams and karst geology—a text never exhausted by a single reading.

Vignette 1. Bell Mountain: John Bunyan on Simplicity

It is late October and I'm bushwhacking my way down a ridge in the Bell Mountain Wilderness Area toward a ribbon of water sheltered by yellow and orange maple trees in the hollow below. I'll camp there beside Shut-in Creek tonight, falling asleep to the sound of running water. I may wake to the cries of coyotes in the night. But I'll recognize familiar stars and go back to sleep with the contentment that only wilderness affords.

Half of the beauty in coming here is the simplicity it demands. Backpacking reminds me of how little I require to be happy, how light I can travel, how many of the resources I imagine I need are superfluous out in the wild. "We need great vigilance in all things," says John Climacus, the sixth-century abbot of Saint Catherine's monastery at Mt. Sinai, "but especially in regard to what we have left behind." He spoke of *haplotes*, the deliberate abandonment of unimportant things, as a spiritual practice that wilderness teaches supremely well. I'll eat simply tonight—bread-on-a-stick baked over an open fire, washed down with creek water and the guilty pleasure of a little Jameson's Irish Whisky. I'm reduced here to a life that John Climacus described as "simple and uncompounded."[4]

I've brought along on the trip a copy of John Bunyan's *Pilgrim's Progress*, an apt choice for reflecting on simplicity and non-attachment. In Bunyan's allegory of the Christian life, his pilgrim undertakes a long trek through the wilderness of this world to the Celestial City. He passes through the Slough of Despond, where he nearly drowns. He loses the trail in opting for an easier way through By-pass Meadow. He trudges up the Hill of Difficulty and through the Valley of Humiliation. Disoriented again and again, he rediscovers the path in sighting the distant wooded slopes of the Delectable Mountains.

I think of his difficulties as I remember how many times I myself have been tricked in hiking through this winding hollow at the foot of Bell Mountain. The similar-looking ravines leading into it twist in different directions. I've often been convinced I was on the right one, only to find myself an hour later several miles from where I'd expected to be. You have to trust the compass in hiking such terrain. The most obvious path is often the wrong one.

Hiking the Ozark wilderness is never quite what one expects. It requires your leaving behind all your preconceptions, the baggage that keeps you from being fully present. Bunyan speaks of Christian starting his journey with a heavy burden. This isn't a backpack with the basics needed to sustain him on the trail; it's a heavier, inner burden that falls from his shoulders only as he passes overhanging cliffs, ascending a hill to the place of the cross.[5]

Hikers invariably carry two packs on traveling into wilderness. I can adjust the straps of the one easily enough, but releasing the other is beyond my skill. It holds the things I've come to relinquish—my stubborn insistence on going the wrong way, the fragile reputation I try to nourish back home, a failure to hold myself accountable as husband, father, and friend. The work of the trail loosens my grip on this inner load, reminding me how little control I have of anything out in the wilderness. "A snake can shed its old skin only if it crawls into a tight hole," John Climacus wisely observed.[6]

Bunyan penned his classic tale from a tight place of his own, having spent twelve and a half years in a Bedfordshire prison between 1660 and 1672. He had been convicted of preaching without a license as a nonconformist Protestant in Restoration England. His jail cell was located on a bridge overlooking the River Ouse. Deprived of everything but a Bible, the sound of flowing water, and his own dreams, he wrote from a place of forced simplicity. He gradually learned what this Ozark hollow tries to teach me as I work my way over moss-covered rocks toward the creek below. The path toward wholeness demands a stark simplicity, a letting go of things I once thought important. Book and landscape alike are co-conspirators in teaching an unsettling backcountry truth. They both ask how much I can leave behind.

John Climacus and a Desert Reading of the Spiritual Life

The desert saint I've found most helpful in relating the power of the text to the place of its reading is John Climacus, one of the later Desert Fathers. Years ago I spent a week with his *Ladder of Divine Ascent*, trekking through the desert toward his monastery at the foot of Jebel Mussa, the "Moses Mountain." The words of the book echoed in my dreams every night, reverberating through the rock-strewn desert where they had been written. I was hiking the upper Sinai massif with a group of European climbers, trudging through its lunar landscape of red and black granite, swept by blowing sand.

The Sinai is an unforgiving place. Dangerous slot canyons and ragged peaks pepper its terrain. The little vegetation that grows there is as fierce as the desert itself. The waxy leaves of the caper bush, for instance, keep their edges turned toward the sun during the day, exposing the least possible surface area to its heat. The plant's root hairs secrete an acid that eats into the sandstone cliff, anchoring the shrub against relentless winds. In the Sinai, nothing survives without adapting to hardship.

We walked twelve-hour days through the desert, following our Bedouin guides with camels. At night we boiled tea and ate simple meals of flat bread, feta cheese, couscous, tomatoes, and onions. Largely cut off from the others by language, I read John's *Ladder* each night before collapsing into a sleeping bag. The nights were restless, with wind whipping the tent flaps, camels grumbling, and imagined cries coming from nearby graveyards. Yet all the while, John's dusty, dog-eared book ate its way into the sandstone cliff of my unconscious mind.

John Climacus himself had spent forty years in this expanse of nothingness, his cell located beneath a huge boulder at a place called Tholas. When the monks chose him to be their abbot, he wrote the book I carried with me, urging his brothers to "leap with him into the fire," embracing the "marvelous, tough, and painful" life that the bleak environment afforded. He loved it. Despite its challenges, so did I—finding encouragement in his charge to "Keep running athlete and don't be afraid."[7]

His book is the most widely read spiritual classic in Eastern monasticism. I'm intrigued by the correlation it suggests between physical survival in a rugged landscape and the hardy exercise of monastic virtues. John was fascinated by Jacob's dream of a ladder ascending into heaven, using this image to describe the spiritual life as a pattern of thirty rungs leading up a *Ladder of Divine Ascent*. Each chapter offers instructions for monks struggling to live their faith in a wild and desolate land. The book lays out a model of wilderness spirituality I've adapted as a framework for this book.

John focuses on the monastic ascent of the *spirit*, yet he understands that this also involves the descent of the *soul* into the commonplace. The wilderness path to God embraces the dark way of the cave as well as the luminous route up the mountain.[8] The angels on Jacob's ladder move in both directions. Each involves a discipline, an awareness of the body as teacher, and the need for a spiritual guide. John wants to lead his brothers to the heights of perfection, but he knows this begins with the grounded and earthy character of all spiritual practice.

Three of the most important virtues, or rungs, on John's ladder illustrate how he perceived these spiritual values as being taught by the wilderness itself. The three rungs include what we've described already as *haplotes,* the simplicity of moving through the world without being attached. The other two he called *agrupnia,* a watchfulness or vigilance about everything around and within oneself, and *aphobia,* a fearless resistance to all threats, real and imagined.[9]

These are virtues cultivated by a desert landscape. In John's mind, the Sinai wilderness taught them as effectively as the words of Scripture. Unadorned simplicity (*haplotes*) is literally a delight in "non-abundance," making do with available resources. It resists the temptations of an urban life marked by redundancy and excess. In an environment of scarcity, the monks learned that less is more.

The acacia tree supplied most of their basic necessities, for example. They drew medicine from its sap, food from its leaves and pods, shelter from its branches, and water from the direction indicated by its roots. Papyrus plants afforded them paper for writing, mats for their cells, ropes and baskets to trade with desert travelers. They learned to do much with little, taking care to preserve the plant in using its resources. My experience with John Bunyan in the hollow near Bell Mountain reminded me of this stark simplicity.

The alertness of *agrupnia* was a second virtue the desert monks pursued in keeping vigil through the long hours of the night. It helped them resist the grogginess of sleep in the silence before the dawn. The wakeful monk, says John, remains as attentive to the Psalms in the night office as he is in walking the rocky terrain outside the monastery walls. For safety's sake, the monks cut three thousand "steps of repentance" into the granite slope leading to the top of Mt. Sinai. They recognized the perennial danger of falling, both physically and spiritually, for pilgrims like themselves. An awareness honed by desert experience was essential.

The third virtue of *aphobia* emerged from a familiarity with the terrors of a bleak terrain. John knew how easily minds are unhinged by the rasping sound made by horned vipers just before they strike. These highly poisonous snakes have devil-like horns above their eyes and hide camouflaged in rocks along desert paths. But by practicing a holy mindfulness, John said, the soul can be unafraid "even when the body is terrified."[10] Hence, he urged, "Do not hesitate to go in the dark of the night to those places where you are normally frightened." Fearlessness emerged as a consequence of their familiarity with the desert landscape and their growing trust in God. It carried over as well into the monks' ability to speak prophetically to the culture from which they had separated themselves.

For the Desert Christians, simplicity, attentiveness, and courage became three of the most trustworthy rungs on the ladder of the spiritual life. They knew that the landscape taught these virtues as readily as any monastic rule. In my own experience, wilderness backpacking—despite its limitations as a weekend exercise—makes a start at teaching many of the same things. I never understand so well what the Desert Fathers wrote about discipline in the spiritual life as when I'm carrying a thirty-five-pound pack down a winding path into dark trees.

I don't want to give the illusion, however, that entering into wilderness is, in itself, a guarantee of spiritual growth. Virtue is never an automatic result of backcountry experience. Far from building character, the wilds sometimes simply terrify. No one hikes or canoes the wilderness of north Georgia without thinking of James Dickey's *Deliverance*. Human beings, invariably, are the scariest things in the wild. *We* are the alpha predator most to be feared. The rest of God's world, by comparison, is fundamentally safe. I'm far less at risk in wilderness than on the public highways that take me there. Yet there are never assurances of protection in wilderness hiking . . . or in the life of the spirit. Risk-taking is intrinsic to both.

Vignette 2. Whispering Pines Trail: Jean-Pierre de Caussade on Attentiveness

Several months after the Bell Mountain trip, a January thaw makes possible another foray into the Ozarks. I've camped this time in a stand of red cedar trees on a bluff overlooking the River Aux Vases. This is a site along the south loop of Whispering Pines Trail in Hawn State Park. Filled with sandstone cliffs and canyons, it's a landscape shaped by thousands of years of rushing water.

Clouds have been rolling in since I set up camp this afternoon. The temperature is dropping, and I wonder if I've attended to everything necessary as a cold night threatens. I've tucked the ground cloth under the edges of the tent, suspended the bear-bag from a distant tree, even tucked a Nalgene bottle of hot water in the bottom of the sleeping bag. It's important to pay attention to details out here, especially in winter.

At home I'm easily distracted. I'm an absent-minded professor with ADD, inattentive to little things. Surviving in the woods forces me, however, to a "practice of the now" that carries over to home as well. I took joy this morning in shagbark hickory and ironwood trees, stripped of leaves . . . the "bare ruin'd choirs" of a Shakespearean winter forest. Deer tracks stood out in sandy glades, alongside gray-green lichens with stunning red markings. I kept an eye out for the bald eagles that nest here at this time of year. Attending to the world around me is a virtue the wilderness teaches very effectively.

The Desert Christians called it *agrupnia*, the discipline of "not sleeping" even when one is awake. Being fully present to where I am is a rare experience of irrepressible delight. It makes me notice far more details than I normally would. It keeps me from making mistakes that might be unsafe in the wild.

This time I've brought along an eighteenth-century Jesuit named Jean-Pierre de Caussade. His little book on the contemplative life, *Abandonment to Divine Providence*, speaks of what he calls "the sacrament of the present moment." He's convinced that the Holy hides in every single detail. As he once said in praying to God, "You speak to every individual through what happens to them moment by moment." If only we could "lift the veil" and attend with all of our senses, "God would endlessly reveal himself to us and we should see and rejoice in his active presence in all that befalls us." But instead, we are "bored with the small happenings around us." We can't imagine God's presence in "the most trifling affairs."[11] Yet this is precisely where mystery lurks.

Attentiveness is hard to sustain, however. That's why backpacking remains an essential practice for me. It requires a consistent mindfulness and self-presence. It demands my keeping an eye on the trail, attending to variations in the terrain and weather patterns, noticing changes in my body as weariness rises or blisters start to form. It necessitates a reading of the entire landscape, learning to dance and flow with the interconnectedness of its details.

But the discursive mind works against this sensitivity. It is easily distracted, says John Climacus, like a "cur sniffing around the meat market and reveling in the uproar." We need an exercise of quiet perceptiveness to "keep the mind clean," he adds.[12]

De Caussade had learned this truth as a philosophy professor who left the academy to become a spiritual director of Visitation nuns in the mountainous region of Lorraine in northeastern France. He was quick to recognize the limits of intellectual analysis, urging instead an alert sensitivity to the present moment. "We need know nothing about the chemistry of combustion," he said, "to enjoy the warmth of a fire." One simply needs to be present. But staying in the moment, John Climacus urged, means resisting the arch enemy of attentiveness—the *anesthesia*, or thoughtless negligence that so easily anesthetizes the soul, dulling its perception.[13]

Falling asleep to the words of the French Jesuit, I manage to stay warm through a night that steadily gets colder than expected. I resist leaving the tent to catch a glimpse of Orion's belt through the trees. Nor do I hear any sound of the bobcats or wild turkeys that regularly make their home in these woods. In fact, I hear nothing through the night, waking at dawn to a stillness that is almost unnerving. Opening the tent flap, I'm astonished by four inches of snow blanketing the landscape and covering the tent. It had fallen silently through the night, a white coverlet softening the edges of everything. I sit at the tent door looking out onto a world that summons me to radical amazement. The wonder at the heart of things is suddenly, patently apparent.

Outdoor Reading as Transformative Experience

I've learned from experiences like this that reading, in the history of the saints, is more than an indoor affair pursued in the shelter of monasteries and libraries. There are books best read outside the enclosure of walls, where their pages get dirty and have to be held down against the whipping of the wind. When I read the sayings of Abba Macarius in a wilderness setting, it is the next best thing to reading them in the desert west of the Nile where he spoke his words. They ring with an added forcefulness.

Indeed, the reading process itself changes when I'm far from the nearest road, unprotected from weather, relying entirely on what I've brought in my pack. I read more furtively, attending at the same time to birdsong and the movement of the wind. I pause more often, testing the truth of the text against the presence of conifers and lichen-covered rock. The smell of sagebrush and flicker of fireflies become part of my understanding. The book may abruptly burst into life with a whole new intensity. When I toss it back into the rucksack, the forest threatens to explode into flames.

St. Augustine, in his *Confessions*, speaks of this as a potential hazard in any provocative reading. He uses the metaphor of fire to describe what happens when you encounter a spiritual text. Being a teacher of rhetoric, he knew there's always the danger of being burned, or set afire, by what you read. This is especially the case, he observed, in reading outside.[14] He understood how the ambience of one's reading can stir the embers of a smoldering text.

When he described his conversion experience, for example, he focused on what happens when you submit yourself to a particular text within a context that heightens your susceptibility to it. He prefaced his narrative with the story of an acquaintance named Ponticianus. This man had read Athanasius' *Life of Anthony* while strolling through a garden outside the walls of Trier.

The book changed his life. Augustine notes that the *location* of his reading ("outside the city walls") sharpened his attentiveness, connecting him to "the fecund wastelands of the desert" where Anthony had practiced his faith.

Going on to relate his own experience of reading the letters of the apostle Paul in another garden in Milan, he mentions having retreated "as far from the house as possible," finding refuge "under a fig-tree." There he hears a child singing, "Take and read." What he reads in that moment from the book of Romans cuts him to the quick. The biblical text calls him, as it had Anthony, from his compulsive self-absorption into a new desert freedom. The book's invitation to radical abandonment proves transformative, in part at least, because of reading it outside the safety of city walls. The place suggests a vulnerability that matches the prompting of the text.[15]

In the final book of his *Confessions*, Augustine explains what makes outdoor spiritual reading so potentially life-changing. It touches the human soul with such power because it occasions the simultaneous reading of *two* books—God's truth inscribed in writing and God's voice proclaimed in nature. These two different "texts," when read together, ruthlessly cut through human defenses and draw the soul to beauty. "We know no other books with the like power to lay pride low and so surely to silence the obstinate contender," the Bishop of Hippo insists. He knows how the majesty of a Mediterranean thunderstorm, stretching across the vault of the heavens, can be as compelling (in its own "veiled" and "tantalizing" way) as the voice of God spoken through biblical writers.[16] The book of nature communicates a danger and beauty that stirs the senses, opening the soul to a corresponding truth found in the text of Scripture.

Vignette 3. Lindsay Mountain: Julian of Norwich on Fearlessness

Spring has finally come and I've hiked up the trail through tall strands of Queen Anne's lace to Lindsey Mountain in the eastern section of Mark Twain National Forest. A streak of unseasonably warm weather has led me to throw a few things in a pack and head to the mountains. At 1,662 feet, Lindsey Mountain admittedly isn't much of a peak, even by Ozark standards. But these are mountains measured by age, not height. They have their own charm, and their surprises.

As I set up camp under the blackjack oaks at the top, I noticed I've forgotten to bring along a fly for the tent. With the nice weather we'd been having, I hadn't expected rain. But now as midnight nears, I hear distant thunder rumbling through the hills and begin to regret my negligence. Flashes of lightning multiply quickly and a stiff wind suddenly brings torrents of rain. It comes right through the old tent walls as I huddle on a sleeping pad, wondering what possessed me to think of camping on a mountaintop in the middle of a thunderstorm. Wilderness offers abundant opportunities for an exercise of fearlessness, but I'm not up for it now. Counting the lessening number of seconds between flashes of light and cracks of sound, I reflect instead on the correlation between stupidity and wisdom on the learning curve of backcountry experience.

The next morning I lay out wet gear to dry in the sun, eating breakfast overlooking the rolling hills to the west. Serviceberry trees are in bloom. Dogwoods and redbuds won't be far behind. For this morning, at least, all is well once again in the Missouri Ozarks. I relax by reading a few pages of an old favorite brought along on the trip, Julian of Norwich's *Showings of Divine Love*.

For three days and nights in the spring of 1373, this English solitary was stricken by an undiagnosed illness. No one expected her to live. When she finally recovered, she spoke of having participated in a profoundly intimate way in the sufferings of Christ. A refrain echoes again and again through the visions she recounts in her book. There is nothing to fear, she insists. "All will be well. All manner of things will be well."[17] Her truth is easy enough to acknowledge as I stir a cup of hot chocolate with the morning sun on my back. I notice how alive and tranquil everything seems after the storm of the night before.

But as I place the book on a nearby rock to finish my breakfast, I hear movement in the brush behind me. Thinking another squirrel is scratching in the leaves, I turn to see a half-grown black bear coming through the trees only twenty feet away. My mind goes numb with a mixture of terror and awed delight. The bear, however, is as surprised to see me as I am to see him. He quickly turns and runs as I reach for a pan, beating on it with a spoon to alert his mother of my presence. Over the next half hour I calm down enough to imagine Julian laughing at me. Only in the midst of terror, she insists, can anyone *truly* confess that "All will be well."

I'm learning from her that a life of theological reflection, like backpacking, demands fearlessness and risk. It isn't entirely "safe." Metaphorically, it pushes me into unfamiliar terrain where the threat of snakebite (in taking an ethical stand) or a twisted ankle (in articulating the political bite of biblical truth) is always possible. That's why Johann Baptist Metz argues that "theology has to be done in the face of danger."[18] It necessarily evokes the dangerous memory of Jesus, the altogether subversive character of spiritual texts. It requires my taking chances. It means overcoming my persistent fears and listening instead to the voices of those who suffer in a remote place like this.

The economic and ecological precariousness of these depressed counties in southeastern Missouri is readily apparent. I can't hike this section of federal land without being aware of its fragility as an ecosystem, the various dangers that confront the bear I've just met, for example. These include recent plans to sell parts of the Mark Twain National Forest to huge logging companies. Mining interests also pose a threat to wilderness land and to those who suffer from poverty in the surrounding area. Lead mining has endangered the health of children in this region for years. On the drive to the trailhead yesterday, I passed the Doe Run Company in Herculaneum and huge mounds of mine tailings near the old, abandoned smelter in Leadington. The land and its people here cry out for justice, even as the wilderness itself evokes a fearlessness in speaking on its behalf.

Julian of Norwich knew the imperilment of everything in the natural world. Her visions speak of creation as sharing in the sufferings of Christ. The earth, she claimed, is as fragile as a hazelnut held in the palm of a woman's hand. It amazed her that it exists at all; so easily it can fall into nothing.[19] Yet she knows ultimately that all will be well. There is nothing to fear. A mothering God who commands the work for justice holds everything in her hand.

The storm-swept top of Lindsay Mountain, the black bear coming through the brush, the economic threats facing the land and its people—all these elicit the fearlessness that John Climacus expected of his desert monks. In late antiquity the practice of *aphobia* provoked controversy. It made the Desert Fathers politically dangerous. Not a few of them were draft dodgers and tax resisters, sought out by magistrates who tracked them into the desert. In its early usage, the word implied a "lack of reverence," a refusal to defer, for example, to the authority of Imperial Rome (or to the intimidating power of companies who neglect their social responsibilities).[20] What are the implications of *aphobia* for someone hiking in a place like this? As I go back home, I'm uneasy about what it may demand of me.

Backpacking as a spiritual discipline is both rewarding and unsettling. Few experiences in my life are as total—or as demanding. It carries me through a wide range of emotions, from exhausted weariness and overpowering dread to ecstatic joy. Wilderness regularly occasions an experience of "limit" in my life. Camping alongside thousand-year-old bristlecone pine trees at 11,000 feet in the Colorado Front Range, I'm touched by a palpable mystery. I lack any language for describing what it's like to be surrounded by a wild majesty . . . that feels strangely akin to home.

Bill Plotkin suggests that wandering in nature may be "the most essential soulcraft practice" any of us can have in a society like ours. It connects us with a solitude, simplicity, and vulnerability that we've lost in our fully wired, technological world. It fills a hunger we didn't know we had.

Yet backpacking with the saints isn't an exercise for the faint-hearted. It exacts a willingness to travel light (jettisoning one's preconceived ideas), a readiness to listen to other voices (in the surrounding terrain as well as in the text), and a courage to act without fear. When you read a dangerous book in an unfamiliar place, your life may be changed by the words of a wise elder and the even wilder wisdom of the land. Who knows what might happen?

PART TWO

The Pattern of Wilderness Spirituality

People need wild places. Whether or not we think we do,
we do. We need to be able to taste grace and know again
that we desire it. We need to experience a landscape that is
timeless, whose agenda moves at the pace of speciation and
glaciers. To be surrounded by a singing, mating, howling
commotion of other species, all of which love their lives as
much as we do ours, and none of which could possibly care
less about us in our place. It reminds us that our plans are
small and somewhat absurd. It reminds us why, in those
cases in which our plans might influence many future gen-
erations, we ought to choose carefully. Looking out on a
clean plank of planet earth, we can get shaken right down
to the bone by the bronze-eyed possibility of lives that are
not our own.

BARBARA KINGSOLVER, Small Wonder[1]

Each of the following chapters offers an account of a backpacking trip to a particular place, along with the writings of a saint and a theme from the Desert Fathers associated with the experience of the journey. I try to let the places (and the saints) speak for themselves, but the essays are also shaped by what I bring along on the trail with me. I've organized the chapters after a pattern of wilderness spirituality drawn from the early Desert Christians.

Their understanding of growth in the spiritual life is similar to Joseph Campbell's journey of the hero, Bill Plotkin's passage from egocentric to soulcentric identity, and Richard Rohr's path of ascent and descent in negotiating the two halves of life.[2] The desert monks spoke out of a particular context of cultural resistance, a communal exercise of spiritual direction, and the imitation of Christ. Yet they shared a more universal pattern of the spiritual journey that can be characterized by four stages: (1) the call to adventure and risk, (2) the assumption of a necessary discipline, (3) the descent into darkness and loss, and (4) the return to a freer and more responsible life.

The four subsequent sections of this part of the book probe the dimensions of these stages, building on the metaphor of the wilderness journey. Chapters 3, 4, and 5 deal with the choices one makes in launching out on the trail, sensing the call of the wild. Chapters 6, 7, and 8 address the disciplines necessary for sustaining a wilderness practice. Chapters 9, 10, and 11 speak of the experience of being undone in threatening terrain. And Chapters 12 through 15 attend to the joyous and prophetic freedom that can arise from a sustained spiritual practice.

First Leg: Departure (Leaving the Trailhead)

Any new beginning in one's life involves a dissatisfaction with the past and a call to something new. It can be as unsettling as it is exciting. The Desert Christians learned that wilderness had a way of abruptly putting them in their place. It awakened them to a mystery that had no regard for their self-importance, yet welcomed them with an astounding love. Their entry into a life shaped by the desert required a stout readiness to commit, a weathering of disappointment, and a birth of an irresistible desire. These are the themes explored in this section of the book.

Part of the grandeur of wilderness is that it cares so little about the things that absorb us so much. We find a glorious, disarming indifference in its grand vistas and hidden niches. It shares its gifts with a prodigal extravagance, even as it ignores our imagined self-importance. John Burroughs delighted in the generous beauty of a sugar maple in the Catskills, knowing that it lacked any personal regard for him whatever. "What the old maple holds for me is maple-sugar, but it was not put there for me; it is there just the same, whether I want it or not; it is a part of the economy of the tree; it is a factor in its own growth; the tree is not thinking of me (pardon the term), but of itself. Of course this does not make my debt to it, and my grounds for thankfulness, any less real."[3] Accepting what is—for what it is—is the place to start.

3

Venturing Out: The Irish Wilderness and Columba of Iona

*The path I walk, Christ walks it. May the land in which I
find myself be without sorrow. May the Trinity protect me
wherever I stay, bright angels walk with me, the ninefold
people of heaven come with me. May I arrive at every place
I enter. Well does the fair Lord show us a course, a path.*

From a sixth-century hymn attributed to St. Columba[4]

*The voyage tale in the Celtic tradition may be attributed
to the impact on the Irish imagination of peregrinatio (pilgrimage), the monastic practice of voluntary self-exile as a
form of devotional austerity.*

JOHN T. KOCH[5]

I PUT IN at Greer Crossing, planning to float the twenty-one miles to River-
ton over the next three days. Canoeing the Eleven Point River—a National
Wild and Scenic Riverway near the Arkansas border—is a quintessen-
tial Ozark experience. The stream skirts the western boundary of the Irish
Wilderness, a 16,500-acre area of the National Wilderness system. It's a pocket
of dense forest, sparkling creeks, and limestone caves as wild as the wooded
glens of Ireland's Wicklow Mountains. The place abounds with white-tailed
deer, bobcats, raccoons, gray foxes, brown trout, and songbirds galore. A
Celtic mystery lurks in this secluded Missouri landscape.

I like to think of the Irish Wilderness as connecting me with my family
roots in Ireland and Cornwall, near Land's End in southwest England. It
takes me back to a spiritual practice of wilderness wandering firmly rooted
in the Celtic tradition. The Druids would have loved this part of southern
Missouri. A dozen species of oak spread their branches overhead. Colonies
of mayapples thrive along the trail. The limestone bluffs above the river are

scattered with dolomite crystals. Canoeing downstream, you hear the sound of a beaver tail slapping the water to warn its kits as you round a bend. Ducking under the branches of an overhanging sycamore tree, you're surprised by a harmless rat snake resting on a limb. With each stroke, the paddle dips into crystal-clear water rising from underground springs.

There are times in your life when you realize you need a discipline. You have to decide about where you're going (or not going). That's why I'm here— to renew a spiritual regimen in my life, venturing out so as to find my way back in again. Salmon do it instinctively as a part of their life cycle, swimming upstream to their source. Naturalist Freeman House says that humans and salmon are a lot alike: "We are related by virtue of the places to which we choose to return."[6] I, too, need to revert from time to time to the primeval wonders of great blue herons and hazelnut trees . . . to an untamed Celtic landscape.

As salmon know, there's a certainty of risk involved in going back to one's beginnings. Reclaiming a spiritual discipline can be dangerous. It demands change, even utter loss, in exchange for a new generativity. In the case of Columba, the sixth-century Celtic saint, it meant trusting himself to the Irish Sea in a rudderless boat made of animal skins, going wherever the winds carried him.

Getting started in the spiritual life isn't easy. In Twelve-Step work, one's natural resistance to the first step is overpowering. It takes an enormous stretch to admit you're powerless to change what has to be changed in your life. That's why a wilderness discipline may be necessary. Now and then we need something arduous to shake us out of our lethargy. We need the harsh candor of a poet like Hāfez. "Love wants to reach out and manhandle us," he says, "breaking all our teacup talk of God. . . . It wants to drag you by the hair and rip from your grip all the toys in the world that bring you no joy." The Sufi mystic insists there are times when we're "tired of speaking sweetly." Pluck and plain-spokenness are demanded of us: "The Beloved wants to hold us upside down and shake all the nonsense out."[7] It's time to wake up.

In rites of passage I help to lead (in connection with Richard Rohr's Men as Learners and Elders program), I see men at midlife struggling to be accountable in their lives.[8] They want to act decisively, venturing out. But walking away from what isn't working in their lives is difficult. Columba realized this himself as he left Ireland under a cloud of copyright infringement and bloodshed. Familiar patterns were no longer an option for him. He was forced to start all over again.

Launching on a Wilderness Discipline

Now and then order has to be imposed on the chaos of our lives. A crisis initiates it. Or a bottoming-out in our addiction, even a crushing weariness with the struggle. The discipline we choose at the time may lead us to a wise teacher. It might engage the body (as in Tai Chi) or involve deliberate reading (like *lectio divina*). It may quiet the mind through meditation, fasting, or intensive journaling. My own practice of wilderness backpacking has been a way of incorporating all of these disciplines.

Every time you renew a pattern of intentional training you do something good for yourself. The body and the spirit both delight in exercise. Discipline is a deliberate way of recalling what it is you really want. It is a choice to be what you know you *have* to be. Yet it's disconcerting, too—demanding that you remain true to yourself even when you're not yet sure what that means.

In my case, launching out on a wilderness discipline is a way of returning to my Celtic roots, adopting a regular practice of pilgrimage. It's also a way of being true to the names I've been given—Belden Curnow Lane. I *am*, by virtue of my given names, a "beautiful green hill in Cornwall." In Old English, the name *Beildin* means "beautiful hill," the hill of Bel (the shining one), a Celtic deity connected with fire and the sun. He was honored on Beltane, the May Day festival observed each spring. *Kernow*, in turn, is the Gaelic word for Cornwall. I'm named, oddly enough, after a great-grandfather I never knew *and* after a place of Druidic worship. My very identity calls me out to the edge . . . to the wild Celtic regions beyond the reach of Roman civilization, to green hills wherever they may be. In a mystery I can't fully grasp, my discipline is to draw strength from the greening, life-giving power of a place on the margins. Every green hill glimpsed from a ridge-top trail is a reminder of home.

I went to Cornwall with my family years ago in search of a hill I might be able to call my own. I don't know of any relatives still living there. My family history is largely a mystery; my father changed his name long ago to escape his past. But for three weeks we hiked and camped through southwest England, Ireland, and Scotland, looking for geographical roots I might be able to claim. Along the Cornish coast near Boscastle one evening we were looking for a B & B to spend the night. We'd been camping in the rain for several days and could think of nothing better than a warm, dry bed.

Stopping at a cottage with a room to let on the road to Tintagel, the woman of the house showed us a small room overlooking the sea with an eleventh-century Norman church nearby. Between where we stood and the ocean beyond was a beautiful green hill. I knew it instantly as home. It was as if I had stumbled onto my "resurrection place," as they say in the Celtic tradition. We stayed there for three days and three nights and we loved it . . . drawing on the deep peace of the running wave, the deep peace of the quiet earth, the deep peace of the shining stars.

The very name I carry summons me, therefore, to a wilderness beyond the next bend in the trail. This is especially the case as I enter an important time of transition in my life. For years my journeys into wilderness have allowed me to escape the confines of an academic life, but I'm preparing now to leave the world of the university altogether—approaching retirement. How do I foster a spirit of wild adventure in launching out on new, unmapped trails? How can I retain the values of what I've been, as a critically trained scholar, while plunging into a deeper backcountry I haven't yet dared to explore?

The eccentric air of the Irish Wilderness entices me. It's a place that thrives on unpredictability, scorning all efforts at control. It disdains academic language, ignores reputations, and discounts all credentials. It insists on my writing without the university looking over my shoulder, as if "real theology" could only be done in peer-reviewed journals. This is home for the poet and storyteller, for the Celtic bard who learned to recite his truth in verse, without reducing it to writing. He *sang* it, rather than submit it to the *Harvard Review*.

Columba's courage as a wandering poet sustains me in my quest, as does the ravishing beauty of the island of Iona to which he came. Celtic places have been life-giving for me. I'm enthralled by stories of the wandering saints or *peregrini* celebrated in Irish tales. Brendan was a voyager in search of the mythical "Isle of the Blessed" in the western sea. Cormac set out three times in quest of a "desert in the ocean." On his last trip he journeyed where no one had been before, "beyond the limits of human wanderings" from whence "to return was impossible." That's the fear we inevitably have in venturing out. "Following the flight of the wild goose" in search of God, as Brendan did, we have no guarantees of returning as the same person we were.[9]

From Celtic Monasticism to the Irish Wilderness

Cormac's search for a "desert in the ocean" symbolized the fascination that sixth-century Celtic Christians had for the rigorous life of the Desert Fathers and Mothers in ancient Egypt. Back in the fourth century, Martin of Tours founded a monastery in Gaul imitating the Egyptian model. There

St. Ninian and other missionaries to the Celts were initially trained. St. Patrick himself may have been a nephew of St. Martin. Hence, the line from Egypt to Ireland—from the desert monks to Celtic pilgrims—made its way through central France.

What the two held in common geographically was an affinity for life on the edge. What they shared spiritually was a readiness to start over from scratch. Egyptian monasteries were located "off the map," largely hidden in the desert west of the Nile. Celtic places thrived on the western fringes of Europe, beyond the influence of Roman power. Their coastal outposts stretched from Galicia in Spain and Brittany in France, to Cornwall, Wales, Ireland, and Scotland to the northwest.

Fourth-century Egyptians and sixth-century Celts shared a high degree of social upheaval. Historian Peter Brown says that the desert monk, like the Celtic wanderer, represented the desire to "chuck up everything and just clear off." Reacting (in each case) to Roman authority, they were acting out a dramatic ritual of social disengagement.[10] Their discipline was a quest for personal transformation as well as a critique of social prominence. Their combination of spiritual athleticism, a prophetic voice, and life on the edge has had an enduring appeal in the history of Western Christianity. It's what draws me to wilderness as well.

Desert spirituality in the fourth century was a response to changing social conditions in the church after the emperor Constantine. He dramatically ended Roman persecution, embracing Christianity. But he also brought a new prestige and prosperity to the Christian community. Monasticism consequently emerged as a protest movement, criticizing the growing laxity that came to characterize many Christians. Abba Theodore of Pherme feared the church was becoming sedate and acculturated, lacking the zeal of those who had so recently died for their faith. He lamented that "In these days many take their rest before God gives it them."[11] Their religion had become overly comfortable.

Yet the Desert Christians, in their previous lives, hadn't been great examples of moral rectitude themselves. They went to the desert knowing that their lives needed changing. Abba Moses had been a robber and gang leader before his conversion. Apollo of Scete had knifed a pregnant woman. Evagrius had ended an affair with the wife of a Roman prefect who was trying to kill him. These weren't picture-book saints. Amma Eugenia came to the desert fleeing a forced marriage. Others had resisted mandatory military service or the payment of taxes supporting war. Turning their backs on a previous life, they adopted a strict discipline in beginning anew.

Yet they knew that running away in itself wasn't an answer. "We carry ourselves wherever we go," warned Amma Matrona. "We cannot escape temptation by mere flight."[12] It wasn't a change of place, but the adoption of a discipline that altered their lives. Reaching beyond traditional boundaries of church and society, they chose wilderness as an ideal terrain for starting over. The pattern has kept repeating itself ever since. "Each time there is a spiritual renewal in the Church, the Desert Fathers are present," says Jesuit Irénée Hausherr.[13]

The same was true of the Irish Catholic immigrants who came to Missouri in the nineteenth century, settling in the Irish Wilderness. There they joined the rigors of Desert Christianity with a Celtic fascination for the wilds, seeking refuge from a hostile culture in the Ozark backcountry. These Catholic refugees were led by John Joseph Hogan, a priest from County Limerick, Ireland. He had arrived in St. Louis in 1857. There he wrote in his travel diary of Irish children dying of starvation in shanties outside the city. He documented Irish railroad workers near Rolla who were paid almost nothing and African slaves in iron manacles carried on barges along the Missouri River. Managing to buy land in a remote part of the state, between the Eleven Point and Current Rivers, he invited destitute Catholic families to form a "community in the desert." This was the beginning of the Irish Wilderness in southern Missouri.

"The solitariness of the place seemed to inspire devotion," Hogan wrote in his journal. "Nowhere could the human soul so profoundly worship as in the depths of that leafy forest, beneath the swaying branches of the lofty oaks and pines, where solitude and the heart of man united in praise and wonder of the Great Creator."[14] Some fifty families joined him over the next few years. Protestant circuit riders, however, fearing Catholic influence on the frontier, preached inflammatory sermons about them. When the Civil War broke out, armies of the North and South both occupied the area at different times. Raiders attacked the settlement, burning houses, killing and scattering the people. The beleaguered Irish settlers soon vanished, leaving only stories (and a dark wilderness) behind. Today the Wilderness Free Will Baptist Church stands near the site of their original log cabin church. Yet memories of a Celtic past linger.

Columba as Wilderness Saint

As I paddle downstream, past Graveyard Hollow and the entry of Hurricane Creek, I delight in the emerald beauty of the landscape. I think of the

Celtic saints that Irish immigrants emulated in their flight to the wilderness here. Columba (521–597), nicknamed Columcille, "the Dove of the Church," was a descendent of kings born in County Donegal in northern Ireland. He studied under St. Finian in the monastic school at Clonard Abbey along the River Boyne and was apprenticed to one of the *filidh*, a Christian bard steeped in the wisdom of the Druids. His life suddenly changed, however, in the year 563.

According to the hagiographical *Life of Columba*, written a century later by the ninth abbot of Iona, the Irish monk had been working in the monastery scriptorium, copying manuscripts under the tutelage of his master Finian.[15] A Psalter he was reproducing at the time caught his eye, and he decided to make a private copy for his own use. This led, strangely enough, to an accusation of intellectual property theft. Conflicting parties took sides, and an outright battle ensued over the question of proprietary rights. Lives were lost on both sides, and Columba went into self-imposed exile, grieving over the controversy he had sparked. He embarked in a small leather coracle that washed him up on the island of Iona. There he began a new life.

Columcille was renowned for his love of nature, delighting in the wild beauty of the island to which he came. He was drawn to birds, like all the Celtic saints. The Scots called him "the crane-cleric" for having rescued a crane stranded on Iona. He was probably trained in the skill of ornithomancy, a form of divination and bird lore common in Ireland at the time. To prevent a fire from destroying a beloved oak forest in Derry, he once uttered an incantation drawn from Druidic sources. He even allegedly stopped the Loch Ness monster from attacking a swimmer near Inverness, making the sign of the cross and shouting, "You will go no further!"[16] On the day he died, his old white horse rubbed its head against the monk's shoulder and wept at his approaching death.

Stories of the Celtic saints and their passion for nature readily come to mind here on the edge of the Irish Wilderness. They were so attuned to the natural world that a bird was said to have dropped a feather for St. Molass to use as a pen when he needed to write down his thoughts. A stag rested a book on its antlers so St. Cainnech could read while walking through the forest.[17] Columba, in his own poetic celebration of nature and the Holy Trinity, *The Altus Prosator*, spoke of God as an Irish farmer, the "First High Sower," planting a paradise full of natural delights.[18]

As an apostle to the Picts in Scotland, Columba successfully wove together earlier Celtic traditions with his Christian faith. He once returned to Ireland to speak at a church council in defense of the *filidh*, preventing the

Druid bards from being condemned and banished. Taliesin, at King Arthur's court, had been the most famous of these, serving as storyteller, singer, poet, and diviner. Columba himself wrote nature hymns, was skilled in rhetoric, and possessed the "second sight," being able to read signs and portents of the weather. "My Druid is Christ, the Son of God," he declared.[19] One of his hymns, written on Iona, sings of God's glory in the "heavy waves over the glittering ocean," "the voice of wondrous birds," and the "mighty whales, the greatest of wonders."[20] Joining his faith to a pre-Christian love of nature came perfectly naturally to him.

Floating downriver through this Ozark wilderness, I can hear the sound of a Celtic harp in the lapping water, strumming the music to the hymn "St. Patrick's Breastplate." Tunes like this flourished here 150 years ago. Irish immigrants would have relished the old Celtic bards and their weaving together of story and song. The bards were required to master three noble harp strains: the lament strain (bringing tears to the eyes of their listeners), the laughter strain (replacing tears of sorrow with tears of joy), and the sleep strain (lulling their listeners to the shadowlands of sleep).[21] As I pull the canoe onto a gravel shoal, seeking a place to camp for the night, the music of night birds fills the oaks nearby. They're singing the forgotten tunes of an Irish Wilderness—provoking tears and laughter and sleep even now.

Along the Eleven Point River: Returning to Celtic Roots

After a breakfast of instant oatmeal and dried fruit, I put into the river again. Sunlight dances on the water. Turtles sun themselves on logs; otters play in the current. Black and bright-blue butterflies touch down on the handle of my paddle. Half-gnawed trees stand out along the water's edge, where beavers have been at work. For half an hour a heron keeps taking off ahead of me down the river, flying again every time I catch up. Is he curious, somehow attracted to this solitary paddler? Or is he simply using the sound of my canoe to steer fish in his direction? The river challenges every tendency to put myself at the center of its world.

Negotiating the chute rapids at Mary Decker Shoal is a bit tricky. I have to watch for rootwads in the river, fallen trees with exposed roots blocking the stream. They like to catch and overturn canoes. But nothing seriously disturbs the flow of the river, or myself with it. I draw as little attention to myself as do the water striders treading the eddies along the bank. I begin to savor being part of a world that isn't about me.

Later that afternoon I tie up at the Whites Creek float camp and walk part of the Whites Creek Trail, an 18.6-mile loop providing the only access into the interior of the Irish Wilderness. The tall, dense trees make it a dark and seductive place. Weird things are said to have happened here. In 1861, a Union soldier mysteriously disappeared at Mary Decker Shoal. The ghost of Devil Dick Boze, one of Quantrill's Raiders gunned down by the 7th Kansas militia, still stalks the area around Boze Mill. Leprechauns "mess with people" in the night at Horseshoe Bend. The Ozark Black Howler, a panther of legendary size, supposedly prowls the shadows nearby. I follow the trail to Whites Creek cave, pondering these persistent Ozark tales.[22]

The cave is one of 6,300 underground caverns scattered across the state of Missouri. Far off the beaten track, it is an obscure world of water pools and dripstone, winding 1,600 feet into the earth. I sit inside its opening, waiting for my eyes to adjust to the dark. I'll not wander far inside. Endangered Indiana bats live in its depths, and its fragile rock formations shouldn't be disturbed. But the cave troubles me, too. It hides the deep earth work to which I'm invited at this period in my life.

The earth-based discipline of backpacking carries me back to the earliest roots of my Christian faith. As a child growing up in the fundamentalist South, I needed the stubborn realism of the natural world to keep me grounded. Armadillos and mosquito-filled swamps were a helpful antidote to periodic predictions of the rapture and arguments over inerrancy. Years later, in the radically different setting of doctoral study, I stuffed my head with facts and theories of interpretation, practically living in the libraries of Princeton, New Jersey. My way of escaping its highly cerebral world was to walk the overgrown paths of the Raritan Canal or to hike the Appalachian Trail through the Delaware Water Gap. My soul, in short, required a more grounded Christianity than what I encountered in the otherworldly faith of my youth or in the intellectual abstractions of my training. I've needed roots and wings, the rough feel of pine bark and the reek of stagnant swamp water.

The church of my childhood frowned on any undue attention to the world of nature . . . or the world in general, for that matter. Folks thought it smacked of something pagan, like the name I bore. We were accustomed to singing an old Jim Reeves gospel song:

> *This world is not my home; I'm just a-passing through.*
> *My treasures are laid up, somewhere beyond the blue.*
> *The angels beckon me from heaven's open door*
> *and I can't feel at home in this world anymore.*

We sang it with gusto, but I fought it, too—knowing even then that the world was too beautiful, too full of God, to be so easily dismissed.

But the heady world of an academic life didn't prove any better at connecting me to earthbound experience. Its analytical perspective was freeing, its criticism of naïve faith brilliant, its recovery of ancient traditions refreshing. But its ethereal rationality was as unsatisfying as the rigid belief system I'd known growing up. At both extremes I hungered for wilderness. In each context, I lived a partitioned life—the mind disconnected from the heart. I fought to keep together the vitality of an early experience of God, the judicious eye of a trained theologian, and the pulsing life of a wilderness I couldn't control.

My solution over the years has been to adopt a twofold spiritual practice. Every so often I launch out onto wilderness trails, immersing myself in God's "Green Scripture," finding there an immediacy that I thrive on. I also work at reclaiming earthy traditions in the history of spirituality that are able to sustain such a venture. The one keeps me grounded in nature and the other in a wisdom tradition, a skilled habit of seeing. If backpacking is my discipline, the saints are my teachers.

Bernard of Clairvaux encourages me in his reading the Song of Songs among the oaks and beeches of the French countryside. I resonate with Augustine's conviction that "God is poured forth in all things and God is Himself everywhere, wholly." I'm intrigued by Basil of Caesarea's injunction that "creation must penetrate you with so much admiration . . . that the least plant may bring you to a remembrance of the Creator." I delight in the image of God as a bubbling fountain from which all things come and to which all things return, found in Bonaventure and Eckhart.[23] In the end, I reach back to my family roots, to the Celtic Christ of the crashing wave, to Scots-Irish saints who knew that everything of beauty is on its way back to God.

One such Celtic saint was John Scotus Eriugena, "John, the Irish-born Celt," a brilliant and daring theologian of the ninth century. His most important book explores God's relationship to the natural world. He argues that "God is the beginning, the middle, and the end of the created universe. God is that from which all things originate, that in which all things participate, and that to which all things eventually return."[24] Creation, for him, was a theophany, a stunning manifestation of God as "all and in all" (after I Corinthians 15:28). In his thinking, moth larvae and alpha predators, slow-growing mosses and day-old mayflies, winged pollinators and bacterial decomposers all come bubbling forth from the infinitely networking mind and heart of God.

He found no contradiction between the book of Nature and the book of Scripture. In his love of wilderness, he saw no betrayal of the Jesus of the Gospels, only an affirmation of a Cosmic Christ for whom nothing earthy can be foreign. Eriugena's affirmation of creation helps to anchor the ungrounded and conflicting worlds of my faith experience. Its association of God with the unnerving mystery of an Irish Wilderness points to yet another part of the journey of my life, now unfolding.

Leaving the cool air of the cave, I hike back to the float camp and sit that night by a spritely fire of pine knots, reflecting on the events of the day. I mull over Eriugena's notion of *apokatastasis*, the culminating "return" or "restitution" of all creation to its source in God. All things, he says, come back to love in the end. This was an idea shared by Ireneaus, Origen, the Kabbalists, and Teilhard, among others in the history of the saints. For them, the line between nature and spirit, this world and the next, the Irish Wilderness and the beating of God's heart remains extraordinarily thin. Everything belongs. My journey into wilderness is a pilgrimage shared with everything else. We all swim together upstream, back to our source. I dare not consider any of it profane.

The third day of the trip finds me again tracing the winding turns of the Eleven Point River. Numerous stories are told about how the stream got its name. Some say early surveyors were able to map eleven different compass points for change of direction within a single mile of the river's length. Others speak of a huge eleven-point buck once killed by a hunter on its banks. Still others claim that eleven separate springs feed the river along its length. Names invariably carry multiple meanings.

I pass the Blue Hole at Boze Mill, another stunning spring, and sit for a while among the roots of a sycamore tree overhanging its azure eye of bubbling water. A knotted rope dangles from a high oak limb, awaiting kids with inner tubes . . . or recalling the hanging of a renegade Confederate soldier. The Ozarks are renowned for underground springs like this, welling up from a subterranean world of limestone aquifers. Some years ago my wife and I were caught in a thunderstorm just downriver from here. We pulled the canoe over to the bank, watching the rain and lightning from under trees at the foot of a tall bluff. Our fear shifted to wonderment as the storm passed and a change in temperature raised a ghostlike mist from the water.

The unpredictable "otherness" of this Irish Wilderness is strangely alluring, calling me back to myself. It shares in what Thomas Merton once said of wild places in general:

The Desert Fathers believed that the wilderness had been created as supremely valuable in the eyes of God precisely because it had no value to men. . . . The desert was created simply to be itself, not to be transformed by men into something else. So too the mountain and the sea. The desert is therefore the logical dwelling place for the man who seeks to be nothing but himself.[25]

The Irish Wilderness invites me to marvel at myself as a "green hill in Cornwall," claiming the name and the discipline that allows me to be most fully who I am.

Retrieving Celtic Spirituality

The retrieval of Celtic spirituality has been an important development in religious thought over the past hundred years. It allows us to put back together things that were separated in the English-speaking world after the year 597. That was the year Columba died and a Roman missionary named Augustine became Archbishop of Canterbury. The two events symbolized a vast shift in the history of British Christianity. By the year 664, at the Synod of Whitby, Celtic spirituality was largely overthrown by the power of Rome, its wild mysticism and independence brought under Latin control. In the imagery of St. Bede, the apostle Peter's hierarchical authority triumphed over the apostle John's mystical vision of the Light shining in everyone and everything. Pelagius' sense of the original goodness of human life and Eriugena's emphasis on balancing the book of Scripture with the book of Nature were minimized, if not labeled heretical. Eriugena had declared both books to be integral to faith. He warned that without the large text of creation we miss the vastness of the message and without the small text of the Gospels we miss its intimacy.[26]

With the decline of Celtic spirituality, Western Christianity lost much of its wildness, its uncontrolled and risky edge. It lent itself increasingly to abstract thought, an excessive wordiness, and an authoritarian clericalism. It paid less attention to nature and symbol, focusing more on the correctness of its theological formulations. In the Celtic Book of Kells, the Gospels possessed a magical power of their own, akin to the mystical landscape they illuminated. In subsequent Western thought, the accounts of Jesus' life became instead a basis for rational argument and creedal divisiveness. The diminishment of the earthy Celtic spirit led to an impoverishment of the spiritual life in general. Thankfully, its energy is being rediscovered today. It serves, for me at least, as a complement and corrective to the Roman Catholic and Protestant traditions that have been so influential in my life.

This is the discipline I'm called to practice. I need the wildness of nature to enliven my reading of the sacred word. My soul requires a boisterous exercise of faith, allowing the Spirit to blow where it wishes. Many people today long for an authentic spiritual experience. They *expect* it to be dangerous. They're ready when necessary to "chuck up everything" and venture out, yielding to the longing that arises within. For my own part, even my name demands it.

4

Disillusionment: Laramie Peak and Thérèse of Lisieux

It's always farther than it looks. It's always taller than it looks. And it's always harder than it looks.

The Three Rules of Mountaineering

No great art has ever been made without the artist having known danger.

RAINER MARIA RILKE[1]

MAKING MISTAKES IN the spiritual life is an essential part of growth—as important as forest fires, blow-downs, and insects are to the life of a thriving forest. You grow only in being burnt, bent, and bitten. You have to stumble before you can walk.

My error this time wasn't intentional. I saw no signs at the trailhead and didn't think to ask. I simply hauled my backpack up Laramie Peak in the Medicine Bow Wilderness of eastern Wyoming, planning to spend the night somewhere near the top. Only later did I learn that camping isn't allowed anywhere on the mountain. Sometimes ignorance is bliss. More often it's simply dangerous. Yet I had the mountain to myself that night, or I should say that *it* had me.

I was new to backpacking at the time. But I don't remember *ever* being so overwhelmed by deep silence and a haunting sense of presence as I was that night at 10,000 feet near the mountain's peak. Fallen limbs, rock outcroppings, and thick ground cover made it impossible to venture very far off the trail. It was hard even to find a semi-flat piece of ground to sleep on in the dense, moss-covered undergrowth. Everything resisted my being there. Still more disturbing was the feeling that I was being watched—studied from beyond the shadows by something I couldn't see. I've seldom felt so ill at ease in wilderness. Something was out there, frightening in its apparent indifference to my well-being.

Laramie Peak stands alone on the easternmost edge of the Rocky Mountains. At 10,272 feet, it is smaller than the Colorado fourteeners to the southwest. But it offers an imposing silhouette, jutting up from the northern plains like Mt. Fuji rising above the mountains west of Tokyo. One can see it for miles along Highway I-25 in eastern Wyoming. Nineteenth-century settlers on the Oregon Trail caught sight of it from Scotts Bluff in the Nebraska Territory, 120 miles to the east. It was their first warning of the foreboding mountains that lay ahead.

The six-mile trail to the top, with an elevation gain of 3,000 feet, offers a steep hike through pristine National Forest land. Pronghorn antelope, elk, bighorn sheep, mule deer, even mountain lions and black bears make their home on the shadowy peak. Mark Twain, in his book *Roughing It*, spoke of its "deep, dark, rich indigo blue," looming above the gray-green sameness of the Wyoming plains.[2] The peak (and the larger range of which it is a part) is named after Jacques LaRamee, a French-Canadian fur trapper and adventurer renowned among Western pioneers. He died mysteriously in the early 1800s while trapping in unexplored territory up the Laramie River.

The apprehension I felt that night on the mountain was something my body knew, but my mind couldn't comprehend. In my imagination, I sensed what a fawn might experience being watched by a mountain lion hiding in thick branches a hundred yards away. There are over thirty thousand cougars or mountain lions in the western United States. They are solitary animals who hunt alone, stalking their prey in dense underbrush and rocky terrain. They have lithe, sandy-brown bodies, weighing as much as 180 pounds, with long, heavy tails. Cougars can sprint at speeds up to forty miles an hour, leaping forty-five feet in a single bound. They attack from behind, breaking the neck of their victim by sinking their long incisors into the base of its neck. But they rarely attack human beings. Like Peter Matthiessen's snow leopard, they're shy and elusive, almost never seen in the wilds.

The experience of being seen without seeing in return is an unsettling one, a fear going back to Paleolithic hunters and gatherers crouched outside the caves of Lascaux in southern France. Our bodies retain even now an uncanny capacity to spot instantly if someone is looking at us from across a crowded room. We deeply remember what it means to be hunted.

Wendell Berry's poem, "To the Unseeable Animal," honors the power of what remains unseen in the wilds. His daughter once said to him, "I hope there's an animal somewhere that nobody has ever seen. And I hope nobody ever sees it." Consequently, he wrote an elegy to this invisible creature, hiding deep in the woods. "That we do not know you / is your perfection / and our hope," he concluded.³ But delighting in a child's imaginary "unseeable" creature is different from knowing yourself to be watched in wilderness by something conveying cold indifference, if not menace.

The Initial Encounter of Wilderness

This awareness of unease is a common experience in one's initial encounter of wilderness. It's what Ed Abbey might call a shit-in-your-pants experience of the holy, familiar to novices who make dumb mistakes on rushing into backcountry. In our naïveté, we make a bold assault on the mountain, drawn by illusions of beauty, silence, and solitude. We carry romantic notions of being welcomed by the place, belonging to the landscape, confident of our ability to handle whatever difficulties may arise. We think ourselves naturally adept at the skills of wilderness survival and contemplative solitude that backcountry invites.

But we soon find that we've set too fast a pace, we've stuffed too many things in our pack, we've worn the wrong shoes and misplaced the map. Before long we're disarmed by how the place ignores us—put off by the fierceness of its splendor, the totality of its silence, the horror of its solitude. We realize we weren't prepared at all. Naïveté turns to disillusionment.

Wilderness spirituality classically begins at such a place—with the awkward, disturbing awareness that we have miscalculated our abilities, we are wholly unqualified for dealing with mystery. We're like the religious enthusiasts Rumi described, so eager to *capture* rather than marvel at wonder: "The madmen have seen the moon in the window; they are running to the roof with ladders."⁴ No sooner do they raise their scaffolding to the sky, however, than they realize the absurdity of their presumption.

Our beginning in the spiritual life, like our entry into wilderness, usually involves a passage through disenchantment. We can identify with the spiritual tourists who went into the desert of fourth-century Egypt, enamored by the reputation of the desert saints, seeking the romance of the monastic life. Invariably, their illusions of instant spirituality slammed up against the rock-hard practicality of the monks and the fierce indifference of the land.

A wannabe "holy man" once came to Abba Macarius in the monastery at Scete, seeking a shortcut to sanctification. "I've only got three days to spend here," he said. "But I want to learn how to be a Desert Father just like you." The abbot's amused response was to send him into the desert, telling him to abuse the dead at a nearby cemetery. He instructed him to spend the day there calling the dead people names, insulting them in every way possible. Confused by this assignment, the aspiring saint nonetheless did as he was told.

The next day the abbot assigned him the task of *praising* the same people he had cursed the day before. When the man came back at the end of that day, reporting once again that not a single one of the dead had responded, Macarius remarked that they must indeed be holy people. "You insulted them and they did not answer; you applauded them and they said nothing. Go and do likewise," said Macarius, "and you, too, will be a holy man." The man's spiritual journey had to begin with a good dose of desert detachment, an indifference to what other people think, and a realization of his own inconsequence.

One of the monks' most important tasks was that of disillusioning those who came into the desert in search of an easily acquired spirituality. The Fathers frequently disguised their own sanctity, pretending to be fools or gluttons when gawkers came to venerate their saintliness. They preferred to be dismissed as hypocrites than to be acclaimed as exemplars of piety. They knew the spiritual life wasn't about *them*. Having been stripped of all delusions of grandeur, they required the same of the beginners who came to them for direction.

If the desert teachers were hard, the desert itself was harder yet, disillusioning unwary sightseers and neophytes. A young novice in sixth-century Palestine, trudging up the dry waste of the Wadi Qelt near Jericho, would glimpse Saint George's monastery in the distance with dismay. That's where he would be living—in that daunting structure jutting out from the rock halfway up a cliff in the middle of nowhere. This is what a young Gaelic monk would have felt in tenth-century Ireland, approaching the forlorn and rocky island of Skellig Michael off the coast of County Kerry. His head hanging over the side of the tossing boat, he would fear he'd come to the brink of hell in entering the monastic life. All novices in spiritual things eventually discover as much. They experience dread at a wilderness that proves to be more than they expected, a hollowness at knowing they plainly aren't up for the task.

In each of the great religious traditions, wisdom begins with disillusionment. In Buddhism, it is the invitation to jettison the empty assurances of the past, starting over with Beginner's Mind. In Hinduism, it is the notion of *maya*, recognizing the "illusion" of our attachment to matters of insignificance. Embracing the life of the spirit is a matter of waking from sleep (*satori*, enlightenment) or being released from an imprisonment of which we had been unaware (*moksha*, liberation).

Dealing with Grandiosity

There comes a point in our lives—usually amid the illusion that we've already learned what we most need to know—that we begin, like Dante, our journey

into the dark woods. We proceed with a confident self-assurance, even grandiosity, wanting to prove ourselves. We're eager to test our strength against
the elements, to push the soul to its outer edge, seeking the Ultimate. Risk
itself becomes our measure of success.

Setting off from Friends Campground at the base of Laramie Peak that
morning in July, I had thought to myself: This can't be that hard. I know what
I'm doing. Hiking alone in the mountains is a piece of cake. I thought this,
despite the fact that my previous experiences of backcountry hiking hadn't
been all that successful. They'd been marked by a similar degree of over-
confidence. All my life I'd been trying to prove something, either through
adventures into wilderness or through exploits in the spiritual life.

Years ago, after my wife and I were first married, I couldn't wait to take her
up Kearsarge Pass in the High Sierras, sharing the joy of high country. There
at 12,000 feet, I imagined our gazing onto the sublime wonder of alpine lakes
and granite slopes in the John Muir Wilderness. Another couple we knew
went along with us. They had never been camping at all, but were drawn by
my exuberant accounts of the spiritual experience of mountain hiking. My
naïveté at the time was astounding. From the beginning of the trip, I made
one bad assumption after another, with disastrous consequences for everyone.

I underestimated the effect of rapid altitude change, hadn't anticipated
the possibility of snow coming in late August, and hadn't prepared for any
kind of bad weather. I had assured the other couple that they would be fine in
my extra "tube tent" (a circular piece of plastic). I hadn't known that canister
cook stoves don't work well at high altitudes and low temperatures. Nor had
I brought the kind of food we needed or even pads to put under the sleeping
bags. As a result, we spent a freezing night, cold and hungry with splitting
headaches, the four of us crammed into a two-person tent, covered with tattered plastic whipping in the wind. My wife has seldom gone backpacking
with me again.

A thirst for grandiosity—an expectation of success (usually with minimal
effort)—is a baggage that some of us carry for years. We long to prove ourselves, searching for more than a Walter Mitty world of imagined triumphs.
Our need to excel masks a deep, underlying insecurity. We feel we have to
"shine" even though we know there's no gold within us. Psychoanalyst Alice
Miller describes it as "the drama of the gifted child." I learned it myself in
early childhood.

As a kid growing up, wilderness and spirituality were the two spheres in
which I sought approval. I knew I had to achieve something grand enough
to put at bay the yawning sense of inadequacy that was mine. I was a tall,

skinny kid with glasses, never physically adept (especially at team sports). I was a loner, more comfortable in wilderness. Moreover, my dad was a cop, a "man's man." I needed an arena in which he wouldn't be disappointed in me. Being able to handle myself alone in a scrub pine forest was my way of trying to be good enough. Excelling in spiritual things, on the other hand, was how I gained my mother's approval. She was a born-again Christian. I was able to shine at church, memorizing more Bible verses than the other kids, astounding adults by the depth of my avowed passion for God.

As an only child, in other words, I needed to "stand out," to be what Alice Miller calls a "gifted child." I came late in my parents' lives, representing the promise of a new start after two failed marriages for each of them. Their dream was that I would make up for all the failures they had known in the past. I was the guarantee of the family's future—their "gift." This is the weight a "gifted child" carries. He has to be grandiose to achieve the family dreams, or at least to keep it from ruin.[5]

If and when he fails—when he's thirteen as in my case, when the parents' marriage gets in trouble and the father commits suicide—it's a devastating loss. The child tries to prove for the rest of his life that it hadn't been his fault, but there is never enough he can do to make certain of that. His necessary, if painful, beginning in the spiritual journey is to realize that all his previous efforts at "getting it right" had never been sufficient. Disillusionment is the place where most of us have to start. We learn that none of our efforts can ever satisfy the expectations that were placed on us. Only love allows us to go on from there.

A nineteenth-century French Carmelite, Thérèse of Lisieux, discovered this through the inner struggle of her own spiritual journey. She was able to confess that "God doesn't look so much at the greatness of our actions, nor even their difficulty, but at the love with which we do them."[6] The gifted child learns painfully that she doesn't have to carry the weight of the world. She doesn't have to lead armies and defeat dragons. She only has to love . . . and to accept being loved.

Dealing with my own disillusionment—releasing the dashed hopes that had been attached to my father's dying—has proved to be an unexpected gift. I've had to let go of the need to be grandiose, even at the university where I've been driven to achieve for years. In accepting the courage to be imperfect, I've had to learn that one's worth isn't rooted in one's ability to excel. I can be what little I am, without incrimination. What I accomplish isn't what allows me to be loved. A pint-sized French nun, rediscovered on Laramie Peak, has been my best teacher in this.

Thérèse of Lisieux and the Little Way

Thérèse of Lisieux (1873–1897) isn't what you'd consider a "backpacker's saint." This frail, super-devout Carmelite, known as the Little Flower, died of tuberculosis at the age of twenty-four, spitting up blood in the cloister where she had lived all of her adult life. In spirit, however, she was tough as nails—not unlike the Sisters of Mercy I know who delight in backpacking today. Numerous women's organizations now offer opportunities for wilderness hiking, by the way. These include the Women's Wilderness Institute, Women in the Wilderness, Call of the Wild: Adventure Travel for Women, and Adventures in Good Company. They guide women into the backcountry of Wyoming's Snowy Range, the Great Smokey Mountains, the High Sierras, and the Grand Canyon, respectively. While Thérèse of Lisieux may not have been a hiker, she was certainly no stranger to the wilderness terrain of the spiritual life.

For a long time I thought of her as insufferably sweet. She was known for her sugariness (what the French call *niaiserie*). Catholic theologian Karl Rahner was put off by the "irritating, boring, and repulsive" aura that surrounded her.[7] But I knew she was Dorothy Day's favorite saint and Dorothy had no use for saccharine spirituality. The founder of the Catholic Worker movement considered this French saint's emphasis on "the Little Way" to be profoundly significant, socially and spiritually.

I had been reading both Dorothy and Thérèse prior to the trip up Laramie Peak, and had put notes from them in the journal I carried in my pack. Dorothy was fascinated by Thérèse's emphasis on the importance of being little, attending to little things, valuing little people. "Each small task of everyday life is part of the harmony of the universe," the French saint had said. "It is by little and by little that we are saved," Dorothy added, summarizing her own spiritual journey.[8]

What struck me in reading Thérèse's *Autobiography* was her honesty. She was a hard-nosed realist about herself. I could identify with the contradictions in her character. On the one hand, the woman was driven by an enormous sense of grandiosity. She had been a proud, almost arrogant child, knowing she was "born for great things." She determined early in her life to be a "great saint."[9] Thérèse envisioned herself as a modern-day Joan of Arc, embracing heroic action and martyrdom. In the convent she wrote and performed short dramas in which she played the role of the fifteenth-century national heroine.

Being part of a family with high spiritual expectations contributed to her lofty aspirations. Both of her parents had tried to enter the religious life before they were married but were turned down by the communities to which they had applied. Their subsequent marriage and devout home life produced five daughters, all of whom became nuns. They hoped one might be a saint. Thérèse was the youngest, born when her mother was forty and miraculously surviving severe illness as an infant. She was the golden child of promise, a "little queen" who grew into all that was expected of her. She is known today as Saint Thérèse of the Child Jesus and the Holy Face.

In her autobiography she tells an illuminating story from her early childhood. She was four years old when her older sister Leonie offered her and her seven-year-old sister Celine a basket of hand-me-down dolls and doll clothes. Thérèse says that Celine chose a ball of yarn from the basket and "was pleased" with it. She herself then took all the rest (basket and all), saying, "I choose everything." She explains in recalling the event that she never wanted to do anything half-heartedly. She chose not to live a life of measured increments, to be merely "a saint by halves." She wanted *everything* that God willed, being prepared to suffer anything for God's sake.[10] Like Rainer Maria Rilke's passion for life's totality, she too would have confessed: "I want to love things as no one has thought to love them."[11] She had to do it all, and do it to perfection.

Given the history of her family, one might interpret this impetuous desire to excel as expressing Alice Miller's drama of the gifted child. Her drivenness to succeed was, in part at least, the effort of a daughter anxious to fulfill her parents' dreams. If this was the case, however, Thérèse managed to balance her compulsion for the grandiose with an equal need to be insignificant. The tension between grandiosity and littleness is what intrigues me about her.

At times of disappointment in her life, as for example, when Pope Leo XIII rejected her request to enter the convent at an earlier age than usual, she comforted herself with the assurance that she was loved despite her failure to shine. "Great deeds are forbidden me," she lamented. Yet she came to accept "being little" as enough. She began to realize that she was loved for herself alone, delighting in her role as God's "plaything"—a mere ball in which God takes pleasure, tossing it around happily without its having to accomplish anything. This spawned her attraction to "the Little Way." She found it a great relief that she didn't have to be grandiose. "The splendor of the rose and the whiteness of the lily do not rob the little violet of its scent nor the daisy of its simple charm. If every tiny flower wanted to be a rose, spring would lose its loveliness."[12]

That's the kind of sweet reflection you might expect of a saint. But while her sentimental piety drives me crazy at times, I'm hit between the eyes by the tough, no-nonsense quality of its insight. The woman's fierce intensity is striking, in her contradictory thirst for greatness and delight in insignificance. She boldly claimed as her own "the vocation of the warrior," as well as that of "the priest, the apostle, the doctor, and martyr." The inconsequential Little Flower was at the same time a well-trained soldier, relentless in her courage and obedience. She didn't have to be coddled or rewarded for faithfulness. She relished being inconspicuous. The "gifted child" knew she had nothing to prove. Simply "being" was enough.

The warrior energy of the French saint was especially apparent in the last few months of her life. During this time she went through a period of intense doubt and desolation. She wrestled with a God she wasn't able to know, couldn't see, and wasn't even sure existed. In her dark night of the soul, the nun of the Little Way knew absolutely nothing of consolation. She received no approval, no appreciation of the grand sacrifice of her life. God remained distant and uncommunicative. "If you only knew what darkness I am plunged into," she wrote to one of her sisters. Seeking comfort at least in the thought of dying, the voice of despair dismissed even that as an empty hope, offering "a night darker still, the night of utter nothingness!" "I feel no joy," she wrote, "I sing only of *what I wish to believe*."[13]

Yet in this impenetrable darkness she remained a warrior of disappointment. She later confessed, in fact, that she had never encountered more fully the mercy of the Lord than in the depths of that abandonment. Her account of this season of disillusionment is remarkably akin to the experience of her namesake, Mother Teresa of Calcutta, a century later. The "Saint of the Gutters" who received the Nobel Peace Prize for her work with the poor in India also struggled (for most of her life) with a sense of spiritual darkness. She, too, wrote in a letter to one of her confessors, "In my soul I feel just that terrible loss of God not wanting me—of God not being God—of God not existing." "Within me everything is icy cold," she lamented. "If I ever become a saint, I will surely be one of darkness."[14]

Amazingly enough, both Teresas endured the silence and absence of God, perceiving the experience as ultimately a gift. "I am perfectly happy to be nobody even to God," said the Albanian Missionary of Charity.[15] Neither of them required divine approval to know that their lives counted for something, that they were loved. In disillusionment, they exercised a naked trust, finding love itself to be a harsh and dreadful thing—having nothing to do with previous efforts of achievement.

Wilderness and the Elusive Presence of God

I had opportunity to reflect on this striking defeat of grandiosity—this fierce indifference to approval—while camping on Laramie Peak. I'd been surprised that afternoon at how quickly the trail emptied as the sun began to set. People were anxious to get off the mountain, not wanting to be caught on the peak after dark. There are always more day-hikers on a trail than backpackers, of course. It's not uncommon to pass numerous people during the day, yet have the backcountry completely to yourself at night. But this time the solitude was disarming.

I wasn't yet used to hiking alone at the time. I hadn't learned to take the necessary precautions or acquire the humility that wilderness teaches. My need for solitude in the wilds simply overrode any need for caution. I hadn't yet been disillusioned. I still thought of myself as competent in handling whatever problems might come my way.

With the approach of darkness, however, a sense of being watched began to play on my mind. We all know there are places where humans don't belong, especially as night comes on. The vast loneliness of Laramie Peak was disturbing. Deep in the Medicine Bow Wilderness of Wyoming, my image as professor, spiritual seeker, and self-styled "wilderness backpacker" counted for nothing. I could have been just another stray mule deer, with a lion studying its movements from behind dark firs. It was an unsettling feeling. I would experience it again years later on a trip up Lion Gulch in the Colorado Rockies.

I've never seen a mountain lion in the wilds, but one may well have seen me. I marvel at the possibility. That night on Laramie Peak I felt hemmed in by its shadows. I'd run out of space as the mountain narrowed at its crest. There was nowhere to run. It might have been all in my mind, but imagined dangers are as real to the psyche as those that are genuine.

The persona I'd tried to cultivate as a "proficient outdoorsman" disintegrated. I had no tangible reason for feeling uneasy, but knew I'd gotten in over my head. I had wandered into Mussorgsky's "Night on Bald Mountain," with a felt-but-unseen presence lurking in the darkness. I was at the place where every novice has to begin.

What happens when a "gifted child" finds himself in a wilderness where he's stripped of any way of proving his worth? What does he do when there's nothing he *can* do, when there's no audience to applaud his performance, when he faces a cold, silent indifference, if not hostility? His world falls to pieces. The soul hungry for approval starves in a desert like that. It reduces the compulsive achiever to something little, utterly ordinary. Only then is he able to be loved.

Fully aware of his inconsequence, he awaits the belligerent gaze of the "other," expressing disapproval from across the room or from deep within forest shadows. Yet having expected a disparaging glare, he suddenly glimpses—to his amazement—a smile instead. Everything changes. Instead of rejection, he encounters a radical grace. He has been "seen," unaccountably, through loving eyes, without the slightest hint of hostility.

The Hindus call it an experience of *darshan*, of seeing and being seen by the holy. Tony de Mello speaks of prayer as a matter of "beholding the one beholding you . . . and smiling." He draws on one of Teresa of Avila's favorite exercises in meditation, imagining Jesus as gazing at her. "*Mira que te mira*," she says. "Notice him looking at you . . . with the deepest pleasure." Poet William Cowper put it this way: "I seem forsaken and alone, / I hear the lion roar; / And every door is shut but one, / And that is Mercy's door."[16]

As darkness fell on Laramie Peak, I had little hope of such an outcome. I found an open space between fallen trees where I spread my sleeping bag on a bed of thick green moss. There I burrowed into a makeshift nest, watching and listening as night came on. Pulling the bag over my head at last, I asked to be protected from my foolishness in having come to such a place. To my astonishment, I slept through the night like a baby. Waking at dawn, I knew I had been safely passed by, if I'd been threatened at all.

In C. S. Lewis' Narnia tales, Aslan—the Lion of the Tribe of Judah— walks through the night over the mountains of a newly formed world, breathing its creatures into life. When fear of an encroaching darkness later grips the hearts of those in his care, the great lion speaks "in the low voice which was nearest to his growl," saying, "Peace." In that moment "the earth seemed to shake a little and every living thing in the grove became still as stone."[17] As dawn came, the world broke again into song.

I have no idea whether *any* sort of lion passed by as I slept that night on Laramie Peak. Was it a 150-pound cougar, the Aslan of my imagination, or nothing at all? Whatever I make of the event, I know that trifling with the sacred (and with wilderness) is a dangerous thing. My night there might have ended very differently. You sometimes pay for your mistakes in taking safety for granted. All things wild come without guarantees. Venturing into the wilderness that is God, you never know what you're dealing with, says Rumi.

The Persian poet and mystic tells of a farmer who tied his ox in the stable one night before going into supper. While he was gone, a lion strolled into the stable, ate the ox, and lay down in its place. When the farmer came back later to check on his animal in the dark, he rubbed his hand over its shoulder, down its back, and along its flank. The lion remained perfectly still, thinking to himself, "If a light were lit and this man could suddenly see, he would die of the discovery. He's stroking me so familiarly, because he thinks I'm his ox."[18] There are times when you have no idea of the mystery you've encountered in the wilds. You've met something you cannot fathom.

When it comes to wilderness spirituality, you never know what you're getting into. It may well lead to your undoing. But if you're lucky enough to make the necessary mistakes, and to survive them as well, you may find—at the heart of your disillusionment—that you had been loved all along.

5

Desire: Rockpile Mountain Wilderness and Thomas Traherne

To crave and to have are as like as a thing and its shadow.
For when does a berry break upon the tongue as sweetly as
when one longs to taste it?

MARILYNNE ROBINSON[1]

The thirst in our souls is the attraction put out by the water
itself.

JELALUDDIN RUMI[2]

A WILDERNESS PLACE triggers desire in unexpected ways. It plants an itch that can't easily be satisfied. Take Rockpile Mountain in the Arcadia Valley region of the St. Francois Mountains in southeast Missouri. I've hiked its wilderness area numerous times, taking Little Grass Mountain Trail south to hook up with the loop trail that circles from the rocky shut-ins near the mountain's foot to the strange "rock pile" at its crest. The place awakens desire in me every time I come.

It's nothing remarkable—a 1,305-foot knoll covered by an oak-hickory forest. Its name derives from a circle of blue granite stones atop its ridge. White settlers noticed the oddity in the early nineteenth century. Prior to their arrival, Osage and Illini peoples lived in the area, descendants of earlier Oneonta and Mississippian cultures in central Missouri and eastern Illinois. Whatever purpose it originally served, the place carries a sense of mystery to this day.

The stone circle is fifteen feet in diameter. An anvil-shaped rock stands near its center, with two small cedar trees nearby. Archaeologists have excavated similar stone circles in the upper Midwest. They appear to have been ceremonial sites, possibly used by flint knappers in making stone tools or weapons. It is a good place for cutting to the heart of things—for recognizing desire as one of the soul's hardest disciplines.

Giving yourself to desire isn't an exercise for the faint-hearted. The desert novice who passes through disillusionment is gripped by a hunger for what she has sensed but never seen in the surrounding wilderness. Stripped of grandiosity (her initial confidence in mastering challenges), she's had a taste of something grander yet. But she lacks proof that the "elusive lion" of her deepest desire was anything more than her imagination. Keeping desire aflame in the absence of what one seeks requires stoutness of heart. It demands the relinquishment of lesser longings as well.

A holy desire isn't a warm feeling that sweeps you off your feet. It is a discipline, something you *choose*. The greatest desires are beyond fulfillment. They thrive on the wanting itself. The desolation of "not having" simply enhances one's patience in waiting. "When I am in the cellar of affliction," wrote Puritan writer Samuel Rutherford, "I look for the Lord's choicest wines."[3]

That's why the archetype of the warrior is as crucial to a spirituality of desire as the archetype of the holy fool. The warrior makes a fierce commitment to what is most worth loving, whether it's attainable or not. He cuts through whatever gets in the way. The fool, on the other hand, throws himself with playful abandon into every fleeting taste of longing. He embraces the moment, celebrating the part as if it were the whole. Rockpile Mountain, at different times in my life, has taught me both ways of exercising desire.

I've stood beside the stone circle at its summit, knowing there were things I had to walk away from. I've knelt at its anvil rock, asking for the hardness of stone in cutting through indecisiveness in my life. I've spent a cold, rainy night amid those stones, as part of a vision quest that changed the way I perceived desire altogether. The mountain's stone ring has been a place of sacrifice in my life. It evokes the courage to cut and run, choosing what's most important.

At other times I've camped down below, on the knoll's western side, where rivulets from the hollows run together after a hard rain, cascading through rocky shut-ins. Water tumbles around boulders the size of small cabins, through swirling pools filled with fallen leaves and frog spawn. It's a place of moss-covered rhyolite, granite glades, and limestone caves. Water dances there, on its way to the St. Francois River, the Mississippi, and eventually the Gulf of Mexico. I'm tempted to dance myself in its boisterous playfulness. I think of Mephistopheles' question of Goethe's Faust and wonder if *this* is what it's all about. Sometimes your life comes to a stop in a given moment, and you're ready to say: "Yes, this is all I need. I'm satisfied at last . . . in a rowdy Ozark wilderness." The shut-ins invite you to play the fool. Like I said: Rockpile Mountain triggers desire in very different ways.

The Burden of Longing

Hunger is a weight we bear as well as a joy we celebrate. We hike into wilderness with the accumulated desires of the past. We carry our own twisted longings and those of our parents, our lovers, and our children as well. We're the "walking wounded," battle-scarred by desires we've carried throughout our lives. More than once I've lugged a wounded father on my back up Rockpile Mountain. Father and mother wounds are handed down to us, filled with frustrated desires we still try to satisfy.

Carefully guarded secrets of parents and grandparents, with all their hidden desires, are transmitted from one generation to the next. The children and grandchildren inadvertently act them out if they aren't brought to consciousness. I carry, for example, the secrets of a dad who had been beaten by an alcoholic father, a dad who never became the lawyer his grandfather had dreamed he would be, a dad who killed a German soldier in face-to-face combat on the fields of Flanders. I bear his disappointment and guilt at having betrayed an earlier wife and leaving a five-year-old daughter to run away with my mother. I've inherited the longings of a man who lied about his past, changing his name to escape a life he couldn't bear living.

I also carry—in the pack I tote into wilderness—the anguish of a mother who had been sexually abused by a family member as a child, who had been raped as a teenager and forced to marry the man who raped her. I bear the suppressed longings of a mom who gave up one child for adoption and aborted another, who spent the rest of her life dreaming of starting over again. All these are secrets learned secondhand, of course, never directly from my parents. Unfulfilled longings are passed on through wounds, not words. They have no voice of their own.

John Bradshaw in his book *Family Secrets* says the first sibling in a family will act out the father's secrets. The second will take on the unresolved emotional baggage of the mother. An only child—like myself—will assume both.[4] How, then, do we recognize the hidden desires that we carry for others, and how do we release them? How can I abandon the unconscious need to hide and conceal, to lie about who I am, for example—even when it's unnecessary? These are the wounds of the *father* unwittingly showing up, for some reason, in *my* actions. The things we carry possess an awful inexorability. Tim O'Brien, in his gut-wrenching account of a platoon of American soldiers in Vietnam, says, "They carried all they could bear, and then some, including a silent awe for the terrible power of the things they carried."[5] Many of us do that.

Wilderness backpacking, along with counseling and the men's groups I've been a part of, has allowed me, over time, to release these wounds back into the wilds. I let them go, like injured animals treated at the wolf sanctuary in Eureka, Missouri, and eventually returned to wilderness. It's not far wrong to think of our wounds as creatures who've wandered into our lives from out in the wilds. Doing so gives them the respect they deserve. It also allows us to identify ourselves as separate from them. There is a danger in trying to hold them too close.

The Desert Fathers and Mothers found the wild terrain of the Egyptian desert a good place for doing such work. The desert knows desire, after all; it's a landscape forever thirsty. The monks were remarkably attentive to the wounds (to all the baggage of desire) they brought with them into the wilds. These included the forced marriages or affairs from which they had fled, military service they were escaping, family problems that had been overwhelming. Entering the monastic life, they soon realized they weren't leaving the world behind them. They carried the old desires with them, like shadows in the heart—things they now had to face resolutely.

They spoke with keen insight, therefore, of the "passions" that derived from their inner wounds. These desires continued to bind them in obsessive behaviors as they nursed old injuries from the past. Abba Poemen observed that such wounds (with their unfulfilled longings) have a way of expressing themselves in four stages of unconscious activity. They first appear in the *heart*, as festering wounds that crop up in our dreams and fantasies. They subsequently show up in the *face*, in passing glances of anger, jealousy, or envy. (Abraham Lincoln said that everyone over forty is responsible for his face. It mirrors everything we carry inside.) Thirdly, said Poemen, inner wounds reveal themselves in *words*, in our sniping at others, our passive-aggressive language. And finally, the wounds appear in our *deeds*. We replicate them in our actions, doing to others what had been done to us. What isn't transformed, in other words, *will* be transmitted. That's the danger of unacknowledged desire.[6]

The desert teachers understood that desire itself isn't the problem. Holy desire is necessary and good, emerging out of our deepest humanity. It is rooted physically in the liver, they thought, at the core of our being. Sinful desires, by contrast, arise from the lobe of the liver, that part that God told Moses to burn in offering animal sacrifice (Exodus 29:13).[7] Recognizing the body as a source and teacher of desire, they emphasized the importance of distinguishing between true and false longings. The desert discipline they employed in the stringent training of body and mind aimed at strengthening the one and relinquishing the other.

Evagrius, for example, warned that these passions crop up as nagging thoughts or fantasies (*logismoi*) that crave the satisfaction of inner desires. His list of such thoughts became the foundation of the seven deadly sins. He embraced a discipline that stripped these compulsive longings of their fixation on specific outcomes. He knew that the feverish attainment of any single object of desire can never answer the yearning of the soul. Lesser longings have to be transformed into a larger yearning for *infinite* satisfaction—for something never fulfilled, but continually enhanced by every partial realization of its joy. The goal, then, isn't to eradicate desire, but to enlarge and refocus it, being able to see (and to celebrate) God in all things. Teilhard de Chardin spoke of it as a transition "from simple life to 'Life Squared,'" a multiplication of desire that becomes exponential.[8]

Rockpile Mountain has repeatedly been a place for releasing and transforming desire in my experience. At its stone circle, in a fog-shrouded dawn, I've wrestled with the longings left over from a suicide in the family. I've confronted what I'd learned as a child about men not accepting responsibility. I've acknowledged my reluctance in embracing risk. These rocks, thrust to the surface by years of frost action atop this mound in an old-growth forest, are half-suppressed memories. They signify the geological shifts in my own life.

The night before my father took his life we sat together in a church prayer meeting. I was thirteen years old. The congregation sang his favorite hymn, "The Old Rugged Cross." I suppose I should have noticed something unusual that night, but there were always tears in his eyes on hearing that song. We sat together, my dad, my mom, and myself. I suspect he was fixing in his mind an image of what he'd always dreamed of having but knew was now slipping away. Earlier that afternoon he had been interrogated by the FBI about money missing from the bank where he worked as a guard. I never learned any of the details, but presumably his past had caught up with him. The desires that he and my mother had nurtured in starting over again came crashing down around them. He shot himself the next morning. I was left to pick up the pieces.

It was a .38 Police Special that took my father's life, but the secrets were what destroyed him. He was a victim of wounds (and of desires) that he couldn't acknowledge, much less fulfill. The father wound, the mother wound, whatever wounds we carry in our lives entail far more than any specific event. It's not the suicide itself, the physical abuse, the emotional neglect, or the painful divorce that hurts us most. It's the secretive nature of the wounds, the desires embedded within them. Our deepest pain is that we aren't allowed to talk about it.

This keeps us repeating the agony over and over again in order finally to get it right. But healing doesn't come until we give up the illusion that it's our job to satisfy the unmet desires of the past. Even if we had done everything we could have to satisfy our parents' longings, it wouldn't have been enough. The yearning that lingers in unhealed wounds is insatiable.

What is necessary for wholeness, then, is nothing less than an explosion of desire—a release of these reckless, obsessive longings in exchange for a much larger Desire that is never satisfied, yet endlessly delights. The psychological (and spiritual) importance of wilderness is its ability to model both sides of this exchange. At times in my life, Rockpile Mountain has been willing to accept all the unfulfilled longings I was able to leave on its slopes. At the same time (often on the same trip), its austere beauty has stirred within me a far greater Desire for what I can't even name. It triggers an infinite yearning, the hope of finding an unaccountable love in the shadows I fear most.

Much of the "threat" we experience in hiking into wilderness is our own inner turmoil rising to consciousness. If we can identify what comes up for us, we can use the wild terrain as a vast "sink" for the reception of unfulfilled desires. Its immense emptiness, its seeming indifference, invites the release of things we've been holding too long. Ecologically, the forests around us already serve as a sink for carbon emissions, absorbing the consequences of a consumer society given to impetuous desire. But trees, in their quiet presence, are also able to receive whatever we need to release in terms of misspent passion. We can pour out endless frustration in exchange for an equally endless longing. The welcoming void of wilderness gives birth to inexplicable yearning. It opens us to a mystery we can't get enough of.

Triduum on Rockpile Mountain

This happened for me one year as I hiked into the Rockpile Mountain Wilderness with a book by Thomas Traherne, the seventeenth-century English metaphysical poet. Traherne is one of the grandest celebrants of desire in the history of spirituality. He writes with extraordinary passion about the natural world's ability to arouse a longing for God.

His *Centuries of Meditation* are a series of reflections on God's presence in nature, written over the last few years of his life.[9] The world for him was a laboratory for practicing the awakening and loosening of desire. He knew that wanting is everything in the spiritual life, more important even than having. Spiritual teachers from Gregory of Nyssa to William of St-Thierry had long insisted, in fact, that to want *is* to have. A willingness to live without closure, in the hope of continuously expanding desire, is the end as well as the beginning of one's journey into God. Bernard of Clairvaux had claimed, "The one who seeks for God, has already found Him."[10] Traherne himself knew that the heart's deepest Desire is its own reward.

Yet he also knew that coming to such knowledge requires a studied practice in continually finding (and releasing) God in the beauty of a brown trout breaking the sunlit surface of the River Wye, in the fierce majesty of waves crashing on the rocks at Swansea. That's what the world is *for*, said Traherne: the light touch of enjoyment in any given moment. A "catch and release" spirituality of this sort is how we learn the pleasure of Desire itself. The world is shot full of splendors we're never able to possess. But we *can* enjoy them, and to the hilt, by delighting in the immediate experience of "wanting" as itself a gift.

"You never enjoy the world aright," he said, "till everything in it is more your treasure than a king's exchequer full of gold and silver. You never enjoy the world aright, till the sea itself flows in your veins. You never enjoy the world aright, till you see all things in it so perfectly yours that you cannot desire them any other way."[11] Accepting (and loving) the world precisely as it *is* (without owning a single part of it) provides a practice in the mystery of wanting and not having. It is a pianist's five-finger exercise in learning the love of God.

Traherne spoke of desire as the essence of God's being: "You must Want like a God that you may be satisfied like God. Were you not made in his image?" he asked. "His wants put a luster upon his enjoyments and make them infinite."[12] We don't usually think of God as "wanting" anything, given the distant immutability we attribute to the deity. Yet it is out of this longing, endemic to the Holy Trinity, that the created world emerges. God *wanted* hawksbill turtles and humpback whales, columbines and Queen Anne's lace, angels and human beings, splendors and companions of every sort. All are incurably creatures of desire, wanted into being by the restless ardor of God's own heart.

Everything is an answer to that longing. "The visible world is the body of God," Traherne insisted. A passion for interdependence fills it all. Desire permeates the macrostructure of the universe. Physicist Brian Swimme speaks of the allurement "that excites lovers into chasing each other through the night, that pulls the parent out of bed for the third time to comfort a sick child." We see it in the Hubbell Space Telescope's photographs of the Eagle Nebula, where new stars are being born. Massive clouds of hydrogen atoms come rushing together by gravitational attraction. In the process, they are stripped of electrons, fusing to form helium ions as they release enormous amounts of energy in a burst of brilliant light.[13]

Our planet shimmers with desirability, says cellular biologist Ursula Goodenough: "Fireflies pulse, houseflies beat their wings, moths send out musk, fish dance, frogs croon, birds display feathers and song, mammals strut and preen."[14] These "wants [are] the bands and cements between God and us," says Traherne. Yet they link the universe together as well.[15] Allurement pervades the world at every level. Our panting for God is but an echo of God's own panting for us. Thomas Traherne's universe was aflame with longing. Recalling Augustine's response to God, he exclaimed, "You touched me, and I am set on fire."[16]

I hit the trail with his book in tow on the morning of Good Friday that year. I had two days of backpacking ahead of me, wanting to test the authenticity of his words against a forest of white oak and shortleaf pine. With luck I'd be back in time for the Easter Vigil on Saturday night in the college church at the Jesuit university where I teach. The weather that April weekend had suddenly turned warm. Redbud trees and dogwoods were in full bloom. Spring in the Ozarks is hard to resist.

But it did nothing for me that morning. The pack frame weighed heavy on my shoulders. The trail bent uphill more than usual. I felt a headache coming on. The idea of carrying forty extra pounds on an empty stomach wasn't as appealing as it had been the night before. Besides, I hauled along a lot of other baggage from a busy semester, a host of family concerns (old as well as new), and a need for solitude denied too long.

By the time I reached the creek above the shut-ins, set up camp, and broke fast with a light supper, my headache was worse than ever. The kindness of an evening campfire, a full moon rising, and the loveliness of the night were lost on me. Unable to sleep, I grudgingly read Traherne by candlelight, with little insight and still less pleasure. Exhausted at last, I lapsed into unconsciousness sometime late in the night. I'd encountered the slow, throbbing pain of Good Friday in a way I hadn't anticipated.

The next morning I woke up feeling better, though still listless—wondering why I'd even come on this trip. I walked down the creek through the shut-ins, stumbling over rocks and skirting pools of water. I tore my shirt on the branches of a dead cedar tree and finally sat, disgusted, on a huge boulder overlooking the last and largest of the pools. A noisy waterfall splashed behind me. Sunlight glared on the water below. Bored and irritated, I opened the book once again.

Looking back on it now, Traherne's volume had been a good choice for reading on a Holy Saturday in April. There I was, stuck in the middle of Triduum—the three liturgical days that move from Christ's death to his resurrection. If April is the cruelest month, as they say, a Holy Saturday in April is the hardest day of all. Death lies just behind (still fresh) and resurrection (highly unlikely) is still far off. It's a day of endless waiting, stretching on (it seems) to infinity. Life sucks on a Holy Saturday in April.

Such is the human condition, I suppose: trapped in the middle space—the void of that liturgical eternity. Looking back on trampled hopes, we can't imagine anything better ahead. There I sat, frozen in time, shouldering the collective longings of the past. I had yearned all my life to be the son who might have saved his father's life, to accomplish what a mother had never dared to dream, to discover a forgiveness and healing that had eluded one generation after another.

Wallowing that Holy Saturday in all the unsatisfied longings of the past, I sat on a rock above a shimmering pool at the foot of Rockpile Mountain. Thomas Traherne was inviting me to something crazy at the time, to the fool's celebration of the "now." Amid the riotous beauty of an Ozark backcountry, he was summoning me to reckless abandonment. He was urging that I give myself to Joy . . . in the full awareness of all the *unrealized* joys in my life. To embrace what he called felicity despite a world full of endlessly unmet needs. To choose happiness as if it depended on nothing more than God's astonishing presence in that moment alone.[17]

I yearned for his irrepressible joy, but held back from it, too. The idea of opening myself to love in the recklessness of the moment—against all the evidence of unfulfilled loves in my life—seemed naïve. The wilderness was alive with attractions. A Presence beckoned. I *wanted* to respond. But I was chained to old, unfinished desires. I feared risk, having learned that it's never safe to give oneself to love.

Felicity as Seen Through the Cross

Traherne's abandonment to felicity was a hard-won struggle in his own life. This seventeenth-century Anglican poet was a product of the Welsh borders, like other metaphysical poets of his day—George Herbert, Henry Vaughan, and John Donne. The matchless beauty of a Herefordshire landscape with rolling hills and hedgerows had prompted his quest for a still more perfect Beauty. On an early morning at dawn, he would gaze on the "mythic oaks and elm trees" beyond the River Lugg and be transfixed by what he called *Felicity*. This he defined as our deepest humanity—the breaking open of the soul to beauty, our being stunned by a yawning capacity for boundless enjoyment. Felicity is a down payment on the satisfaction of infinite desire. It is the earth's mirroring of God's own inexhaustible delight.

Traherne had experienced in his lifetime (1638–1674) both the horrors of the English Civil War and the beauty of the Welsh marches where he grew up as a shoemaker's son. Finding God in the space between horror and beauty hadn't been easy. While still young, he had been overwhelmed one night by a sense of terror when caught alone in the open fields as a storm blew up. The threat of the dark night, however, engendered desire as well. He went to Oxford seeking proof of God's existence, but found it only later—among the "ravishing green trees" of Credenhill, where he served as rector of an Anglican parish.

Walking up the steep wooded hill behind St. Mary's old stone church, he glimpsed the meadowlands beyond and marveled at the happiness welling up within him. He imagined himself "the sole heir of the whole world," as if it had been created for him alone. The miracle of felicity—the power of taking exquisite delight—was, for him, the greatest proof of God's existence. It lent a radiance to everything in the world. Our highest nobility as humans, he said, is our insatiable longing for beauty.[18]

Yet he understood that in a universe run by desire, many wants are never fulfilled, or fulfilled only at the expense of others. Not all atoms combine to create stars, nor does every firefly discover a mate. In Traherne's day, wandering wolves attacked red deer in the English countryside. In the shut-ins at Rockpile Mountain, sharp-eyed kingfishers snatch minnows from dark green pools. In a world of tangled want, individual longings are often co-opted by more powerful interests. Satisfied desire in one sphere means loss in another.

How do we embrace God's infinite desire in a world of frustrated yearning? How do we affirm the existence of Love in a cosmos where individual loves go unfulfilled? These were questions I had carried all my life. Traherne's answer was that God shares in all of it. God takes on the thwarted longings of every creature at enormous personal expense. At the heart of his *Centuries*, deeper even than its celebration of felicity, is the claim that God assumes the agony of all twisted desire and unfulfilled yearning. In the cross of Christ we encounter the "silent footsteps of innumerable sufferings." There we discover "the Center of Desires," an "abyss of wonders." At the cross a universe of soul-racking desire is absorbed into the churning heart of God's own love.[19]

Traherne's vision of the world is no Pollyanna celebration of giddy enjoyment. He affirms felicity in a world where we "eat and devour one another."[20] He can do this because he knows that God's grandest moment is the embrace of the world's greatest pain. "God never gained more glory than when he lost all glory," Traherne insists.[21] Felicity emerges out of God's own reckless participation in unfulfilled desire. It's the courage of leaping (with God) into a happiness not yet realized, but firmly rooted in God's relentless passion for love. Only there can we comprehend the dark side of a universe of competing wants, where felicity is God's hard-earned answer to a world of wounded desire.

As I sat on the rock that morning, it proved harder and harder to resist the jubilance of Traherne's poetry, much less the falling water of an Ozark stream on a warm spring day. The poet warned me that those who "put off felicity with long delays are to be much suspected." I felt his rebuke.[22] I knew at last that I had to act on what I'd been reading. My body, at least, demanded a response to the beauty around me, insisting that I forget everything else and jump. In the midst of a pulsing Ozark wilderness—in the face of all the reasons *not* to give myself to desire—I started pulling off shoes and clothes, preparing to leap into that iridescent pool shining in the noonday sun. Scattering clothes every which way, I failed to notice Traherne's book precariously balanced on the sloping rock nearby. That's when it happened!

To my horror, the university library's copy of the Clarendon Press edition of Traherne's *Centuries* began sliding down the rock and into the water ahead of me! As if the author and his book were crying out, "HERE'S how it's done!! THIS is what felicity looks like!! Wheeeeeeee, follow me!!" And so I did, screaming as I hit the ice-cold water, grabbing the book before it sank out of sight. The water took my breath away, but the rescue operation was a success. I spent the next hour sitting on the rock, butt-naked in the April sun, leafing page by page through the book like a fool, wiping off each one with my T-shirt. I imagined Traherne laughing with me on every page.

What happened in that moment as I spied Traherne's book sliding down the rock was my yielding to a mystery of attractiveness apparent in everything around me. The book itself had succumbed to the irresistible force of gravity. The limbs of cedars nearby were reaching for the sun. Chemoattractant receptors on tiny amoebas in the pool below were picking up the scent of nearby food sources. Pheromones secreted by neighboring yeast cells were announcing their sexual identity to the world, seeking a mate. I was summoned in that instant to a holy desire, there in a vast wilderness with room enough to accept all the crippling desires I could leave behind.

Amid all the reasons *not* to leap, not to risk yourself to desire and its anguish—in spite of all the chances of being hurt yet again—you leap! You do it because God leaps first. God risks failure in love over and over again, on the cross and throughout the universe. The clutching and releasing of desire is the pattern of love everywhere. "Remember," says Rumi, "it is by failures that lovers stay aware of how they're loved. Failure is the key to the kingdom within."[23] Traherne proclaimed it "a happy loss to lose oneself in admiration at one's own felicity and to find GOD in exchange for oneself."[24] The honing (and stripping) of desire is the only true measure of progress in the spiritual life.

I left Rockpile Wilderness that afternoon, making my way back in time for the Easter Vigil service on Saturday night. I sat in dirty clothes in the rear of the dimly lit Gothic church, gazing up (as it were) into tall tree branches on the vaulted ceiling. I listened to the sound of creek water trickling in the font behind me. I noticed sparkling stars over Rockpile Mountain in the candles held by people around me. Surrounded there by yet another Community of Desire, I felt as if I were still in the woods—at a place where passion is rooted in want, where the paschal mystery ends in a felicity unrestrained.

A few weeks later I bought the university library a new copy of Traherne's *Centuries*. With some embarrassment I tried to explain the warped condition in which I'd returned the original. I said that I'd like to keep that copy as my own—the dried-out text that I'd swum with that day in the woods. The pages are still wrinkled, but the volume sits now in the office near my desk, a lyrical reminder of felicity. I think of it as a partner in waiting and longing. It stands poised on a high shelf nearby, in readiness even now to slide over the edge once again.

In the final calculus of desire gained and desire lost, Traherne treasured most the insatiability of those who—as often as they fail—are ever ready to leap again. "For giving me desire, an eager thirst, a burning ardent fire," he prayed in one of the last of his poems, "be Thy name forever praised." Catherine of Siena said that our infinite desire is the only thing infinite that we're ever able to give to God. There's a book in my office that won't allow me to forget that.[25]

Second Leg: Discipline (The Practice of the Wild)

Every path to wholeness requires a discipline, especially for those who pass through wilderness. Quaker writer Richard Foster, in his book *Celebration of Discipline*, distinguishes the "inward disciplines" of meditation, prayer, fasting, and study from the "outward disciplines" of simplicity, solitude, and service.[1] All of these can (and at times must) be practiced in wilderness, as the Desert Fathers and Mothers evidenced long ago.

They went to the desert to learn to delight in spending time alone, to see how lightly they could travel, to ask how available they could be to the present moment. These three elements were central to the spiritual practice they adopted. Having set out on the trail, they were obliged to follow the rules of wilderness. They knew, as wilderness travelers learn, that "If we don't discipline ourselves, the world will do it for us."[2]

6

Solitude: Bell Mountain Wilderness and Søren Kierkegaard

Religion is what one does with his solitude.
ALFRED NORTH WHITEHEAD[3]

No one should go through life without once experiencing healthy, even bored solitude in the wilderness, finding himself depending solely on himself and thereby learning his true and hidden strength.

JACK KEROUAC[4]

IT IS AN uncommon gift to have a mountain to yourself. Pulling up to the trailhead for the Bell Mountain Wilderness Area, I saw no other vehicles parked there and began to hope for as much. I noticed that the dirt road into the area hadn't been graded recently. Another good sign was my having to wipe spider webs from my face every hundred yards or so as I hit the trail. Obviously no one had been there for a while. But the real treat was reaching the top of the mountain and finding nothing. A favorite campsite lay empty, nestled in the rocks just above the treetops. From there you can look out onto thousands of acres of oak- and hickory-covered hills to the east. Not a road or a building in sight, nothing but trees.

Bell Mountain is one of eight protected wilderness areas in Missouri. It is named after a family that once lived and farmed along its 1,700-foot ridge. I'd gotten a late start that day and the sun was going down by the time I set up camp. But sunlight on a late April afternoon, filtered through the yellow-green growth of new leaves, can be stunning.

I sat on a rock ledge, cutting up potatoes, onions, and carrots for mulligan stew, watching shadows creep up the hills across the hollow. Putting the vegetables in a pot, I added fresh basil and rosemary, topped it off with ground beef, and washed it down with a shot of Grand Marnier as night came on. I delight in the solitude of these trips, but I'm not always sworn to a monastic austerity.

Bell Mountain is a good place for the study and practice of solitude. I've sat there for hours with only the dog beside me, watching red-tailed hawks and turkey vultures soar on thermals rising from the forest below. Now and then you'll see a lone eagle high overhead, though generally they nest closer to the river. Bald eagles are common in Missouri, especially in winter. They migrate down the Mississippi River Valley from Canada and the Great Lakes, coming here to mate, nest, and bear young. These "sea-eagles with white heads" (*Haliaeetus leucocephalus*) are solitary birds that mate for life. In late January of each year, people drive up to Lock and Dam 24 in Clarksville, where a kettle of eagles fish the open waters below the dam after ice has covered the river. They are sociable birds, food and family bringing them together. But they're lovers of solitude as well.

Bald eagles are easy to spot from the ground because they don't appear to have any heads or tails. Their white head and tail feathers are practically invisible when seen from below. The term "bald" doesn't refer to a lack of feathers, of course; it comes from the Old English word *balde*, meaning "white." These are birds with amazing eyesight. They can spot a rabbit a mile away at a thousand feet up. With a wingspan of six feet or more, they build huge nests of sticks (sometimes weighing a ton) in high trees to which they return year after year.

They glide on wind currents at 20 to 30 mph but can reach speeds of over 100 mph in diving. To watch an eagle soaring above your perch on a mountain that belongs entirely to you in that moment is a rare gift. But when the shadow of a white-tailed raptor unexpectedly sweeps over the rock where you're sitting, it triggers a memory deep in the reptilian brain. You remember that even the finest joys are tinged with a touch of terror.

The apparent effortlessness of an eagle's flight is something fledglings learn with difficulty. A typical eagle has seven thousand feathers, all made of lightweight keratin, trimmed for aerodynamic lift. Yet 40 percent of young eagles don't make it on their first flight. Their parents don't push them out of the nest, as commonly presumed. What the adult birds do is to hover close to the limb, dangling a tempting fish in front of the young fledgling, enticing it to the edge. Hopefully, as the youngster flaps its wings, trying to balance on the lip of the nest and reach the fish, it breaks into flight as it teeters over the edge. Learning to fly is a solitary and risky business . . . for any of us.

Solitude is the first and most important of three wilderness disciplines that the Desert Fathers took seriously. Learning how to accept being alone, not cluttering one's life with unnecessary things, and not being driven by distractions formed the heart of the wilderness pattern of their spiritual training. Solitude was the hardest of all. Today we're so accustomed to the comfort and security of a world filled with other people that being alone is unsettling. We view "loners" too often as objects of suspicion. Danish philosopher Søren Kierkegaard observed that "The majority of the people are not so afraid of holding a wrong opinion, as they are of holding an opinion alone."[5] We fear being singled out, perceived as different, isolated from the safety (and conformity) of the crowd. The desert monks identified a fear of solitude as a major obstacle to any serious spiritual practice.

The life of the soul thrives in community, but it begins with a radical aloneness before God. Kierkegaard said that faith (to be faith) has to reach beyond the certainties and assurances of the masses. It accepts the dread of unaccompanied loneliness, treading water over 70,000 fathoms, risking oneself with passionate abandon for what is found only in inwardness.[6] Taking pleasure in solitude is the lifeblood of wilderness spirituality.

The Four Gifts of Solitude

Through the years I've come to acknowledge that spending time alone is neither an option nor a self-indulgence for me. It's as important to my well-being as food or sleep. I simply have more of myself to give away when I've spent several hours a day in writing, journaling, or riding the bike to work. The solitude of backpacking goes a long way toward restocking my capacity for sharing with others. Each of us has to negotiate our own dance between the solitary and communal life. It differs for everyone. When we ignore the balance of the two, we run the risk of severe loss to ourselves and to others.

Saints, mystics, and prophets have habitually praised the gifts of solitude. It allows them to gain access to their truest self, to experience the holy at the core of their being, even to connect most deeply with the rest of the natural world. Wisdom teachers from Julian of Norwich to Thomas Merton have expounded the benefits of a solitary life. Søren Kierkegaard was an eloquent celebrant of solitude. I've on occasion stuffed a well-thumbed paperback selection of his *Journals* into my pack.[7] The man's passion and sharp wit have been welcome company at the end of a day on the trail.

In the academic and ecclesiastical climate of nineteenth-century Denmark, Kierkegaard acclaimed solitude as the only way he could sustain his soul in a culture ruled by the vapid exteriority of the crowd. He singled out the "professor" and the "prelate" as prime examples of those who practice a passionless objectivity, avoiding the inner life and any personal investment of themselves. He tells the story of a preacher who inadvertently brought his congregation to tears with one of his sermons. Startled by their emotion, he quickly blurted out, "Children, children, don't weep. It might all be a lie." Kierkegaard contrasts this shallow, acculturated religion of his day (concerned mostly with the approval of people outside of it) with the intensity of early Christians in ancient Rome. Christians today, he laments, "are afraid of being laughed at instead of being put to death." [8] They lack inwardness.

The first gift of solitude is its capacity for separating the individual from the crowd. When you're alone in wilderness, you escape the fretful arena where performance and the search for approval govern so much of your life. There are no expectations to meet, no authorities to please, no audiences to impress. In wilderness, you stand outside of the throng, outside of the pressures of admiration and blame. Only there . . . *outside* . . . are you alone enough to resist being defined by anything external.

"Wherever there is a crowd there is untruth," Kierkegaard declared. "Everything that needs numbers in order to become significant is by that very fact insignificant." Under the pressure of the herd we become intensely self-conscious, aware of our words and actions being judged by others. Whether it's the academy or the popular press or even the church, says Kierkegaard, we're obliged to conform, to identify ourselves as members of a comfortable majority. Society scorns the solitary individual as a threat to the public good. "It is a frightful satire and an epigram on the modern age," he laments, "that the only use it knows for solitude is to make it a punishment, a jail sentence." [9]

If the freedom to stand alone before God (escaping the tyranny of the majority) is the first fruit of solitude, the second is its ability to nurture one's true self, as opposed to the artificial self we market to the crowd. Only in solitude can we attend to the work of "soul-gathering" that's so important in a world of endless activity and anxiety over other people's opinions. The true self is what we already *are*, an identity granted by God alone in the depths of our interiority.

If we don't take the time we need to be alone, it is easy to forget who we are, falling into self-confusion and doubt. When I venture into wilderness, I'm surprised by how much I enjoy my own company. The person I travel with there isn't worried about his performance. He sheds the polished persona he tries so often to project to others. Scribbling in my journal under the shade of a pin oak atop Bell Mountain, I'm as happy as a lark. I want to *be* the person that I am when I'm alone in wilderness.

A third result of solitude, and surely the most intriguing, is how it grants access to the mystery found at the core of our being. The outlandish idea echoing through the history of the saints is that we find God most assuredly in the solitude of our profoundest humanity. Teresa of Avila encountered the divine as she descended into the interior castle of her soul. Augustine proclaimed that God is "more intimate to me than I am to myself, ... more *me* than I am myself." Meister Eckhart went so far as to insist that "The eye [the 'I'] with which I see God is the eye [the 'I'] with which God sees me." Catherine of Genoa declared that "My me is God, nor do I recognize any other me except my God." [10] Bayazid al-Bistami, the ninth-century Persian Sufi, rejoiced in his mystical union with Allah, shouting, "Glory be to me! How great is my majesty!" [11]

They were all astonished by the fact that in plumbing the depths of their being they couldn't finally distinguish where "they" ended and where "God" began. Even John Calvin claimed that knowing God and knowing oneself most deeply are, in the end, the same thing. [12] But this only becomes apparent, the teachers affirm, in a quiet solitude where the self touches the ground of its being.

The fourth and final gift of solitude is the way it connects us to the larger, otherwise hidden community of the natural world. In giving ourselves to a silent aloneness, pulling back from the hubbub of human language and culture, we're aware of the interlocking web that embraces the whole of creation. Paradoxically, genuine community is a sharing of solitudes. The only true self we have to give is one that is grounded in a solitary life. We won't appreciate the unity of which we're already a part until we pull back from the frantic crowdedness of our lives. Annie Dillard discovered this when she locked eyes with a muskrat in an ecstatic moment along Tinker Creek. Aldo Leopold first started to "think like a mountain," recognizing his relationship to everything else, when he gazed into the eyes of a dying wolf.

Several years ago I lay in the grass one night in the yard behind my house, lost in the silence of a contemplative practice. My wife and I live on the edge of the city of St. Louis, where encounters with the wild aren't usually expected. So I was startled when something squeezed my foot through the toe of my shoe. Opening my eyes and sitting up, I found myself face to face with a raccoon. He was as surprised as I was, rearing up on his back feet. Perhaps he had been curious about these human creatures he'd only seen from afar. Coming across this one so very still, perhaps even dead, he decided to see what it felt like.

In the quiet of contemplation, I hadn't been generating the static of human thought that's so disturbing to animals. He must have thought me safe enough to investigate. We stared at each other in astonishment. Then he dropped back onto all fours and calmly made his way across the grass and through the fence. My joy in that moment of shared solitude, crossing the boundaries of species, was a gift I'll not forget.

Meister Eckhart said God's joy is what ties together the whole of creation. It is the delight a horse feels in running through a vast, green meadow. God's pulsating life is as present in a stone or a log, he argued, as it is in human beings. If the stone or log were only aware of this, it would be as blissful as the highest angel. Our task as humans, then, is to appropriate this mystery for ourselves and to share it with others, with *all* the others—with stones and trees . . . and raccoons, too—reveling in the common life that binds our separate solitudes into one.[13]

The Danish Prophet as Solitaire

Prophets, by the nature of their calling, are solitary people. We perceive them as dangerously different, dissociated from others by public opinion if not by personal choice. Søren Kierkegaard (1813–1855) was an object of scorn for much of his life. He had a physical deformity of some sort, possibly related to his having fallen from a tree as a child. But he had a brilliant mind, excelling in the study of theology and philosophy at the University of Copenhagen, where he earned the equivalent of a Ph.D.

Having learned to trust the solitude of his inner life, he found himself reacting to the dominant philosophy of his day, seen in Hegel and what Kierkegaard called the other "systematizers." They reduced Absolute Truth to neatly packaged ideas that stimulated the mind. He wanted, instead, a truth that could change one's life. Turning from the academy to the church, he considered entering the ministry. But he found nothing more authentic or alive in the Lutheran Church of his day. It, too, operated out of habit. "The machine continues to go on," he complained, "despite the spirit having vanished."[14] As a result, he became neither professor nor priest, challenging podium and pulpit alike in his zeal as a writer working from the edges.

Kierkegaard remained an oddity in his day, lampooned in the popular press, dismissed by town as well as gown. But he couldn't keep silent. "When the castle door of inwardness has long been shut and finally is opened," he declared, "it does not move noiselessly like an apartment door which swings on hinges."[15] Not until the mid-twentieth century would he be recognized for his genius as the "father of existentialism."

The man's personal life was tragic, as often happens with a prophet. He fell in love as a young man, becoming engaged to Regina Olsen, the only woman he ever loved. But on his twenty-second birthday, he learned of his father's guilt for some hidden sin. Whether this involved the father's having cursed God for his poverty as a young shepherd boy or a later marital infidelity, we don't know. Søren concluded, however, that a curse rested on the family as a result. This "Great Earthquake," as he called it, led him to break his engagement and to "stand like a lonely pine tree" for the rest of his life. If solitude became the source of his passion, it was also the font of his pain.[16]

The Danish prophet emphasized the value of the solitary life in two particular ways. He said that only in the solitariness of the soul does one exercise the existential *risk* required in a leap of faith. You have to stand alone, out on a fragile edge. Faith has to be practiced by an individual—by *me*, not by "Christians-in-general" or a religiously tinged culture as a whole. In fact, "when all are Christians, Christianity ceases to exist," he claimed.[17] At its best, true religion functions as a minority position, a pain in the ass to both religious and sociopolitical establishments.

He argued, secondly, that only an individual before God can grasp the moral *seriousness* of a life of faith. It isn't a body of thought or a point of view to be casually held. Faith demands a deep investment of the self. Kierkegaard complained that Christendom had downplayed the demands of Christianity by turning the Ten Commandments into little more than lifestyle recommendations. The church no longer took seriously the arduous life that Jesus required of his followers. Christians, in fact, viewed the demands of the Gospel as having intentionally been made a little too severe, like setting the clock ahead a half hour to make sure you weren't late in the morning. You could still sleep in a little if you wanted to.[18]

The Copenhagen gadfly insisted that faith can't be a retreat from rigorous action, nor an intellectual construct entertained by the mind. He complained that too many thinkers build an enormous castle of intricate beliefs, then live their lives in a shack nearby. An authentic life, by contrast, demands bold and daring risk. It doesn't keep lists of other people's accomplishments, like Leporello's inventory of the Don's conquests in Mozart's *Don Giovanni*. Kierkegaard admired the character of Don Juan, the sinner who throws himself into life, seducing women right and left, instead of Leporello, his pious sidekick, who merely follows along, "noting down the time, the place and a description of the girl."[19]

No one becomes truly human by sitting on the sidelines, Kierkegaard said. The sad truth is that "the majority of men are curtailed 'I's'; what is planned by nature as a possibility capable of being sharpened into an 'I' is soon dulled into a third person." He dismissed religious people in particular as lacking in passion, despite all of their articles of belief. They had no capacity to endure isolation, to stand alone as responsible individuals. They were "constantly in need of 'the others,' the herd." [20]

Kierkegaard complained that Christianity in his day had been safely (and innocuously) reduced to an idea stored in the dusty pages of Scripture. What it needs is someone "who, in fear and trembling before God, has the courage to forbid people to read the Bible." It has to be *lived*, not footnoted with meticulous reference to chapter and verse. Downgrading it to a matter of doctrinal correctness misses the point entirely. "Christ has not appointed assistant-professors," he said, "but followers." [21] In this he skewered the entire Protestant enterprise, reforming the Reformers in his call for a renewed intensity of faith.

Returning to the Desert Cell

You can understand why Søren Kierkegaard urged a new appreciation of the monastic life. He said that if Luther had found it necessary to leave the monastery in the sixteenth century, "the first and foremost duty" of the church today is to return to it. When you're immersed in the mass culture of the modern age, taking seriously a personal spiritual practice becomes the highest priority. It isn't accidental that Kierkegaard employed the pseudonym "Johannes Climacus" in writing some of his most important works. The nom de plume of this seventh-century desert monk allowed him to write from the perspective of a wilderness ascetic inviting personal risk. To be human, he avowed, is to accept the dread of one's aloneness before God. [22]

He saw the desert monks as prime exemplars of the importance of silence and solitude in the spiritual life. Spending time alone, adhering to the rule of *stabilitas*, staying in one's place so as to listen to what's going on inside—these are non-negotiables in the work of attending to the soul. "Think of yourself as a dog that has been driven away from the crowd and tied up because he bites and bothers people," said one of the Fathers. [23] Adopt a practice of solitude for the sake of the poor people who have to live with you, if not for yourself.

The monks and nuns continually advised the younger novices to stay in their cells. Remain like a bird sitting on her eggs in the nest, said Amma Syncletica. St. Anthony similarly cautioned: "Just as fish die if they stay too long out of water, so the monks who loiter outside their cells lose the intensity of their inner peace." The Desert Christians knew that taking time to be alone allows things to surface that wouldn't otherwise be available to us. Only then do "we become aware that our worth is not the same as our usefulness," said Henri Nouwen. Only in the deliberate choice of the cell do we discern the difference between the spaciousness of solitude and the isolation of loneliness, the glory of the one and the pain of the other.[24]

In his year of chosen solitude in the wilderness of Patagonia, Robert Kull was able to identify the anxiety he had been carrying for years: "I see how misguided my efforts are to 'get' somewhere. I'm already here. There is nowhere else to go. The *aliveness* I seek is everywhere. I'm always in it and it in me, even though I often don't experience it consciously."[25] Only in solitude could he realize that nothing is alone. Everything belongs.

"There is a huge silence and a great quiet here," Jerome said of his fourth-century journey into the desert expanse west of the Nile.[26] There he learned that silence is the older and wiser sister of solitude. Like the other desert dwellers, he fled the noise and bustling crowds of Rome, seeking the opportunity to be quiet and alone. Both possibilities are increasingly rare in our day.

Genuine silence is profoundly at risk in our culture, says audio-ecologist Gordon Hempton. This is a man who has traveled the world recording the sounds of nature in the wild. He bemoans "the unchecked loss of silence" caused by human encroachment on natural habitats. With chagrin, he points to the "one square inch of silence" that remains in the Hoh Rain Forest of Olympia National Park. It is "arguably the quietest place in the United States," he argues.[27] Everywhere else the hum, if not roar, of technology continues to spread.

Solitude is no easier to come by. Catherine Doherty, writing out of her Russian Orthodox tradition, calls for a return to the practice of maintaining a *poustinia*—"a desert, a lonely place, a silent place"—to which one regularly retreats for prayer. The Russian *starets* (or monastic elders) had done this. Doherty urges its importance for lay people as well. She is especially drawn to the quiet, solitary figure of Joseph in the New Testament accounts. "The Word is the adopted son of silence," she alleges, noting that "St. Joseph passes through the pages of the gospel without uttering a single word." Yet the power of his silent and reticent life forms a shelter in which the holy family remains safe.[28]

Our tendency, however, is to be wary of quiet and solitary people. We're apprehensive of the old desert rats that Ed Abbey praised, saying, "They couldn't breathe properly without at least a cubic mile of unshared space about them." We smile at the oddity of Thoreau's reclusiveness at Walden Pond: "I have a great deal of company in the house," he wrote, "especially in the morning when nobody calls." [29] We're uncomfortable about launching out on our own. On those rare occasions when we do try to get off by ourselves, it isn't easy—not even in wilderness. Anywhere you go in the lower forty-eight states you're never more than twenty miles from a road of some kind.[30] Solitude can be a very relative thing, depending on how much of it you need.

Yet even small doses of silence and solitude can be unnerving. This struck me again with the coming of night on the top of Bell Mountain. A hush settled over the landscape as the sun went down and the wind stopped. When you've been without silence for a long time, it's disturbing at first. It speaks with a clamor louder than sound. I can't imagine what it must have been like two hundred years ago, when Lewis and Clark (a little north of here) were beginning their long route to the Pacific or when the Cherokee Indians (a little south of here) were following the Trail of Tears toward Oklahoma. Silence must have been the agony and the solace of people on the frontier. One in four people died on the forced march of the Cherokee. Their voices still whisper in the hills as dusk descends on the Missouri backcountry.

Alexis de Tocqueville, plunging into the American wilderness in 1830, wrote of "a silence so deep, a stillness so complete, that the soul is invaded by a kind of religious terror." [31] I experienced something of what he described that night at the campsite. It was unseasonably warm that weekend. The dog and I slept without a tent, stretching out on a patch of grass beside boulders on the mountain's crest. My dog, Desert, is very good about not wandering off when we're camping. I never have to tie her up. But something woke her in the middle of the night. I heard nothing myself, yet felt her beside me as she stiffened and raised her head. She was aware of something nearby that I couldn't sense. She growled . . . with a low, deep guttural warning I'd never heard her use before. She broke the silence—she *answered* the silence—with a response to the wild that had the adrenalin pumping in both of us. We listened for another fifteen minutes without moving, but heard nothing more. Sometimes, as Sherlock Holmes observed, what you *don't* hear in the night is as compelling as what you do.

The Responsibilities of Solitude

While solitude is indispensable on one's spiritual journey, it isn't an end in itself. Hopefully it increases our sense of accountability to others. Going alone into wilderness awakens me to a larger set of responsibilities than what

I'm accustomed to practicing at home. First, for example, is my responsibility for taking care of myself out on the trail. Solo backpacking, depending on the terrain and the weather, is not always a good idea. It behooves me not to do anything stupid out there. I don't want the local forest ranger's office having to organize a search and rescue team to lift me off the mountain.

I have to observe all the necessary precautions in letting people know where I'll be, registering at the trailhead, being well equipped, and not venturing farther than I should. I need to think twice about every decision I make on the trail. There's always more than myself to take into account. The choices I make out in wilderness affect everyone else back home as well.

A second responsibility that grows out of my experience of going into wilderness alone has to do with the land itself. In the trust we share together, I acquire an obligation to do more than enjoy wilderness. I have to speak and act on its behalf as well. This means more than practicing "Leave No Trace" principles, as important as those are. It means raising hell about logging and mining infringements on unprotected wilderness, for example. I'm indebted, after all, to the time-honored anarchist tradition of Ed Abbey. That "apostate Presbyterian," as he called himself, underscored the sacred responsibility of bellyaching about land development, the factory farming of animals, and industrial tourism. He stressed the moral obligation of the desert solitaire to resist much and obey little. Wilderness necessarily gets your back up when it comes to injustice.

A third and concluding responsibility that arises out of my solo encounter with wild terrain is the need to honor and bless the land. Offering praise along with the other inhabitants there—simply practicing appreciation—is the finest gift I'm finally able to leave. When you're the only human present, you have a particular responsibility to take pleasure in the place. To have a mountain to oneself is to shoulder a responsibility. As the sole occupant of the Chair of Applied Appreciation, yours is the task of blessing white oak trees and swallowtail butterflies, reindeer moss lichen and box turtles. You have to take it all in, make love to all of it, celebrate every blessed thing.

You find yourself traipsing from one serviceberry tree to the next, dipping your nose into every fragrant, white blossom, doing as fine a job of cross-pollination as any self-respecting bee, distributing gratefulness everywhere. You're a kindergarten teacher, rushing to compliment each of your students on their excellent work . . . until you realize *you're* the kindergarten student yourself, surrounded by stunning teachers at every turn.

Solitude has to bring us back at last to community, says environmental ethicist Holmes Rolston, back to a connection with everything else. The spaces for solitude in our lives are essential. They help us identify our unique identity. "Without such spaces there is no togetherness—merely fusion and homogeneity. Alone we cannot be human. Yet we cannot be human until we are alone." [32] Our forays into the solitary life, in the end, make us better lovers, more passionate in embracing the fullness of a world that stretches us beyond ourselves.

As D. H. Lawrence wrote:

> *When we get out of the glass bottles of our ego,*
> *when we escape like squirrels turning in the cages of our personality*
> *and get into the forests again,*
> *we shall shiver with cold and fright*
> *but things will happen to us*
> *so that we don't know ourselves.*
> *Cool, unlying life will rush in,*
> *and passion will make our bodies taut with power,*
> *we shall stamp our feet with new power*
> *and old things will fall down,*
> *we shall laugh, and institutions will curl up like burnt paper."* [33]

We'll delight, with Søren Kierkegaard, in the passion that binds us to the source of life itself.

7

Traveling Light: Gunstock Hollow and Dag Hammarskjöld

He who would travel happily must travel light.
ANTOINE DE SAINT-EXUPÉRY[1]

For all that has been—Thanks! To all that shall be—Yes!
DAG HAMMARSKJÖLD[2]

IT WAS NEW to me. *Backpacker* magazine had listed Gunstock Hollow as the "best Southern hollow in America," and I was curious. The dog and I set out one weekend, hiking the middle fork of the Ozark Trail into this hollow nestled between two ridges. Three days remained in deer hunting season that year, so I tied a red bandana around Desert's neck and wore a bright orange vest myself. With a name like Gunstock Hollow we figured we ought to be careful.

Gunstock Hollow is typical of a lot of closed-in wilderness sites in the Ozarks. Thickets of densely growing trees give it a secluded and mysterious air, muffling sound. A wandering stream runs through it, leading down to Neal's Creek below. Two huge cedar trees, a couple hundred years old, stand watch in the middle of the valley. The haunting trees and a series of knoblets that pepper the area give the place its character. You find deer tracks everywhere.

I wouldn't call it the "most beautiful hollow" in the Ozarks, however. I suspect its *name* drew the attention of *Backpacker* magazine as much as anything else. "Gunstock Hollow" fits the hard-core romanticized image that people have of rural Missouri—a place where moonshine distillers have been replaced by meth cookers, where desperados like Jesse James have morphed into the criminal mania of backwoods communities steeped in the drug culture. The stereotype of the illiterate, inbred, shotgun-wielding hillbilly is reshaped today in the stark and violent world of *Winter's Bone*. All this is certainly part of the history (and reality) of the region, yet I'm intrigued by the tendency to make wilderness more sensational than it is. Tourist boards and backpackers alike are prone to fabricate a backcountry of the imagination, something more colorful, edgy, and dangerous. Exaggeration attracts tourists. It enhances the image of those who brave its dark wilderness trails and points up the stark simplicity of the people who live there.

The Ozark Mountains lend themselves to tall tales as it is, but storytellers like to accentuate the dark, eccentric, and scandalous. Maverick places delight us. Gunstock Hollow, like Wolf's Den Hollow nearby, shares the colorfulness of other place-names in rural Missouri. Remote communities include Tightwad, Peculiar, Useful, even Pucky Huddle and Toad Suck. Ozark tales celebrate outlaws and questionable characters from the James brothers and Dalton Gang to Johnny Ringo and Calamity Jane. Others tell of giant cave bears hiding in deep caverns and hoop snakes holding their tails in their mouths as they roll down hillsides.

I'd like to think of my own ramblings into wilderness as part of this dodgy, romantic mix. But my ventures into the wild have very little to do with danger or high adventure. They're vast exercises in simplicity instead. Backpacking as a spiritual practice demands traveling light. This means leaving behind the ego's need for ostentatious achievement as well as unnecessary equipment. In traveling light you not only relinquish the comforts of home; you go without an agenda—without needing to chalk up another sensational "experience," add another spiritual writer to your list of books read, or check off "the most beautiful Southern hollow in America" on your list of trails hiked. It's about accepting whatever comes, and not having to celebrate your having "done it" when it's over.

Backcountry hiking as a spiritual exercise doesn't give itself to summit fever. It doesn't have to gain the highest ridge or reach the farthest lake at the end of the trail. It's not about breaking a record in pushing the Scout troop up a hundred miles of high country at Philmont. It's not about rushing to finish the four hundred miles to Santiago de Compostela, so as to arrive by July 25, the feast day of St. James. The *journey* is the destination . . . as pilgrims come to know. The spiritual practice isn't the success one achieves in the end, but the process itself.

Traveling light, therefore, is more than limiting the number of things we carry. It calls into question the consumerist mentality of the entire culture: our incessant thirst for experience, personal achievement, endless distraction, boogie fever. It challenges the passion for "peak-bagging" that preoccupies climbers in the high country of the Rockies. Like other trail freaks, I'm tempted myself to reduce backpacking, and the spiritual life as well, to a breathless series of accumulated experiences. I keep echoing the mantra—"Been there, done that!"—trying to do it *all* without being changed by any of it.

The Economy of the Trail

That's why discipline is so important: slowing down, embracing simplicity, traveling light. "Economy" is the title Thoreau gave to his first chapter of *Walden*. There he listed the basic materials he needed to begin a life of simplification, limiting himself to "the gross necessaries." He found that "most of the luxuries, and many of the so-called comforts of life, are not only not indispensable, but positive hindrances" to genuine human growth.³ You have to lessen the load you carry, he insisted.

Backpackers constantly deal with the question of what to take and what to leave behind. Thoreau trimmed it down to four basic categories of food, shelter, clothing, and fuel. When you leave the car at the trailhead and walk into wilderness, your comfort (and survival) are defined entirely by what you carry on your back. You're stripped to essentials, with room for just a few "luxuries"—maybe a chocolate bar, something to read, a small pair of binoculars. The process demands careful choices. Packing for the trip is an exercise in values clarification.

Yet the soul discovers a deep joy in being self-sufficient, relying on resources you didn't know you had. You realize how little you really require to be happy. You sense an affinity for tortoises, turtles, and terrapins, moving slowly and close to the earth, carrying their houses on their backs. There's a lightness of being in abandoning the frantic haste of a consumer society. It's the power of less as more.

In practical terms, deciding on what gear to take depends on when and where you're going and how long you'll be gone. The weather forecast, the season of the year, the altitude and nature of the terrain all determine what goes and what stays. At times you don't need a tent; just a sleeping bag will do. In cold weather you'll want more layers of clothes, on longer trips more freeze-dried food. Experienced hikers generally recommend "Ten Essentials" that ought to be included in any pack:

- Map (in waterproof plastic bag)
- Compass (or GPS)
- Flashlight or headlamp
- Food

- Water (with purification tablets or filter for backcountry water sites)
- Extra clothing (including rain gear)
- First-aid kit (with sunscreen lotion)
- Matches and firestarter (a cheap butane lighter)
- Pocketknife
- Basic survival kit (emergency moon blanket, signal mirror, whistle, and 8×8-inch square of heavy-duty aluminum foil for makeshift cookpot)[4]

Ultralight purists will cut the ends off their toothbrushes and trim map edges to save weight. Backcountry hikers never get tired of sharing new ways of traveling more lightly and practicing their craft more simply. There's a *gnosis* (a knowhow) that's distinctive to any community of knowledge. It's the esoteric wisdom that's passed on by those who have embraced the discipline, those able to initiate newcomers into its mystery. Knowing how to read a topographical map, for example, or how to load a pack and stay warm on a cold night, how to keep a tent from leaking and operate a PUR water filter to prevent giardia—all these are part of the arcane world of backcountry travel. They make up a cluster of simplicities that are basic to wilderness comfort and survival.

Serious hikers will also emphasize "Leave No Trace" principles in introducing others to their practice. When I take groups of students into the Ozarks we make a point of using established campsites, keeping water sources clean, and packing out everything we take in. Digging "cat-holes" and hauling out used toilet paper in Ziploc bags sounds a little disgusting at first, but it's a way of honoring the earth and respecting the habitat of those living there. Leaving as light a footprint as possible is part of the discipline.

Harvard environmentalist Lawrence Buell identifies two kinds of relinquishment that have perennially fascinated American environmental writers. There's a relinquishment of *goods*, exemplified in Thoreau's plain life at Walden Pond, and a relinquishment of *self*, seen in John Muir's mystical identification with the mountains of the Sierra Nevada. Thoreau feared that adding the convenience of a door mat to his cabin floor might signal the "beginnings of evil," for instance. He thought of material possessions as traps, not treasures.[5] Muir, on the other hand, affirmed his unity with the "psalm-singing, lichen-painted trees" around him. He renounced his illusion of a separate human identity, as if he could stand *over* the natural world, "experiencing" it without being a part of it. Both relinquishments are dimensions of traveling light. We leave behind unimportant "things" as well as the need of the ego to collect noteworthy "experiences."

What matters most is simplicity. I like to mention this when I'm talking to friends from Colorado. They're inclined to brag about their mountains, and rightly so. They have fifty-four "fourteeners" scattered over the state—beautiful mountains, all exceeding 14,000 feet in height. I'll point out, however, that here in Missouri we happen to have six "seventeeners": six very old and majestic mountains over seventeen *hundred* feet high! Their youngsters in Colorado, a mere one hundred million years old, don't begin to have the wisdom of these old-timers. Our specialty is primeval mountains, made remarkable by their plainness, their minimalist beauty. When we climb, we like to travel light.

Hammarskjöld and the Discipline of the Desert

My teacher in Gunstock Hollow that weekend was Dag Hammarskjöld, the Swedish diplomat who served as Secretary-General of the United Nations from 1953 to 1961. I'd been using his book *Markings* in a course that semester. This was a journal he left at his death, tracing a series of "trail-markings" in a life that sought out the plain and unadorned amid a world of incessant activity and refined taste. "To be free," he said, "is to be able to stand up and leave *everything* behind—without looking back / to say '*Yes*' to whatever comes."[6]

The man's gifts were a study in contradictions: urbane intellectual and wilderness backpacker, polymath and lover of simplicity, eloquent public speaker and practitioner of silence. Henry P. Van Dusen, his friend at Union Seminary in New York, described him as a man of

> immense and wide-ranging culture, at home in the literature of half a dozen languages and a dozen nations and all periods, an ardent and highly literate connoisseur of drama and music, painting and sculpture, both classical and contemporary, himself a poet and translator of poetry, a lover and interpreter of nature, a mountaineer, withal "the best of comrades," all his life surrounded by admiring companions of the most diverse types and outlooks and cosmopolitan interests—in sum, a Renaissance man.[7]

Hammarskjöld's quiet temperament, joined with a self-effacing and unpretentious manner, readily drew others to him. He loved a solitary day of hiking in the Swedish mountains. People described the sparse Scandinavian decor of his apartment on the Upper East Side as almost monastic. His passion for haiku poetry expressed an appreciation for a stark leanness in language. Drawing on wellsprings of simplicity, he carried about him the aura of a Desert Father at mid-twentieth century.

Dag Hammarskjöld's position with the U.N. kept him at the center of the world's attention. He knew that self-absorption was ever a danger as a result. Like the Desert Christians, he was wary of the machinations of the "false self," given its need for constant approval. "Praise nauseates you," he wrote, "but woe betide him who does not recognize your worth."[8] Using his journal as a way of holding himself accountable, he practiced a spiritual discipline not unlike that of the desert monks in ancient Egypt. Yet his interior life remained hidden from public view. When the manuscript of *Markings* was found at his death, it surprised even people who knew him well. Like the Abbas and Ammas of late antiquity, he wasn't one to flaunt his own piety.

The highly reflective, pared-down, and celibate life of the U.N. Secretary-General offers an interesting parallel to the values of early Christian monasticism. This chapter, along with those that immediately precede and follow it, focuses on the contours of the spiritual practice they shared. This helps to elaborate the larger pattern of wilderness spirituality I'm trying to delineate in these pages. I argue that the virtues taught by these "athletes of God" in the remote deserts of the Roman Empire find an echo today in the learning curve of wilderness backpacking. Hammarskjöld happens to connect all of these interests—in his uncluttered life, his quiet self-restraint, and his love of wilderness.

In Chapters 3, 4, and 5, we've looked at the necessary venture, disillusionment, and clarification of desire that the Desert Christians thought essential in starting one's journey. You can't begin without knowing your limits and what it is you want most deeply. Having identified the fundamental desire at the core of their being, the monks went on to assume a discipline that allowed them to sustain it. This involved, among other things, a practice of welcoming solitude, traveling light, and pursuing mindfulness. These form the intrinsic discipline of what I'm calling wilderness spirituality.

The early monks of Egypt and Palestine gave themselves to stark simplicity and silence. They wove palm fronds into mats, kept a garden, attended to prayer, and offered spiritual direction to those who sought them out. They lived close to the land, staying attuned to its plant life, animal patterns, and geography. Their relinquishing of goods as well as self was evident in their non-attachment to the few possessions they owned and the humility for which they were acclaimed.

Abba Macarius returned to his hut one day to find a thief in the process of stealing everything he had. His whimsical response was to help the man load the goods onto his camel. In a similar story, Abba Euprepius ran after robbers who had just emptied his cell. They had missed a good walking stick standing in the corner and he hurried to give it to them, lest they leave something of value behind. Euprepius relished poverty as the best of gifts. "If we happen to lose something," he said, "we must accept it with joy and gratitude, realizing that we have been set free from care."[9] Things must be held lightly, if at all.

The desert monastics were just as eager to renounce their acquisition of superlative "experiences" as they were their accumulation of goods. Take the story of Abba John the Short. He announced to his brothers one day that he was leaving the weariness of his cell to become an angel. He wanted to serve God unceasingly—achieving the highest ecstatic experience, becoming a spiritual giant. A week later he came plodding back, knocking on the door. "Who's there?" an elder asked, before opening it. "It's me, John." The older man promptly shouted, "John's gone off to be an angel; he doesn't live here anymore." He then left him outside until the next morning. On finally opening the door, the old man said to the chastened monk, "If you're an angel, keep going; if you're a man, simply get back to your work."[10]

The monks insisted that what was being achieved (or *not* being achieved) in their spiritual practice was none of their damned business.[11] It didn't matter where it got them, how it "paid off," or what attention it drew from others. The discipline was an end in itself. These desert teachers were adamant that a habit of traveling light—letting go of results entirely—is crucial to any spiritual exercise. Dag Hammarskjöld continually reminded himself to "act without thinking of the consequences, or seeking anything for yourself."[12]

He was able to honor this directive in his inner life, not worrying about what people thought of him, while simultaneously weighing the geopolitical consequences of every action he took as Secretary-General. His private life served as a check on the temptations to despair (and grandiosity) that were so much a part of his public life. He wasn't always successful at this. In his *Markings* he speaks of wrestling with an exaggerated sense of self-importance, anxieties over his work, and loneliness bordering on depression. Nonetheless, in the churning vortex of world affairs, he managed to work from a quiet center. He lived in the city, but his heart remained in the desert.

No cracking of the whip of words
disturbed his peace
in a space that sang.[13]

These seventeen syllables of the haiku pattern gave voice to his love of a sparse simplicity in language. It was part of the frugal Japanese wisdom he cherished along with his Lutheran roots. He loved the *Tao Te Ching* and other early Chinese classics. In 1954, at a time of intense shuttle diplomacy, Chou En-Lai was impressed by his polite and unaffected manner, almost Asian in style. On Hammarskjöld's birthday, as a tribute to his negotiating skill, the Chinese premier released American pilots who had been captured over North Korea.

What fed this inner tranquility in the Swedish diplomat's life was a spiritual practice that included the solace of mountain hiking. He retreated as often as possible to Europe's most dramatic and untamed wilderness in the Lapland province of northern Sweden. There, with "the wilderness for a pillow" and "a star his brother," he celebrated the "sacrament of an arctic summer night." In a letter to a friend, he wrote of "longing to drown in the silence and light of the mountain moors." There's nothing better than "a night spent in the high mountains," he said. There he could travel lightly enough to lose himself in the landscape. "Here [one] is no longer the center of the world, only a witness, but a witness who is also a partner in the silent life of nature, bound by secret affinities to the trees." In the mountains he learned "to preserve the silence within—amid all the noise . . . ." Drawn to "the deathly gleam of ice blocks in the slanting rays of the sun," he was able to relinquish pride of accomplishment, the acquisitive self, and spiritual attainment alike. Wilderness alone was enough.[14]

Traveling Light in the Spiritual Life

I thought of Hammarskjöld while sitting with the dog in Gunstock Hollow as evening shadows gathered. I leaned back in my Crazy Creek chair with the dog between my legs, watching water flow and listening to the call of whippoorwills in the trees. You seldom see these elusive birds ("nightjars," they're called), yet their haunting cries are clear and lovely as night comes on. Desert, my dog, is an old German shepherd. Like a desert monk herself, she attends with ears cocked to every sound in the wilds. She's been my teacher and occasional hiking partner for years. We delight in the shared solitude of an Ozark evening.

We're surrounded here by a typical Missouri landscape, marked by a deceptive simplicity. Along the banks of an intermittent woodland stream, everything seems ordinary, even monotonous—what you'd *expect* to find in the woods. But a thousand different species of trees, wildflowers, vines, shrubs, herbs, and berries are native to this part of Missouri. Another two thousand species of mosses, lichens, liverworts, and fungi grow on its rocks and trees. Still another three thousand species of aquatic insects (from springtails to mayflies to whirligig beetles) thrive in and around its ponds and creeks.[15]

Once you start paying attention to a place as full of diversity as this, you'll want to read every field guide you can get your hands on. You can't wait to learn the names of things. You're eager to master the vast body of knowledge that others have collected, listening to their tales. You're tempted, in short, to *grasp* everything—assigning labels to each detail, duplicating the experience of others who have been there before. You're eager to identify yourself as an accomplished "backwoodsman," literate in the lore of the wild. You forget that knowledge is the servant of wonder. It allows you to settle back in a folding camp chair with a dog leaning against you, delighting in fading sunlight as the katydids begin an evening serenade.

"In the point of rest at the center of our being," says Hammarskjöld, "we encounter a world where all things are at rest. . . . Then a tree becomes a mystery, a cloud a revelation."[16] But we won't arrive there so long as we have to label every cloud as altocumulus or cirrostratus, every tree as deciduous broadleaf or evergreen conifer. Our primary task is to be present to whatever is there before us. We don't have to pigeonhole it in our minds, turn it into a memorable event, or copy what others have found significant in it. Our lust for experience-in-general often leads to the tyranny of *other people's experience*. We imagine theirs to be far superior to our own. If *only* we had Wendell Berry's sensitivity to nature or Anne Lamott's experience of God! When we imitate someone else's way in the world, we lose touch with the quiet center that is ours.

I'm invariably tempted by this passion for accumulated data and canned experience when I'm out in the woods. I expect vivid encounters with the saints, dramatic happenings on the trail, peak experiences I can add to my list of accomplishments. I forget that my goal in backpacking isn't to achieve some iconic outdoor spiritual experience. At best, I'm focusing without judgment on whatever is happening right here, right now. That's what Robert Kull learned in his year of solitude on a remote island off the coast of Chile. His craving for experience had often kept him from experiencing reality itself. "As long as I want to be in the flow of Life, that very desire prevents me from seeing that I'm *always already here*."[17] Coming to rest at the core of one's being is the hardest task in the spiritual life. I practice it all over again on every trip into backcountry.

The problem is endemic to life in a postmodern age where every experience is up for grabs. We have a penchant for "trying on" other people's reality, leading anyone else's life but our own. We experiment with a continual exchange of lifestyles, viewpoints, and endlessly engaging activities. The consumption of experience has virtually replaced the consumption of goods as a primary determinant of personal identity in American cultural life. A recent article in *Time* magazine speaks of a $10.5 billion industry focused on self-improvement through assorted spiritual and meditative practices. An "unofficial religion of personal transformation" thrives on our culture's passion for novelty, for the next potentially life-changing experience.[18]

In religious circles, this means adding Hāfez and Rumi to one's previous reading of Merton and Nouwen. It's about working through the Four Agreements and doing guided meditation with Deepak Chopra. It involves retreats to desert monasteries, Kabbalah study, and the use of Buddhist mandalas. These can all be helpful tools, of course, but when they turn into a list of accouterments in the spiritual life they lose their power to change us. We run the risk of becoming "tools of our tools," as Thoreau cautioned in *Walden*. Techniques become an end in themselves. We search for the next new teacher, the latest fad that will finally make the spiritual life easy. Consequently, we lose the freedom to affirm what is spare and good. We amass an all-encompassing catalog of experiences without being present to any of them.

This thirst for stylized experience is subtle. It's rooted in a genuine yearning for transcendent meaning, a desire to stand in reverence before Mystery. But it's easily boxed into predictable patterns. In the Bible church where I grew up in central Florida, the mark of a truly "spiritual person" was her ability to point to a date (even an hour) scribbled on the front page of her Scofield Reference Bible. This was the precise moment of her conversion experience, when she had been "born again." I envied these people, feeling inferior because I never had a dramatic experience of the kind they described. I sought it. At summer church camp, like other teenagers, I committed myself to foreign missionary service—the highest possible expression of devotion. We were answering the challenge thrown down by D. L. Moody that "the world has yet to see what God can do through a man wholly yielded to him."[19] We were set afire by the possibility that one of *us* might accomplish that task.

But in responding to the allure of total commitment, we were also calling attention to our devotion, stunning others by the power of our experience, joining the elite ranks of "the higher Christian life." Creeping into the process of absolute surrender came a subtle degree of competition, self-promotion, and imitation of other people's ways of encountering God. We yearned to achieve stardom in the spiritual life, at the expense of a primal impulse to exaltation and praise.

What wilderness backpacking has taught me through the years, with its insistence on traveling light, is that great accomplishments (and other people's spiritual experiences) count for nothing on the trail. Wherever you've hiked in the past—whatever saints or nature writers you've read—there's no substitute for being present in this moment, in this place. On every trip into wilderness I'm obliged to witness nature's wonder as if for the first time. The only indispensable item I pack is a capacity for amazement. That's all I need.

The best thing that happened that weekend in Gunstock Hollow was that nothing happened. There were no revelations, nothing to report. I had no melodramatic sense of being watched in the night by an animal I couldn't see. There were no books leaping into the water, inviting me to felicity. The dog and I were merely present to a wilderness place—content with whip-poorwills, the shadows of a Missouri hollow, and cedar trees older than the Civil War.

You don't have to exaggerate the exotic character of an Ozark wilderness in order to enhance your presence within it. It is what it is. People in these parts like to embellish tales of sinkholes appearing out of nowhere, caverns into which you can throw a stone without ever hitting bottom. They say drinking Missouri branch water from a gourd can cure your rheumatism. Slippery-elm bark boiled in water can ease your hangover. Down in the hill country even pileated woodpeckers supposedly have supernatural powers.[20] But none of these mysteries are essential to the discipline to which I give myself.

I'm charmed by the art of water dowsing that Ozark folks still practice. Old codgers argue the relative merits of different species of trees to use in cutting a divining rod. Some insist on wild cherry (green, with the sap still running); others say peach is better. They all swear you can see the stick bend when it passes over water underground. But I don't require any of this to locate the sort of magic I'm looking for.

I need only the ability to glimpse the wonder in the ordinary. Adoration is all that matters, says Catholic theologian Hans Urs von Balthasar. Sitting at dusk by the creek in Gunstock Hollow, I watch the coming of the night. I marvel that nothing is "happening," yet *everything* is happening. I rest in a container larger than myself. Whatever I experience in that moment is out of my hands. It's none of my business. My task is simply to adore.

Sweden's snow-capped mountains served to remind Dag Hammarskjöld that the world wasn't about him. What happened or didn't happen there (or anywhere in his life) was beyond his control. In wilderness he was part of a grander mystery. It reduced him, in the end, to open-mouthed astonishment. "I am the vessel," he confessed. "The draught is God's. And God is the thirsty one."[21] He learned finally to travel lightly enough to abandon even himself.

8

Mindfulness: Moonshine Hollow and Thich Nhat Hanh

Once the Buddha was asked, "Sir, what do you and your monks practice?" He replied, "We sit, we walk, and we eat." "But everyone sits, walks, and eats," his questioner responded. "Ah," said the Buddha. "When we sit, we know we are sitting. When we walk, we know we are walking. When we eat, we know we are eating."

Ancient Buddhist Legend[1]

Life is available only in the present moment.

THICH NHAT HANH[2]

THE LOCALS CALL it Moonshine Hollow, or Mooner's Hollow, partly because of the haunting character of the moonlight in this small, isolated valley. It forces you to pay attention to the thousand shades of shadow and light you'd never thought to distinguish before. The phenomenon has something to do with the curvature of the ravine here, as light reflects off stone cliffs above and the lithe, white limbs of sycamore trees below. Whatever accounts for it, Moonshine Hollow is well named.

Up from Coonville Creek in St. Francois State Park in southeast Missouri, it lies along the eleven-mile Pike Run backpacking trail. A small trickle of water flows year-round from the base of the cliff where I usually camp. During Prohibition it's said that bootleggers operated a still in this remote hollow, making hooch, white lightning, or panther's breath (as it was variously called). Hidden deep in the Ozarks, with cornfields nearby, a steady supply of cold water, and sufficient wood to keep a fire going, it was an ideal site for producing "mountain dew." In fact, Missouri law still allows its citizens to distill up to two hundred gallons of whiskey a year for personal and family use. All of this lends Moonshine Hollow its unique appeal.

What creates the ambience or "sense of place" that we associate with a singular locale? For Moonshine Hollow, it's a combination of sheltered seclusion, the distinctive play of shadows on a moonlit night, even an edge of lawlessness. It's a place where time has stopped. It invites you to linger. The moonshiner's art is a slow and demanding one. The corn has to soak in a wet burlap sack for ten days. The mash has to be fermented with water, yeast, and malt for another ten days or more. Then, in being gently heated over a low fire, the alcohol has to evaporate, passing through a copper coil inside a barrel of cold branch water, dripping leisurely into a stoneware jug. The process can't be hurried. Nothing should be rushed in Moonshine Hollow.

Several times I've hiked into this glen on a Friday afternoon halfway through the semester, needing to escape the city and the university—seeking what Gerry May calls "the power of the slowing." I come to practice mindfulness, a habit that isn't easy to sustain amid the distractions of academic life. Simone Weil argued that school studies can be an aid in the exercise of prayer. If you think of praying as primarily a matter of *paying attention*, then memorizing geometric theorems and mulling over Anselm's argument for God's existence might help. She was right, up to a point.[3]

Prayer *does* involve a discipline of practiced attentiveness, but it's more than a concentration of thought, a knitting of one's brows. Contemplative prayer is what gets you out of your head entirely. That's what I come to wilderness for—a deeper practice of mindfulness, a virtue that Buddhists and Desert Christians have both held in high esteem. The mindfulness that wild terrain evokes is actually a sort of "mind*less*ness," an end-run around rational analysis that seeks an immediacy of presence.

Moonshine Hollow questions my habit of defining reality before experiencing it. It urges me to marvel at the subtlety of moonlight without scrutiny or critique. It resists my tendency to "script" my experience there—to create a personal drama of what's happening around me, conjuring up images of moonshine stills from an exotic past, nursing disgruntlements over the job back home, projecting mystical encounters onto a landscape that sings.

The mindfulness that wilderness provokes is able to draw me out of the buzz of my incessant, internal conversation with myself. Like Vipassana meditation in Buddhist practice, it urges my seeing reality as it truly is. Doing that requires being present to the moment, apart from the expectations and interpretations I bring to it. Once I stop shaping reality into a theatrical performance with myself at its center, mindfulness allows the world to surprise me. The universe becomes delightfully open-ended. Shunryu Suzuki Roshi remarks with a wry smile that "The secret of Zen is just *two* words: not always so."[4] That's Moonshine Hollow, too. It's unpredictable. When I'm there—if I'm really alert—I can witness the unexpected *wonder* of nightfall and sunrise. I "wake up" to what *is*, as the Buddha would say.

Thich Nhat Hanh: The Monk as Observer and Activist

Small, provocative books are ideal for backpacking—books like Brother Lawrence's *The Practice of the Presence of God* or Thich Nhat Hanh's *The Miracle of Mindfulness*. The latter is one I've dropped into my pack on numerous occasions. These are books that insist that anything worth doing is done better with consciousness. Thich Nhat Hanh is a Vietnamese Buddhist monk, widely revered for his work on behalf of world peace, inter-religious dialogue, and the practice of meditation. He's known affectionately by his students as Thây (meaning "teacher"). "Thich" is a title given to all Buddhist monks and nuns in Vietnam. He was heralded by Thomas Merton as a man uniquely able to join the teachings of Jesus and the Buddha.

Merton first met Thich Nhat Hanh in 1966, at Gethsemani Abbey in the hills near Bardstown, Kentucky. As they walked the monastery grounds together, Merton was taken by the parallels between Thây's Buddhist monasticism and the spiritual practice of the Desert Fathers. Both emphasized the importance of mindfulness. The Vietnamese monk considered it so rare, in fact, as to be miraculous. "People usually consider walking on water or in thin air a miracle," he said. "But I think the real miracle is not to walk either on water or in thin air, but to walk on earth." To do anything ordinary with a totality of consciousness is nothing less than extraordinary.[5]

The Desert Christians knew that such clarity in being available to the present moment is possible only when one pauses to exercise awareness. Indeed, the Egyptian monks declared that "unawareness is the root of all evil." One observed that even the murkiest jar of water becomes clear when allowed to sit undisturbed. "So drink your tea slowly and reverently," advises Thây, "as if it is the axis on which the world revolves—slowly, evenly, without rushing toward the future."[6] In Merton's effort to relate Christian and Buddhist meditation, practicing mindfulness across cultural and religious divides, he found a common spirit in this Vietnamese monk. He said he first recognized Thây as a true monastic because of the way he opened and closed doors.

Thich Nhat Hanh was born in central Vietnam in 1926. At the age of twelve, he climbed a mountain as part of a school excursion, seeking out a cave where a hermit was known to live. Four years later he entered the

Tu Hieu monastery, deep in the pine forests near Hue. In the 1950s, as editor of the journal *Vietnamese Buddhism*, he wrote critically of the dictatorial regime of Ngo Dinh Diem, supported by the United States at the start of the war in Vietnam. Three years later, Thây spent a year on a fellowship studying comparative religion at Princeton University. He was invited at the time to lecture at Cornell and Columbia Universities as well. Returning to Vietnam in 1964, he set up relief organizations and founded the equivalent of a Peace Corps for Vietnamese young people. Speaking out on behalf of social justice and peace became an expression of what the activist monk has promoted as "Engaged Buddhism."

Thich Nhat Hanh returned to the United States in 1966, urging an end to the war. There he met Martin Luther King Jr. (as well as Merton) and was recommended by Dr. King for the Nobel Peace Prize. Denounced by the Vietnamese governments on both sides of the conflict, he was forced to live in exile for the rest of his life. In 1975, he took refuge in a hermitage south of Paris and subsequently founded, amid the orchards and vineyards of Bordeaux, a retreat center called Plum Village. There refugees find sanctuary to this day, as retreatants study meditation while tending plum trees in the orchards around the monastery.

The wisdom of this quiet Asian monk is apparent in his emphasis on Buddhist walking meditation. He cautions that in contemporary culture we perennially face the danger of "going without arriving." Given the frantic pace of our lives, we forget that the steps we take are as important as the destination we seek. Learning to walk slowly with conscious awareness is a first step toward mindfulness.[7]

Wilderness as a School of Attentiveness

When you're backpacking, the act of walking becomes a natural form of meditation. You don't have to think about it. Giving your body to the trail, you breathe rhythmically with every two steps (in and out), moving more slowly as changes in elevation may require. This steady pattern of breathing and moving is almost trancelike in its repetitiveness. It offers an exercise in mindfulness. After hours of hiking a wilderness trail in this way, you *become* the trail. You're alive to everything around you.

Mindfulness is simply the heightened awareness that backcountry travel demands. In wilderness terrain your senses are more carefully attuned. You're conscious of the season of the year, the movement of weather patterns, the sounds of the forest, the lay of the land. Your brain's hypothalamus and frontal lobes are in high gear—accessing and integrating data, watching for danger, controlling body temperature, staying alert to what is happening.

Moonshine Hollow may not occasion this alertness any better than other wilderness places. But I remember sitting there one evening, motionless enough to watch a red fox work its way down the cliff above the spring. I've been quiet enough in the night there to hear the throaty, high-pitched sound that deer make, calling to each other in the woods. Filling up a Nalgene bottle at the spring, I've been aware of the distinctive ecotone (the transitional space between one ecological zone and another) where swimming and crawling insects converge on wet, green moss.

The world is full of natural wonders that we notice only when we take time to attend to details. We marvel at how mockingbirds delight in hopping and wing-flashing on the top of a dead tree, how the leaves of an aspen tree flutter in the least bit of wind, how the cracks in the bark of ponderosa pines smell of butterscotch pudding, how flying hawks use their shadow in hunting mice (the fear of their passing silhouette causes the rodents to run in panic). The world on the edge of our awareness wants to fill us with amazement.

The Missouri Conservation Department publishes a calendar each year that alerts duffers like myself to seasonal events occurring across the Ozark landscape. It teaches me to watch for great horned owls nesting in February, for red maples beginning to bloom in early March, for ruby-throated hummingbirds arriving in April. I learn about cicadas singing in late June, wild blackberries ripening in August, a first frost due by late October, and—come December—the outstretched arms of Orion in the night sky. Thoreau used such knowledge to tell him not only when and where he was, but *who* he was as well. Psychologists tell us that the biological and meteorological cycles of land and sky play a role in forming human identity. We know who we are as we participate in our surroundings. Our sense of self goes through phases like the seasons. A Tennessee mountaineer, celebrating the familiar peaks and hollows of the Smoky Mountains, can say: It's "where you can feel you're you, and no one else."[8]

Attentiveness involves more than accruing a body of information about local flora and fauna. It isn't a gathering of data so much as a practice of being present to where and who you are. Paying attention is about paying attention. It's a preconscious openness to wonder that shapes (and exceeds) the boundaries of individual consciousness.

It's one thing to know intellectually that walking down a mountain is physiologically harder than walking up it. (Coming down, you shift your body weight before actually planting your foot, making descent a kind of controlled fall.) It's another thing to move with the rhythm of a downward slope, placing your foot with mindful awareness even when you're tired. You may have memorized the dictum that, in survival situations, you can go three minutes without air, three days without water, and three weeks without food. But it's something else to move without panic when trapped under a snagged, overturned canoe in fast-moving water. You may know how to identify white Navajo sandstone, red/brown Keyenta formation, and purplish Chinle rock. But it's another skill entirely to recognize a canyon cliff as "having a face that returns your gaze."[9]

It isn't what you know in your head, but what you've *become* that matters most . . . in backpacking as well as in life. The goal of mindfulness is to be present, to "participate" in body, mind, and soul with everything going on around you. When the apostle Paul urged his readers to have "the mind (*nous*) of Christ" (in I Corinthians 2:16), he wasn't talking about rational perception, but a deep exercise of reflective consciousness. To respond out of *that* mind is to exercise a compassionate sensitivity, blurring the fixed distinctions you'd previously made between yourself and everything else.

The Buddhist Practice of Mindfulness

Thich Nhat Hanh's deceptively simple little book *The Miracle of Mindfulness* reflects on this mystery. In summarizing the dimensions of the Buddhist practice of attentiveness that he teaches, I risk missing the point of what he's trying to say. You can't reduce mindfulness to a list of ideas. You don't condense to thoughtful analysis what "thought" is finally incapable of comprehending. Mindfulness is an exercise, not a concept. You have to live it, not mull it over in your mind. What follows, then, can only be understood through practice.

The Welcoming of Awareness

The Buddha says that our deepest happiness is to know we are fully alive. That's the first step in practicing mindfulness. Being present to the wonder of each moment—whether we're smelling plum blossoms in a French countryside or feeling the pain of arthritis in an aching leg—that's what the spiritual life is about. Our finest act as human beings is to welcome the moment, whatever it may be.

From a Judeo-Christian perspective, if we are truly the temple of the Holy Spirit—the dwelling place of the Most High God—then being present to ourselves in any single moment will be an act of prayer. We find happiness in that instant alone, in whatever it contains. If we can say, "Welcome," without needing to change what may (or may not) require changing, we proclaim with our every breath that life is good.[10]

On the other hand, we'll remain *unhappy* to the extent that our personal conditions for happiness are *different* from the conditions of the present moment. If we need anything more than what's happening right now—if we resist being present to what is going on in this instant—to that extent we will be unhappy. Contentment in life is choosing to be who and where we are, no matter what else is occurring at the time.[11] Christians like Thomas Merton would agree entirely, defining happiness as a matter of discerning God's presence in every moment, whatever it contains.

Mindfulness is the fleeting instant of awareness we experience just before we begin to conceptualize reality and make judgments about it. When I hike into Moonshine Hollow, I may hear the song of a bird in a distant glade. In the moment, I don't have time to label it as a cardinal, to associate it with the color red, even to distinguish it from my own consciousness in listening. There isn't any "me" pausing to think that I'm pleased with the sound, wishing it might continue. Nor is there any "theological conception" of God's presence filling the moment. The bird, the song, the glade, and my preconscious participation in the shared reality are all . . . simply . . . one. I accept their *happening* in that moment.

On the other hand, as I hike into Moonshine Hollow on that same morning, I may also hear the distant whine of a truck engine on Highway 67 or an F-15 on a practice run screaming overhead. In the instant before feel resentment and start making judgments, I can choose to accept this sound as well. I can receive it as another part of the "now," without trying to drown it out of my hearing. What is happening is simply happening. I'm able to accept it, with compassion in that initial moment of nonjudgmental awareness, not wishing it were anything else. I may choose later to work for a world that makes tactical fighter jets unnecessary (or truck engines less noisy), but in that moment on the trail, I can simply observe, "Ah, this comes up . . . and now this . . . and now this, too." Mindfulness is a rigorous practice of *welcoming* the moment, whatever it brings.

Intentionality

A second aspect of the mindfulness that Thich Nhat Hanh teaches is the extension into one's daily actions of that moment of naked awareness. To live one's life well is to practice a continuous series of choices in being alive to what occurs. Thây would propose, for instance, that the ordinary act of washing dishes can be an end in itself, not simply a means to the end of restocking your kitchen cabinet with unsoiled tableware. It's another opportunity for being present to the now. "There are two ways to wash the dishes," he explains. "The first is to wash the dishes in order to have clean dishes and the second is to wash the dishes in order to wash the dishes." Scrubbing one's pots and pans after dinner—accepting that task as the most significant thing in your life at the time—makes it an exercise in consciousness, a religious act, if you will.[12]

Doing things for their own sake and not just to get them done is a spiritual practice too subtle for most of us to appreciate. The Vietnamese Buddhist teacher insists that "Each act is a rite, a ceremony." You shouldn't do any task in order to get it over with.[13] Hard as that is for me to practice at home and at work, I find it easier when I'm backpacking. The transient nature of a weekend trip into backcountry—entering a new place and dwelling in it for a few days—models a shorthand version of my life as a whole. It serves as a rehearsal-in-miniature for what I do back home, but with the added intentionality that wilderness brings.

Camping in Moonshine Hollow, for example, I attend to the intricate routine involved in making breakfast. I pump up the fuel canister of my 14-ounce WhisperLite stove, wait for the wick-cup to fill with gas, light a "strike anywhere" match on a nearby rock, watch the orange flames warm the stove's circulating system, then trim the gas flow to a low blue flame ready for boiling water. It's a ritual act different from the one I'm more familiar with in operating a microwave oven at home. It lets me recognize how much of my life is ordered by unconscious, ritualized activities.

Formal rubrics are a part of everything I do in backpacking. There's a fixed pattern for putting up and taking down the tent, hanging the bear bag in a tree, cleaning up crumbs so as not to invite animals, remembering the order in which everything goes back into the pack. There's a methodical and unhurried motion to it all—one that assures my safety and convenience, but also slows me down, allowing me to be present to what I'm doing.

The routine of setting up and breaking camp is a reminder of the impermanence of everything. Shouldering my pack and pausing to bless the campsite at the end of a trip, I marvel at how my time there has been so immediate and real. The place has become a "home," giving shape to my existence. Yet when everything is packed up, it's all gone again, leaving no trace of my having been there.

Jesuit Nick Webber identified this quality of impermanence as central to the ministry he embraced for many years. Working with the Royal Lichtenstein Circus, a troupe of clowns and performers, he traveled around college campuses, using the ephemeral character of the circus to speak of life itself. Itinerant carnivals had always charmed him as a child. A huge tent, full of wonders, would go up one day on a vacant lot across the street. Then the next day it would be gone again, as if it had never been. The whole thing smacked of mystery, he said, making you pay more attention to vacant lots in general. That's the point, of course . . . learning to attend to the unexpected in all the empty places of your life.

Many spiritual traditions, wanting to encourage this attentiveness, make use of short poems, verses, or blessings that punctuate the day, calling the faithful to a deliberate mindfulness in doing ordinary things. In the Buddhist tradition, these are called *gathas*; Thich Nhat Hanh, for instance, will recite the following *gathas* when beginning to wash dishes or drive a car:

Washing the Dishes	Before Starting the Car
Is like bathing the baby Buddha.	I know where I am going.
The profane is the sacred.	The car and I are one.
Everyday mind is Buddha's mind.	If the car goes fast, I go fast. If the car goes slowly, I go slowly.[14]

Orthodox Jews have *brachot*, or particular blessings, they employ in putting on clothes, breaking bread, or cleansing their hands. *Barukh atah Adonai eloheinu*, they intone, "Blessed art Thou O Lord our God, who allows us gratefully to do these things with consciousness." In the Celtic tradition in ancient Ireland, there were blessings (*beannachtai*) for milking the cow (blessing each teat), for making one's bed, and washing one's face. When the simplest actions are ritualized, they become brushed with magic.

Non-Attachment

A third dimension of the practice of mindfulness is the importance of *letting go* whatever it is one has experienced or accomplished in the passing moment. "Releasing what has come" is as important as initially welcoming it. I take pleasure in watching the red fox work its way down the rocks near my campsite, coming closer and closer to where I sit. But when I shift my weight slightly, causing the animal to flee, I kick myself for being fidgety. I cling to the moment, not wanting it to stop. When it's gone, I lapse into irritation, missing the wonder of what I'd just encountered.

This is the nemesis of our efforts at mindful action—our leaping from the simple awareness of the moment into judgments about it. I do it all the time. Walking into Moonshine Hollow, I notice empty beer cans scattered along the trail into paradise. I can choose to let it be what it is (and stuff them into my pack). Or I can lapse into anger over irresponsible rednecks getting wasted on a Saturday night, trashing the environment. Getting worked up over a few beer cans, I lose mindfulness altogether. Whether we're trying to ignore what won't go away or craving to hold on to what can't be kept, we cease to be present to the passing moment.

Non-attachment is a decision not to allow our thoughts and emotions to carry us away from what is now happening. We don't have to transform it into a personal drama, filled with petty distractions. Twenty minutes into a short walk from his home, poet Dan Gerber realizes he's been taking the house with him, along with unanswered letters and telephone calls and windows that needing caulking. "My feet have been taking a walk without me," he laments.[15]

This is the danger of "machine thinking," says Thich Nhat Hanh. It's the opposite of mindfulness.[16] It happens when we're absorbed in what we *should* be doing or *wish* we were doing and, consequently, fail to be present to what we *are* doing. We operate on automatic pilot. At Plum Village in southern France, a gong is sounded several times a day, calling everyone to a moment of "mindful silence." People stop hoeing weeds in the plum orchard. They put down their hammers in repairing the guest house. They even cease talking about peace in the conference center, dropping whatever they are doing. It's a reminder that nothing is more precious than the present moment. Only then are we fully alive.

The Desert Fathers recognized the importance of this in their counseling younger monks. One elder told an antsy young novice to simply stay in his cell and pray. The novice came back the next day, reporting that he'd noticed the door to his cell was old and needed replacing. The old man again sent him back to pray. The following day he returned, saying he'd noticed that the roof of his cell was old and needed replacing, too. The master finally told him that what most needed replacing was his wandering mind. This alone kept him from being present to God, or to anything else for that matter.[17]

"The essential thing," says Thầy, "is not to let any feeling or thought arise without recognizing it in mindfulness, like a palace guard who is aware of every face that passes through the front corridor."[18] When distracted, we need to be *aware* of being distracted—stepping back to notice the feelings of restlessness or anxiety that arise within us. We can't prevent the feelings from coming, but we can choose what we'll do with them.

Engaging the Body

A final dimension of mindfulness relates to the role the body plays in facilitating our presence to the passing moment. Thich Nhat Hanh emphasizes conscious breathing as our most effective tool in focusing a scattered mind. Drawing on the Sutra of Mindfulness, he observes that "feelings come and go like clouds in a windy sky. Conscious breathing is my anchor."[19] Breath is our most dependable link to consciousness. Since it's always happening, attending to it is always a possibility, bringing us back to ourselves each time. As Thây intones, "Breathing in, I calm body and mind. Breathing out, I smile. Dwelling in the present moment I know this is the only moment."[20] *Choosing* to do what the body does naturally makes it a distinctive exercise in attentiveness.

Even the subtle act of smiling can be a means by which the body nudges us toward mindfulness. A smile signals to the brain that all is well in any given moment. Whether we feel like smiling or not makes no difference. The brain doesn't distinguish. Amazingly, the act of smiling itself creates an openness to the moment. "Sometimes your joy is the source of your smile," says Thây, "but sometimes your smile can be the source of your joy."[21]

The same is true of walking meditation. He urges his disciples to walk with deliberateness, "as if you are kissing the earth with your feet." Indeed, the very act of compassionate walking *produces* this sense of reverence, even if it isn't felt. To put the body into motion is to engender the feeling we might have thought necessary in order to act in the first place. The American psychologist William James knew this from his own experience of depression. He learned that in choosing to walk (*as if* he were alert and alive), he could generate the very intentionality he lacked. Going through the outward motions, even in a cold-blooded way, made possible the inner disposition.[22] This is the extraordinary truth of the body as teacher of the spirit. The body can take the initiative in prompting what our thoughts and feelings hold us back from doing.

In the Zen tradition, the time-honored practice of *zazen* involves sitting in an erect, meditative posture as a way of stilling the judging, emotion-filled mind. With the body brought under control, the mind follows its lead. The Desert Fathers understood this in their practice of *ascesis*, an athletic bodily discipline that trains the spirit. All these teachers knew that where the heart longs to go, the body already knows the way.

Moonlight and Mindfulness

Under the gaze of a full moon, I camped in Moonshine Hollow one late September night. A harvest moon can be unnerving, intoxicating in its own right. You can't stop looking at it. Sleep is impossible, unless you're boxed inside a tent. The contour of Moonshine Hollow seems to multiply its impact, reflecting moonlight from every angle.

Restless and unable to sleep that night, I walked through the trees toward the top of the ravine overlooking the hollow. I didn't need a flashlight. Everything was already lit, as if from within. If beauty evokes fear as well as desire, I felt both in the sharpened awareness of the night. The luminous quality of tree branches and rock formations gave the hollow a strange new life. It made the skin crawl. Things on the edge of my field of perception assumed an otherworldly character.

Seeing the world by moonlight is very different from daylight vision. Moonlight is 400,000 times fainter than direct sunlight, and the human eye adjusts to it in fascinating ways. The retina has two kinds of photoreceptive cells. Its "cones" allow us to see color and resolve fine detail by daylight. Its "rods," by contrast, are remarkably sensitive (a thousand times more so than cones), allowing us to see more readily at night. They enhance peripheral vision and heighten our sensitivity in detecting motion. But they can't discern color. For the brilliance of pigmentation, the rods substitute the subtle articulation of shadow. They astound us with all the shades of gray that appear in a black and white landscape. Artists and photographers are able to identify a remarkable range of hues from ashen, cinereal, dappled, pearly, griseous, and mousey, to leaden, smoky, glaucous, Quaker-colored, and taupe.

In an earlier part of our evolution, surviving on the African savannas, we needed the skills that night vision provides. Noticing movement in the brush on the periphery of the campfire where we huddled at night could mean the difference between life and death. Still today our bodies know that, in attending to our surroundings, we have to work from the edges as well as from the center. Not all things are accessible to direct, head-on vision. One of the oddities of night vision is that we have a blind spot at the center of our gaze. We aren't able to count the seven individual stars that make up the Pleiades cluster, for instance, by staring directly at them. Only in looking to the side do they come into view.

Mindfulness involves the recognition of these blind spots in our lives. It attends to the periphery of things, nurturing sensitivity to what is perceptible only by moonlight. The play of light and shadow in Moonshine Hollow that night reminded me that the world is seldom what I expect.

While a luminous experience of night vision can startle us into a sudden, mystical awareness, our deepest hope is to be as immediately present to *every* moment—the mundane as well as the extraordinary. We long to experience the miracle of saying in any instant of our lives: This moment, right now, is what my life is about. I choose not to miss it. "Meditation is not about trying to get anywhere," says Jon Kabat-Zinn. "It is about allowing yourself to be exactly where you are and as you are, and the world to be exactly as it is in this moment, as well."[23] Only in that instant do we discover our deepest humanity.

Third Leg: Descent (When the Trail Gets Rough)

It can, and often will, happen. You forget to bring the matches. You fail to notice the poison ivy surrounding your chosen tent site. Mosquitoes send you home, or blisters make it impossible to go any further. You spend a night without sleep, seeking warmth in a wet sleeping bag as wind whips through your torn and tangled tent. Every backpacker has a story like this to tell.

In your wilderness journey, the Desert Christians warned, you *will* be wounded. The desert will take away everything you hoped to keep—your reputation, your confidence in your ability to achieve, your sense of who you are. You'll know fear. You'll fail. You may even have to die to what you'd counted on most, being dragged out feet first from that wild terrain (at least metaphorically).

But in the process, you may discover your greatest joy in having survived the night, in finding resources you never knew you had, falling back on a strength that was more than yours. You experience a new identity, a fearlessness in the face of terror. You know a love that would never have been yours without passing through the dark night. From then on, you look back on every failure as a gift, every mistake as an occasion for the miracle of grace.

9

Fear: The Maze in Canyonlands and John of the Cross

Always in the big woods when you leave familiar ground and step into a new place there will be . . . a little nagging of dread. It is the ancient fear of the Unknown, and it is your first bond with the wilderness you are going into. What you are doing is exploring. You are undertaking the first experience, not of the place, but of yourself in that place.

WENDELL BERRY[1]

Fear is the cheapest room in the house. I would like to see you living in better conditions.

HĀFEZ[2]

IT'S ONE THING to wake up in the middle of the night to an imagined terror. It's another thing to be wide awake and feel the hand of fear creeping up your spine. Camping alone one winter night above Ghost Ranch in New Mexico, I heard (or did I *dream* I heard?) scratching on the wall of the tent and the heavy breathing of an animal outside in the snow. I was so frightened I couldn't voice the scream stifled in my throat. Or was it in my *dream* that I wasn't able to make any sound? On waking I wasn't sure what had or hadn't happened—or whether it was all in my mind.

An even more uncanny experience came on another moonlit night in the depths of the Maze in Canyonlands National Park in southeast Utah. A friend and I had walked a mile down the canyon from our campsite, under the shadow of the towering walls within that vast winding labyrinth. Hiking in the light of a full moon without flashlights, we felt a sense of wild, animal abandonment. With reckless exuberance we'd been howling like wolves at the moon. But then we found ourselves standing before a canyon wall covered with ancient figures painted by archaic artists some two thousand years ago.

These were spirit beings standing vigil—long, ethereal shadows hovering on the surface of the rock. Whether they were guarding, witnessing, or offering protection, I didn't know. But in the hollowed-out world of moonlight and shadow that formed the Maze, I sensed the presence of something I couldn't name. It's a place about as far away from other people as you can get in the lower forty-eight, yet for an instant I had an uncanny awareness of a finger lightly touching me on the back of the neck. I'd been taken into a profoundly deeper meaning of fear.

Three days earlier we had driven seven hours from the Hite Marina on Lake Powell along a tortuous dirt road, part of the old Flint Trail. It was a belly-scraping, wheel-spinning, bronco-twisting ride, with hairpin turns around huge boulders and narrow rocky ledges. We averaged seven miles an hour in 4WD. George Hayduke, in Ed Abbey's *The Monkey Wrench Gang*, once used this route to escape a posse that was chasing him after a bit of eco-sabotage along the Colorado River. People call it "the roughest road in Utah," but it got us as far as Chimney Rock and the trailhead leading down into the Maze.

The Maze is a thirty-square-mile area of carved sandstone, cut into five major canyons and dozens of smaller side canyons—the result of ten million years of flashfloods twisting their way toward the Colorado River. "Think of five nests of snakes suddenly released at the same time and you begin to visualize the writhing convolutions" of the place, says a veteran hiker there.[3] The narrow 400- to 500-foot walls dividing these sunken canyons are topped with a bizarre collection of mushroom rocks, chocolate drop formations, and bulging rimrock. Down below, the meandering canyon floor suggests the half-heard music of swirling water. The Park Service issues only eleven permits into the area at any given time, so the place is guaranteed to be lonely.

From Chimney Rock the next morning we scrambled down the slickrock, following small cairns that mark a winding route to the bottom, our toes jamming into our boots. There were places where we had to lower our backpacks by rope, carefully maneuvering our way over sections covered with ice. A guidebook into the Maze had said "there's just enough difficulty to make it fun." Yeah, I thought: *Backpacker* magazine's description of the Maze as "the most difficult/dangerous trail in America" seemed a little more apt to me at the time.[4]

That evening, as shadows quickly fell in the depths of the canyon, we camped beside a scraggly old juniper tree, eating goat cheese on sesame crackers, with dried fruit and chocolate bars. By candlelight we took turns reading aloud from Gary Snyder's *Mountains and Rivers without End*. Its staccato, noun-heavy style offered a lean Buddhist affirmation of the world we had entered. We rolled out our sleeping bags on the 250-million-year-old Cedar Mesa Sandstone from which the Maze is sculpted. Carl Jung would have called our first day in the Maze the stuff of dreams, numinous and strangely unnerving.

Fear Along the Trail

Fear is an animal more terrifying than any other creature you find in wilderness. "To him who is in fear everything rustles," Sophocles observed.[5] Panic is the worst danger one faces on the trail, or anywhere else for that matter. "Fear is the mind-killer . . . the little death that brings total obliteration," intones Paul Atreides in Frank Herbert's *Dune*.[6] Being able to distinguish fantasy from reality becomes as important as it is difficult in a wilderness setting. The bona fide as well as imagined terrors of a darkened landscape trigger nightmares. The mind races with "what-if scenarios," leaping from one dreadful possibility to another. Night comes sooner than expected, bringing the possibility that Pan the goat-god may yet have his way with you.

Fear is the great attention-getter, the insistent voice of the reptilian brain concerned above everything else with survival. You've got to respect it. Not heeding its cautions can lead to your undoing. Yet Americans live in a culture rampant with fear, where projected dangers are multiplied everywhere. We thrive on the adrenalin of fright and are no longer able to discern what is truly worth fearing. We arm ourselves against every imagined threat, presuming our reaction to be normal instead of paranoid. In 2011, the Utah legislature adopted a "state firearm" (the Browning .45-caliber semiautomatic pistol) as a symbol of its preparedness in the face of terror. The Utah "state gun" now joins the sego lily as the state flower and the blue spruce as the state tree. Our symbols, sadly, define us. Fear locks us inside ourselves, shutting doors against threats we envision lurking in the darkness.

Fear of the "howling wilderness" leads people to exaggerate the physical dangers of backpacking as well. I don't know how many times I've been warned of venomous snakes waiting to attack and kill innocent hikers. Yet of the seven thousand snake bites reported each year, two thirds of them are the result of victims having intentionally provoked the reptile and only six cases lead to death. Violent wilderness stories fascinate people. Popular magazines tell of skull-crunching grizzlies with four-inch claws savagely attacking sleeping campers. (Most attacks are due to human carelessness with food or other inappropriate behavior.) We read of brain-sucking amoebas lurking in the hot springs and warm-water lakes of the Southwest, crawling up the nostrils of unsuspecting swimmers.[7] Horror is a recurring theme in the mythos of the American wilderness.

And of course, there *are* dangers. But the worst ones are those we carry inside. Imagine a typical scenario: Having launched on your initial wilderness adventure, you're eager to get to that picturesque, remote campsite described in the guidebook. Plunging deeper into the woods, you notice the trail becoming harder to follow. You've not been paying attention to where you've been walking. It's been a while since you've seen any diamond-shaped trail markers on the trees, and the forest looks thicker than it did before. You decide to double back for a hundred yards, but still nothing looks right. You shake your compass, wondering if it might be broken. You suspect the map you have is old. Then suddenly it happens—that proverbial "Oh shit!" moment. The amygdala in your paleomammalian brain alerts the hypothalamus, putting the autonomic nervous system into emergency mode. This in turn tells the pituitary gland to signal your adrenal glands. Within an instant, your heart rate increases, shallow breathing begins, your palms start to sweat. "RUN, don't think," the brain shouts. "For God's sake, you don't want to be lost out here."

Search and rescue teams tell us that fear is by far the most common killer in wilderness. Unseasoned hikers stubbornly deny what is obvious, pushing themselves to exhaustion without thinking, yielding to panic. Statistics show that macho men, in fit condition, are even worse at this than women and children. Brute strength counts for nothing where fear is the mind-killer. That's why National Outdoor Leadership School Wilderness First Responders say, "The first thing you can do in an emergency is to quietly open your jar of calm and pour it over everything." "Panic is like getting lost in your mind," notes psychologist Reid Wilson. "You have to find your mind first, before you can find your way out of the woods." Otherwise, the paralysis of fear brings disaster.[8]

The terror of being hopelessly lost, wandering in ever-widening circles, is an archetypal fear in the roots of human consciousness. We find it pictured in the ancient symbol of the maze. Mazes have been found in the inner chambers of Egyptian pyramids, in ancient rock carvings and Roman mosaics, in the myth of Theseus plumbing the depths of the palace at Knossos, and in elaborate Victorian hedge mazes in nineteenth-century Britain. The human mind is haunted by the horror *and* the enthralling mystery of being lost.

What I experienced in the moonlit wonder of the Maze in Canyonlands was more than a fear of shadows or the lingering presence of a people long dead. It was closer to what Kierkegaard describes as dread, "a *desire* for what one fears."⁹ The soul hungers for a mystery that comes rushing into the vacuum occasioned by the mind's loss of control. We shrink from experiences of self-abandonment and loss, yet something in us yearns for them too. We sense the possibility of being "met" in that aching moment of desertion. The darkness becomes strangely alluring, threatening to disturb but also to befriend us.

Saint John of the Cross observed that being lost in the night is a very different experience for *lovers* than it is for solitary people. For those who risk themselves deeply to another, the narrow canyons of fear have a way of widening out onto unexpected vistas of love. There are no guarantees, of course. Both love and fear dwell in regions beyond all proof. Yet they share a darkness that offers promise as well as peril.

A hundred years ago, Rudolf Otto penned a classic work on the nature of religious experience. He observed that the primeval human response to the "holy" is often terrifying and mesmerizing at the same time—a *mysterium tremendum et fascinans*. It is "the hushed, trembling, and speechless humility of the creature" in the presence of what it cannot name. The experience may involve the horror of Pan—"something uncanny or eerie." Yet it's also a response of thrilled wonder.¹⁰

Otto mentions darkness, silence, and an expanse of spatial emptiness as the distinctive bearers of this mystery. He points to "the semi-darkness that glimmers in vaulted halls, or beneath the branches of a lofty forest glade." It grips the soul through its "mysterious play of half-lights." The retreating distance of "the wide-stretching desert" has the same affect, he says.¹¹ The Maze district in southern Utah would have left him speechless, putting all of his senses on alert. It would have underscored for him the ambiguity of one's fear in the night—its ability to touch the heart simultaneously in altogether different ways.

Loss and Love in John of the Cross

In the history of spirituality no one has explored more thoroughly the symbolism of the dark night than the sixteenth-century Spanish mystic, John of the Cross. He was a man smitten by beauty, yet formed by suffering and loss. He found his highest joy in the poetic images of the Song of Songs. There the bride walks a thin line between fear and love in her search for the Beloved. For her, the dark night is full of terror and gift alike. In the journal I'd brought along on the trip, I had copied a few lines from John's short poems on "The Dark Night" and "The Spiritual Canticle."

The Baroque spirituality of this Spanish friar was marked by the exuberance and excess characteristic of his age. Some people have dismissed him as overly drawn to renunciation, wallowing in the dark night as a pathological state of mind, embracing *nada* (or nothingness) as an end in itself. But in truth he was an extraordinarily sensuous man, a lover (Spanish to the core), taking exquisite delight in nature's beauty, relishing his work with wood and stone as a carpenter, even carrying around with him a picture of his soul friend, Teresa of Avila. The dark night was, for him, not an experience of psychological distress, but a profound state of being-in-love. The sensory deprivation that he embraced in his spiritual practice was a route to a yet deeper affirmation of the world of the senses, to an even greater love. His life was scarred by poverty and suffering, but he was driven in everything by a passion for God's beauty.

Juan de Yepes y Alvarez (1542–1591) was born of the fleeting rapture of love and raised in the agony of poverty. His father came from a wealthy family but was disowned when he fell in love and married a poor weaver in a small Castilian village. Juan's father died when he was only two, leaving his young mother penniless, forced to beg, rejected by her husband's family. An older brother also died at the time, possibly due to malnutrition. Juan himself was placed in an orphanage.

Growing up, he worked with the poor and sick in a local hospital and attracted the attention of benefactors who offered him a Jesuit education. Eventually he entered the Carmelite order and was ordained at the age of twenty-five. That year he met Teresa of Avila, a Carmelite sister who was fifty-two at the time. She was immediately taken by this diminutive friar (he was only four feet eleven inches tall) and shared with him her dream of revitalizing Carmelite spirituality. Together, they modeled devout simplicity in the religious life, founding a movement of Discalced (or shoeless) Carmelites. Their collaboration is one of the finest examples of spiritual friendship known to us. Juan de la Cruz, as he came to be known, went on to serve as a spiritual director, master of novices, rector of a house of studies, and reformer extraordinaire.

The Spanish Inquisition, however, was wary of religious excesses and particularly of any signs of disobedience to authority. Teresa and John's call for greater seriousness in Carmelite devotion aroused the ire of those within their own community who were resisting reform. John was soon caught in the crosshairs of the guardians of the status quo.

In December 1577, he was kidnapped (blindfolded and handcuffed) and thrown into a prison cell in Toledo. The anti-reforming Carmelites accused him of "renouncing his shoes, inventing a new habit, and sowing discord among the friars."[12] For nine months, he sat in the darkness of a six-by-ten-foot cell. His only light came from a two-inch slit of a window high on one wall. It was a world of shadows, known more intimately by touch than by sight. He wore the same ragged habit in winter cold and summer heat, endured floggings, and survived on bread and water much of the time. John kept his sanity by reciting the Song of Songs, composing poetry, and gradually finding in the darkness a still deeper entry into the beauty for which he longed.

Sitting in the dark, he was initially encouraged by the rightness of his work, the assurance of God's care, the memory of the lustrous world of the senses beyond his cell. But as the days wore on, he came face to face with the harsh rejection of his community, the apparent abandonment of God, and the hollowness of his spiritual life. Months passed, as he knew only waste, boredom, ennui, and despair. He encountered day after day of pointlessness, lethargy, the aridity of *acedia*.

Eventually he began to accept (and not to fight) the relinquishment that was forced upon him. In the process, he found a new freedom. He let go of his attachment to the approval of others, his pride in personal achievement, his desire for "spiritual experiences" of one sort or another. He came to realize that he'd spent most of his life, as others do, "trying to get some feeling and satisfaction," to engineer a profound religious encounter.[13]

What came to him, at last, was the Buddhist-like paradox that "in order to possess all you desire, you have to give up all desire for possession. To gain everything, you have to want nothing." Looking back on his life, he was able to say at last, "Neither this, nor that" to every attachment that had bolstered his identity. In the negation of everything he had trusted, he discovered a love he couldn't fathom. He realized that all of his life God had been hiding in the dark night, in the last place he might have looked, in the hiddenness of his own soul. He marveled that he could now say, "You yourself are his dwelling and his secret inner room and hiding place."[14] By the end of the next summer—having been set free in spirit—he found a way to escape physically as well, loosening the screws on the lock of his cell and lowering himself over a wall with a rope of torn bed sheets. The poems he carried with him would change the shape of Spanish literature and Christian spirituality to this day.

He spent the rest of his life secluded in remote mountain monasteries, writing commentaries on his poetry and taking his brother monks up into the foothills of the Sierra Nevada for days of solitude and prayer. This frail Spanish friar had the heart of a poet and a passion for the high desert country of Andalusia. He knew that the language of love is inherently sensuous. "My Beloved," he wrote, is "the mountains and lonely wooded valleys, strange islands and resounding rivers, the whistling of love-stirring breezes, the tranquil night at the time of the rising dawn, silent music, sounding solitude."[15] Yet his prison experience had taught him that the senses must be carefully honed and disciplined in order to taste the still more sensuous life of the spirit.

Discerning a Pattern in the Journey of the Night

In the years after his imprisonment (1582–1587), the Carmelite reformer penned his greatest works while living in a monastery in Granada. These included *The Dark Night*, *The Spiritual Canticle*, *The Ascent of Mount Carmel*, and *The Living Flame of Love*. In these books, he identified a pattern that people commonly pass through in the movement of the spiritual life. He traced the ups and downs that are an inevitable part of any spiritual journey.

1. Initially, John says, one might experience a sense of assurance and attainment in following a spiritual practice. There are joys to be had in a world full of good things. Every creature is "a trace of God's passing." Yet contentment may gradually turn these gifts into ends in themselves, attractions in their own right. As time goes on, "small attachments become great." You run the risk of becoming as little as the things you've learned to love.[16]

2. But then, by a "lucky chance," you may be brought into a disconcerting period of what John calls a "night of the senses." This is a dark and frustrated condition of having lost all consolations, seemingly abandoned by God, finding no pleasure in the things that had previously offered comfort. This "night" isn't an indictment of unbelief; nor does it come as a punishment. Actually, it's a gift. You've been thrust into the arms of God without knowing it. You're being purged of lesser desires so as to increase your thirst—in your emptiness—for what you've really been wanting all along.[17]

3. In some cases, John says, you might be led into an even deeper "night of the spirit," where nothing satisfies the soul in its desolation. You find no joy whatever in the beauties of nature or any of the gifts that had once been messengers of God's glory. Your soul is weaned of *everything* except a love-starved longing for God alone. "Do not send me any more messengers," the bride of the Canticle declares in her anguish. They "leave me dying of,

ah, I-don't-know-what behind their stammering."[18] She's dissatisfied with anything less than total union with her Beloved, unable to put into words the desolate longing she feels.

4. On the other side of this dark night, as desire is radically realigned, you are able to savor the world again with unattached delight. Creation springs anew into life. In the darkness your imaginative powers had dried up, but in rediscovering love, everything blazes forth again in all of its splendor. The "woods and thickets . . . bright with flowers," the groves where God "pours out a thousand graces," become for the soul "a harmonious symphony of sublime music."[19]

This unfolding pattern of initial confidence, attachment to lesser things, disillusionment, and reorientation of desire is one we've seen already—in the spirituality of the Desert Fathers and Mothers. The similarity is no coincidence. Carmelite spiritual discipline was deeply shaped by desert experience. It descended from a cluster of monks living in caves and huts atop Mount Carmel in twelfth-century Palestine, in imitation of the early Desert Christians. John of the Cross was moved by his reading of *The Golden Legend*, a collection of stories about the Desert Fathers and other saints. He made a habit of writing "sayings" after the pattern of the desert monks, 175 of which are preserved in his *Collected Works*.

The Carmelite saint's desert-tested pattern of growth in the spiritual life isn't a normative expectation for everyone, however. John and Teresa explore the upper reaches of the spiritual life. They offer the equivalent of "higher math" in the advanced levels of spiritual attainment. They've gone places where most of us never go. We have to be careful, therefore, in trying to map the movements of the dark night in our own experience. It's usually only in hindsight that we're able to discern the gift in any of the wounded places of our lives. The help of a spiritual director is indispensable.

It is never easy, for example, to clarify the operations of fear and love in the soul. What terrifies you may be a legitimate fear. But it may also offer entry into unaccountable love. John observed that among the "fears, imaginings, and struggles" of the dark night, there are two terrors capable of frightening a person to death, one imagined and one real. The first is the basilisk, a legendary reptile, the king of serpents, whose very glance can kill. The Spanish friar may have associated it with the deadly asp viper in the cobra family, a poisonous snake occupying the mountains of the Pyrenees and the nightmares of Spanish children.

A far more significant (and authentic) terror is the "vision of God," a heart-striking awe that ultimately dissolves into love. "Since the delight arising from the sight of your being and beauty is unendurable," he said to God, "and since I must die in seeing you, may the vision of your beauty be my death."[20] He knew this fear to be one that overwhelms all others (real and imagined). Astonishment in the face of irresistible beauty was what John yearned for most, to be joined in ecstatic union with the Divine.

Call it wishful thinking, the sublimation of fear, a neurotic craving for love, what you may. But John of the Cross knew that perfect love not only casts out fear, but perfect love is the *completion* of all fears . . . the shocking disclosure that we are most affirmed in the midst of what frightens and disarms us most. Fear isn't the opposite of love. It's the gateway to a trysting place where love finally triumphs. There the love-sick bride finds, to her amazement, that what she had desired most was closer than she ever imagined. There are times, it seems, when fear is nothing more than love waiting to be discovered.[21]

In the Canyon Depths

Getting to that awareness, however, may require a dark journey into wilderness. The wonder of any sort of "wilderness experience" in our lives is its alchemical ability to transform fear into love. What frightens and confuses is able also to heal. But the convoluted path from the one to the other will take you where you don't want to go. In the moonlight of the Maze that night, I stood before a panel of Barrier Canyon–style rock art painted by a people older than the Anasazi. They had disappeared centuries earlier, yet the memory of the dead was alive and well in that place. In the "Harvest Scene" depicted there, a figure holds a sheaf of freshly cut rice grass while ghostly images with horns on their heads stand nearby. The ordinary and mysterious are joined together in a beauty wrapped in death. As one desert backpacker in the Maze has put it, "On the spooky and cool scale of 1 to 10, the Harvest Scene rates a 12."[22]

The convolutions of any maze are deeply unsettling to the soul. That's how it differs, strictly speaking, from a labyrinth. The one disorients, while the other offers comfort. You can't be lost in a labyrinth. Its winding path leads assuredly to a safe center. But in a maze you are condemned to aimless wandering. It remains unpredictable, full of false leads and dead ends. It intentionally confuses. Walking a labyrinth is a spiritual practice observed in many traditions for thousands of years. Yet the maze pattern may be more characteristic of the path many of us tread. Far from meditative or lyrical, it rambles haphaz-ardly toward peripheries rather than systematically toward a center.

That certainly has been the case for me. As I stood before the stone wall in the heart of the Maze, thinking of people who had wrestled with imponder-able questions in that desolate place, I was taken back to a fear more terrify-ing than anything aroused by desert canyons. I'd been wandering through a maze myself for years, trying since childhood to understand a father's in-explicable death. I'd grappled with a mother's descent (years later) into the dark night of Alzheimer's, a beloved teacher's untimely death from cancer, the suicide of a best friend, the heart attack of a rabbi I'd learned to love. The haunting, elongated figures on the sandstone wall took me back to earlier encounters with death. The wall was scribbled with memories of loss, mine and that of many others.

For two thousand years these ethereal figures had borne witness to the recurring mystery of harvest and planting, the dying and the budding of new life. They'd wrestled with the problem of good and evil, light and darkness, love and fear. A tangle of desert canyons is an appropriate place for doing that work. It forces you to probe dead ends, seeking Ariadne's thread in moving out of darkness into a mystery deeper still. But you may also find resources there that you didn't expect. Ed Abbey discovered in the desert an empower-ing anger at injustice, a fearlessness in defending beauty. It either kills you or gets your back up, he said. If you're lucky, maybe you stumble onto the wall-scratchings of others who had been that way before. There in the night, you feel the touch of a finger on your back . . . and you know it's time, at last, to face what you fear.

All through my life I'd been going back to that first encounter with death at the age of thirteen. Guilt had been my earliest effort to explain it. Riding home from the hospital with my mother on the day my father died, I watched rain hitting the car window as words welled up from a hollow place inside: "God took my daddy because I'd been a bad boy." It was the forlorn response of a newly rebellious teenager, fearing that his bid for independence had pushed his dad over the edge.

There was no opportunity to process any of this at the time. My mother was hospitalized with a "nervous breakdown." I had to be "the man of the house," suppressing any needs of my own, retreating into the energies of a number "two" (a helper) on the Enneagram scale.[23] I've always taken refuge in my ability to fix things that are broken. I can take care of mothers who are falling apart. I can handle just about anything—except what is going on inside myself.

It was a long time before I began to access my feelings of fear (and anger) over my father's death. The first effort came in a Marriage Encounter weekend years later. Working with my wife, I recognized the fear of death that I'd carried for so long . . . and the *anger* that simultaneously welled up inside. "Death, you goddamned son-of-a-bitch," I cried out in my grief, "why did you take my father?" I didn't need answers . . . only to voice the pain. The anger rising in that moment was a gift allowing me to identify and confront the fear. It even gave me permission to be angry at my *father* for the first time, asking how he could leave me when I needed him most.

To my amazement, my outpouring of rage was accompanied by a sudden and overwhelming sense of my father's love . . . for the first time. Love arrived in the moment I allowed anger to vanquish fear. Love, fear, and righteous anger are sisters that walk side by side in the hollows of the night. Fear says, "This can kill you. Be careful." Love replies, "But we're in this together." And Anger, made wise by the one and courageous by other, takes both of their hands and says, "Bring it on!" When we access an energizing anger, love may come rushing in, putting fear to rout.

Teresa of Avila, John's sister and teacher in the religious life, knew the value of a holy anger in resisting the devil's temptations to fear and despair. With confidence in God's love, she could boldly exclaim, "A fig for all the devils, for they shall fear *me*." She rebuked her culture's preoccupation with the powers of darkness. "I don't understand these fears, 'The devil! The devil!,' when we can say 'God! God!,' and make the devil tremble."[24] The "fig," by the way, was an obscene hand gesture of the sixteenth century, similar to "giving the finger" to someone today. When one of Teresa's early confessors feared that her visions of Jesus were from the devil, he ordered her to "make the fig" at the image when she saw it again. She did this with great reluctance, of course, but the gutsy Carmelite also knew that her Lord wouldn't take offence at her obedience to uninformed authority.[25]

We can be more daring and outspoken in our relationship to God than we imagine. A rabbi named Arnie Asher taught me this. Over coffee one day he told me the story of a massive heart attack he'd had a few years earlier. It left him in a hospital bed, partially paralyzed, with no hope of recovery. All the deaths and losses of his life weighed heavily on him at the time—the illness of his children, the strains of serving a congregation, a sense of defeat in many spheres of his life. In the anguish of a lonely hospital room—up against the wall in the dark canyons of fear—he suddenly cried out of the depths of his despair, "Fuck you, God!" Suddenly, to his astonishment, the room was filled with light, the *shekinah* glory of God's presence flooding his darkness. Never before had he poured himself out to God so completely . . . with no holds barred. Nor had he ever before known such love. It came, strangely enough, in the convoluted experience of a prayer that bordered on blasphemy.[26]

John of the Cross suggests that there is an elusive mystery about God's way of hiding in darkness, waiting to be found. Just because you don't "understand, taste, or experience" God's presence doesn't mean it isn't there. God may not be as absent as you think in times of "dryness, darkness, and dereliction." On the contrary, that's when God may be closest, just on the other side of your loss of control.[27]

Not long before my trip into the Maze, I'd witnessed my mother's experience of this, sitting beside her bed in the nursing home where she was dying. She had slipped into the utter vacancy of Alzheimer's. To borrow John of the Cross's imagery, she might have entered into a "night of the spirit," a time when "God leaves the intellect in darkness, the will in aridity, the memory in emptiness."[28] But I also sensed that she had moved into a deeper peace than she'd ever known. Gerald May says that finding our heart's greatest desire often involves being "taken where we could not and would not go on our own."[29]

There in the dark night, wandering through a maze, the impossible may happen. You find yourself moving beyond the fear and confusion you've been carrying for years. It's no longer necessary to "fix" what was unresolved in your parents' lives. You can leave the past—there at the canyon wall, on the floor of the Maze, finally and for good. NOTHING ELSE NEEDS TO HAPPEN in order for you to go on with your life. What IS, right now, is enough.[30]

Some of us feel responsible for resolving the unfinished stories that have been passed on from one generation to the next. "Nothing has a stronger influence psychologically on the child than the unlived life of the parent," says Carl Jung.[31] To finally let that go can be a miraculous thing. However and whenever it happens, it won't be by any effort of your own. It probably will have to be *taken* from you, in a dark place where you hadn't intended to go. To your astonishment, love is what you discover left in its place.

The sun rose that Utah morning, a few hours after we had walked back in silence from the Harvest Scene to our campsite. I sat on a red rock ledge thirteen stories above the canyon floor, writing in my journal—trying to make sense of what had happened.

The silence of the canyon depths was unsettling. The only sounds I could hear were those of my own breathing, blood pumping in my temples, the glide of the pen on the page. Sitting there, absorbed in my scribbling, I was vaguely aware of a raven on the other side of the canyon, breaking the silence, chattering at me. Every time I stopped writing, the raven stopped, too. It took me a while to realize what was going on. A voice from the canyon was inviting me to give up the writing, to abandon the effort to explain things. I didn't have to resolve my father's death or produce any final analysis of fear. I didn't have to understand . . . or even to be good. I had only, as Mary Oliver says, to "let the soft animal of my body love what it loves."[32] The scholar in me had nothing left to figure out. "At the end of the day," says John of the Cross, "the subject of examination will be love."[33] Love alone. Laughing with the raven, I put the journal away, closed my eyes, and leaned back against the red rock in the warmth of the sun.

The next afternoon we hiked out of the Maze, made our way back to the SUV, and maneuvered once more the rocky route of the Flint Trail. Turning up the music as loud as we could, we listened to the grinding beat of Bruce Springsteen's "The River." We'd been "down to the river" ourselves, that's for damned sure, having survived more than a writhing nest of Utah canyons. We'd been reintroduced to our deepest fears and apprehended by a love we couldn't imagine. We had been taken through the Maze and we were going home again.

10

Failure: Mt. Whitney and Martin Luther

A monk was asked, "What do you do there in the monastery?" He replied, "We fall and get up, fall and get up, fall and get up again."

TITO COLLIANDER[1]

Mistakes are the portals of discovery.

JAMES JOYCE[2]

THERE ARE TIMES on the trail when you have to turn back. Nothing is more discouraging. Maybe you've done something stupid, like losing the map. Changing weather conditions may have made it dangerous or foolhardy to go any further. Maybe your gear is soaking wet or the black flies have become unbearable. Sometimes you simply don't have it in you to go on. Whatever brings you to that point, you admit defeat and grudgingly head back toward the trailhead.

Yet there are times when *not* reaching one's goal on a pack trip may be even better than having done so. At least that's what I've always told myself about my failure to climb Mt. Whitney. It was my second year at seminary in California. My roommate Eric and I wanted to cap off our previous trips into the Sierra Nevada by hiking the highest peak in the lower forty-eight. We had made mistakes on earlier hikes, as we would on this one. That's always easy to do in the Sierras.

One afternoon on an earlier trip, for instance, we'd been returning to our base camp on the High Sierra Trail when we got tired of the interminable switchbacks. We decided to take a "shortcut" down through the rocks. But within ten minutes we were in trouble, facing a level of rock-climbing for which we weren't prepared. We soon were separated, each of us fearing the other had fallen as we heard rock tumbling in the distance, then nothing but silence. Hours later we stumbled onto each other on the trail in the dark far below, grateful to be alive—knowing how foolish we had been. That's what wilderness does for you, says Gary Snyder. It lets you make all the mistakes you need in order to get where you're really going.[3]

The trail we took up Mt. Whitney, peaking at 14,505 feet, was a grueling one. The average elevation gain is 550 feet a mile, though the altitude makes it seem twice that. But the beauty is incredible. Hidden lakes appear and disappear on the winding trail. Wind-blown firs and deep grass at Bighorn Meadow are overshadowed by towering granite cliffs with snowfields plunging a thousand feet down. The sky is as close as you'll ever get to flying. It's a landscape that hangs from the roof of the world.

It's also a place where things can go wrong. Mistakes increase in danger in proportion to the altitude. At the highest reaches of Inyo National Forest, you can't hike much before July (when the snow melts) or after August (when thunderstorms come and winter returns). For duffers like myself, the mountain affords a narrow window of opportunity, fraught with the unexpected. There are risks of dehydration, twisted ankles, and altitude sickness. Sunburn and frostbite can threaten on the same day, not to mention quickly rising storms and the onslaught of galloping fear.

It was early June that summer when Eric and I camped at the trailhead for a day or so to get acclimated. We set out from Whitney Portal on the eastern side of the mountain, hiking past Lone Pine Lake and establishing our base camp near timberline at Mirror Lake. I knew nothing about hiking in snow and ice at the time, and a recent storm had left more of both on the trail than we expected. We had started earlier in the summer than was wise that year, hadn't checked on recent weather conditions, and had arrived without all the equipment we needed. Early the next morning we stopped at Consultation Lake to tie instep crampons onto our boots; we should have had twelve-point mountaineering crampons and trekking poles. We didn't know how much the world changes at two and a half miles above sea level. I felt the full weight of my inexperience.

The trail became increasingly hard as we made our way up the ninety-nine switchbacks between Trail Camp and Trail Crest (at 12,777 feet). This is a two-mile section of the trail that hikers remember most. The higher you go, the more you're taken by the desolate beauty of gray granite, white snow, and blue sky. But the desolation works its way into the soul as well. This was ultimately where I had to turn back, some 1,700 vertical feet from the summit.

Stumbling off the path at one point, clinging to a rock over a steep precipice, I felt the numbing terror of heights for the first time in my life. Worse yet, a cloud bank suddenly moved in, bringing fog so thick I could hardly see beyond my feet. I was scared to death. When we later came to a place that required my stepping over what seemed a sheer drop into an abyss below, I couldn't do it. Eric went on without me, returning to report how close I'd come to the stunning view of the Sierras to the west and the final route to the peak. Yet nothing could have enticed me to go any further at the time.

Later that night, as we returned in exhaustion to our campsite, a group of Boy Scouts passed through, coming back down from the peak. I asked them how far they'd gotten, thinking they wouldn't have made it much beyond the switchbacks. To my chagrin, they announced that they'd all reached the top, even the youngest of them, who was twelve years old. I was blown away. Failure felt like an indictment of my worth as a person, confirmation of a deeper defect in character.

Not making it to the summit of Mt. Whitney has become over the years a metaphor for something profoundly important in my life. The unclimbed mountain is often the most beautiful. Its capacity to teach is supreme. What we *aren't* able to attain at times proves more powerful than anything within our reach.[4] Thomas Merton, on his trip to Asia, was struck by the compelling power of Mt. Kanchenjunga in the Himalayas. He could see it only from a distance at Darjeeling, knowing that the truth of the mountain lay in its inaccessibility. "There is another side of Kanchenjunga and of every mountain," he said, "the side that has never been photographed and turned into postcards. That is the only side worth seeing."[5] It is also the side that remains forever unclimbed, lying beyond all human effort to achieve.

The most important "mountain" in one's life offers no pride of accomplishment, only the unwelcome gifts of inadequacy and incompletion. Whether you face a physical inability to make it to the end of the trail, a failure in meeting the expectations of others, or a realization that you've betrayed someone you love, whatever it is . . . you learn over time that it isn't the end. Every failure is an invitation to growth. Mistakes are occasions for grace, opportunities to choose a different path. They make forgiveness possible. Only in the absence of success can you know yourself to be loved without cause.

Martin Luther: A Theology for Times of Failure

No one has taught me this better than the sixteenth-century Augustinian monk who inadvertently launched the Protestant Reformation. He was a life-line for me as I tried to climb yet another mountain in my first year of doctoral study at Princeton. Had it not been for Martin Luther and his theology of radical grace, I wouldn't have made it across that perilous academic terrain.

My first year at Princeton was one of the hardest of my life. No one in my family had ever been to college, much less attempted graduate work in an Ivy League town with a tradition to live up to. My mother hadn't gotten past the seventh grade and my father had only made it through high school. I was intimidated by professors and classmates alike. The other student admitted with me into the program that year had done his earlier work at Harvard and Yale. I'd been to Florida State and Fuller Seminary. While I had read theologians like Reinhold Niebuhr and Paul Tillich, he knew "Reinie" personally and had been to dinner at Paul and Hannah's home.

I felt painfully out of place. In seminars, graduate students bragged about their connections and told jokes with the punch line in Latin. I tried to laugh credibly and not appear a fool, but it was obvious I didn't belong. By the end of the year I was taking tranquilizers to ward off panic attacks and talking weekly to a heavily accented German psychiatrist at a nearby hospital. I wouldn't have survived without the help of Luther's deliverance from the need to be perfect.

Martin Luther (1483–1546) was born into a German peasant family. His father, an iron and copper miner, had aspirations of moving into the middle class. As an only son, young Martin had high expectations to fulfill. He grew up feeling he could never do enough to please his parents or to prove his worth. He didn't succeed in law school, as his father had hoped, and in subsequently becoming a monk (and later a theology professor) he wasn't able to please God any better. Hard as he tried, young Luther failed (at least in his own eyes) to earn the approval of family members, teachers and superiors, even God. He simply wasn't able to measure up to the demands placed upon him.

But one night in 1512, as he read Paul's letter to the Romans in the tower room of the cloister at Wittenberg, he was stunned by the insight of a gracious God. He suddenly realized that God's acceptance of him wasn't based on anything he could *do*. He was accepted solely for what he *was*, inadequate and incomplete as that might be. Theologically, he spoke of this as being justified by faith rather than works. All he had to do was "accept his acceptance," as Paul Tillich later put it.[6] Luther discovered a relationship to God that wasn't based on Law (and the meeting of expectations), but on Gospel (the surprising assurance that God delights in sinners even more than saints).

He remembered his time as a young student at Erfurt, where a large, apron-clothed butcher ran out of his shop one day, chasing him and several other boys who had been looking through his window. The butcher was furiously waving sausages in the air as he pursued them, eager to give them away, but the boys mistook his enthusiasm for anger and ran in the opposite direction.[7] All of his life, Luther had feared an angry, demanding God, only to discover in the end that God had been wanting to love and forgive all along.

Gripped by this truth, the young theologian began criticizing the theology of merited grace that was prevalent in his day. He questioned the presumption that divine favor could be obtained by "keeping the rules"—making pilgrimages to visit the relics of the saints, buying indulgences, observing religious obligations of one sort or another. He feared the church had become a vast approval system, focused on earning outward religious points while neglecting the interiority of the heart. Luther ruled out on principle any notion of perfectionism in the spiritual life.[8]

"Learn to know Christ," he advised a friend, "so as to despair of yourself and to say: 'You, Lord Jesus, you are my righteousness, but I, I am your sins: you have assumed that which is mine, and you have given me that which is yours.'"[9] Unable by his own willpower to fulfill the demands of God's law, he accepted by faith that God had pronounced him righteous on the basis of what Christ had done for him. Hence, when God looked upon him, God saw only good. This confidence set him free to *become* what he had been *declared* to be. He was able to live into the vision that God had of him instead of polishing a vision of himself and offering it to God as proof of his worth.

The Wittenberg theologian's criticism of shallow devotional practices and his subsequent questioning of the church's role in dispensing grace led to controversy. In 1517, he posted his Ninety-Five Theses for theological discussion, protesting the selling of indulgences—assurances that lessened one's temporal punishment in purgatory for sins already forgiven. In the heat of scriptural debate, Luther went on to question the power of the papacy in his emphasis on the authority of the Holy Spirit speaking through the larger Church. He was excommunicated in 1521.

The hierarchy perceived Luther's theology as permissive, even cavalier, in its treatment of sin and disobedience. His view of a gracious God threatened to undermine the need for effort in the spiritual life. It seemed to condone, even encourage, failure. Luther's response was to quote the apostle Paul, who acknowledged that the shocking character of God's grace naturally raises the question: "Do we sin, then, that grace may abound?" (Romans 6:1) "Of course not," Paul answered. But in effect he added, "You're on the right track in even asking that question." Failure is what occasions the extraordinary gift of God's grace. *O felix culpa* (O happy sin), the medieval liturgy proclaimed—this tragedy that makes possible such astonishing forgiveness! Julian of Norwich was so bold as to affirm that, in heaven, sin becomes a badge of *honor* rather than a matter of *shame*. There the sinner recognizes her sin as having been a "necessity," the only thing that could have brought her to the brink of such love.[10]

Luther never denied that conscientious effort becomes a *subsequent* expectation in the life of the believer. Faith, he said, has to be active in love. It isn't a Pollyanna exercise in wishful thinking. Good works arise naturally out of our freedom in being forgiven, *not* out of a sense of guilt, a need to please, or an effort to obtain merit. The moral life consists of our living our way into the reality that God already sees us to be.

Luther's theology of grace played itself out in a very earthy and practical spirituality. He argued that, since believers are already saints in the eyes of God, everyone has a holy, even priestly vocation to assume in the world. They naturally express the joy and zeal of forgiven people in the everyday details of their lives. Luther and his wife Katie Von Bora, a former nun, took delight in their six children. Those who live a celibate, "religious" life, he insisted, aren't the only ones capable of exercising a divine calling.

One evening Luther and his wife were entertaining students from the University of Wittenberg where he taught. After dinner they were discussing theology over good German beer (no doubt), when Luther noticed that the baby he was holding had messed its diaper. Warmly embracing the child, he said jokingly, "Look at all we put up with in loving you! How much more does God have to put up with in loving us?" He then excused himself to change the baby, returning to remind his students how a father's work in changing diapers is just as holy a vocation as that of a monk in a monastery reading the holy office.[11]

I love Luther's earthiness. On a typical afternoon, he could be found talking theology over a beer down at the Black Eagle tavern in Wittenberg. According to tradition, he had a tall stein with three lines drawn on it—one for the Ten Commandments, one for the Apostles' Creed, and one for the Lord's Prayer. He prided himself on the fact that he could drain his glass all the way to the Lord's Prayer while his colleague Agricola couldn't get beyond the Ten Commandments.[12]

Luther had a coarse, outspoken manner about him. He called the pope a Florentine bastard and his prejudice against Jews was appalling.[13] Yet despite his flaws, he possessed a down-to-earth practicality, a sense of humor, and a casual grace in putting people at ease. All this grew out of his theology of a gracious God. He placed far greater emphasis on forgiveness than on judgment, much like the early Desert Fathers.

Desert Fathers and the Lapses of Younger Monks

The Desert Christians were renowned for their strict discipline of prayer and fasting. Yet at the same time they were gracious to the extreme in dealing with the failures of others . . . especially those who were new to the spiritual life. In fact, says Dominican theologian Simon Tugwell, "The Desert Fathers seem to be rather casual about morality." To the consternation of those more rigidly moralistic, they appeared almost reckless in the way they excused the mistakes of their brothers. Tugwell suggests that the monks practiced a "spirituality of imperfection," putting a far higher value on humility than on achievement. As one of the early Fathers said, "It is better to fail with humility than to succeed with pride."[14]

Numerous stories in the *Sayings of the Desert Fathers* speak of the sensitivity of the older monks to the weaknesses of the younger ones. The elders refused to judge or to shame them, always putting the finest possible interpretation on their behavior, whatever it might be. In one of the narratives, a young monk stole a valuable Bible from the cell of Abba Gelasius and took it to a bookseller in a nearby town to see how much money he could get for it. The bookseller told him, "I'll have to ask around to see what it's worth and then I'll get back to you."

When the monk returned a week later, the shop owner explained, "I had to ask Abba Gelasius, since he knows the worth of these books more than anyone else around here. He said you shouldn't accept less than eighteen pieces of silver for it. This is a valuable book. You've got something precious here." The young monk asked with chagrin, "Is that *all* he said? He didn't ask you about *who* was trying to sell it?" "No, he didn't say a thing," responded the bookseller. The young monk then took the Bible back to the monastery *and* to Abba Gelasius, knowing he'd found something more precious than a valuable book. He'd found the forgiveness of an older brother.[15]

In an even more interesting story, some of the elders approached Abba Ammonas one day on their way to confront a lapsed brother over his moral failures with women. They asked Ammonas to join them. Now the young monk *had* been getting into trouble. In fact, there was a woman in his cell at the time when he heard that the elders were coming. So he hid her in a large barrel in the corner. When Ammonas came in, he realized what was going on and sat on the top of the barrel while the rest of the monks searched every-where for the guilty party they expected to find.

Ammonas finally said, "What is this? May God forgive you for unjustly accusing this poor man." After praying, he made all the others leave. Then he took the erring young monk by the hand and simply said, "Brother, be on your guard." That was all. No lectures. No shaming. He spared the young man's reputation in front of the others, so that the erring man might live into the confidence that Ammonas had in him. The wise old monk knew that in nurturing younger souls "what you see is what you get." They grow most readily into the goodness you affirm them as already having. We don't know, by the way, whether Ammonas also prayed for the woman, sending her away with a blessing as well. We can only hope that he did.[16]

John Climacus, abbot of the monastery at Mt. Sinai, insisted on giving everyone the benefit of the doubt. "Don't judge anybody, ever," he said. "Even if you see them doing something wrong with your own eyes!" Appearances can be deceiving. You may be wrong. Don't judge.[17] The monks' compassion brought out the best in those who might otherwise have been justly accused. Their insight into human behavior was profound. They knew that criticism invariably shuts us down. But the confidence others express in us spurs us to become what they see us to be.

Rudolf Dreikurs, the Adlerian psychiatrist and educator, regularly urged his clients to embrace "the courage to be imperfect."[18] He thought that in our culture perfectionism had become far more than the pursuit of personal ex-cellence. It had become, for many, the only way to gain personal acceptance. To resist judging oneself, therefore, is to foster a compassion that sets others free as well. Criticism eats into the soul like an acid. Generosity of spirit mul-tiplies itself over and over again.

One of the more rigorous monks once complained to Abba Poemen, "What do you do with these lazy young novices who fall asleep during the holy office? It bothers me to no end." Poemen responded by saying, "To tell you the truth, when I see a brother falling asleep, I like to place his head on my knees so as to let him rest more comfortably. I'm sure he's been awake all night praying and the poor man needs his sleep."[19] Poemen persisted in seeing only the good in others. If anything captures the grace of the message of Jesus of Nazareth, it must be this.

The point here isn't that moral failures should be taken lightly—as if no more significant than falling asleep in church or turning back on the trail. When we sin we choose *not* to be who we are, the most dangerous of all pos-sible choices. Moral failure is a denial of one's truest self. In Robert Bolt's play

A Man for All Seasons, Sir Thomas More explains to his daughter Meg that there are times when a man holds his own self in his hands, like water. "If he opens his fingers then—he needn't hope to find himself again."[20] To betray the core of one's being is to put one's very soul at risk.

Yet even then . . . *especially then*, as individuals in Twelve-Step programs know so well, God remains eager to forgive. Where the least desire for authenticity and change remains, the most egregious faults can be healed . . . because the desire itself arises out of what is already there in the hiddenness of the soul. One wouldn't long for wholeness were it not a previous God-given reality. Sin, therefore, is never the last word. Grace refuses in the end to admit defeat.

For Luther and the Desert Fathers before him, sin doesn't define a person's identity. Our truest self is rooted in God's prior affirmation of us, not in the sin that distorts what God affirms. Only in the living out of that certainty are we finally set free to become more fully what we already are. Failure no longer determines one's selfhood. It becomes a route to greater wholeness instead.

An Invitation to Vulnerability

In our consumer-driven society, an image of flawless proficiency is crucial to success. To admit failure in a world that judges value by polished surfaces is to lose your edge as a commodity in the marketplace. This is as true, sadly, in higher education and religion as it is in business, sports, and politics.

We're expected to exhibit a quality of perfection we know we don't possess. All we can do is attempt to hide our sense of insufficiency. The "imposter syndrome" leaves us juggling multiple strategies for concealment while warding off a nagging fear of being "found out."[21] We know we aren't as capable as people assume (or expect) us to be.

My effort to maintain this masquerade nearly destroyed me in my first year of doctoral study. I couldn't do enough to impress my teachers, even to feel adequate as a human being. Day after day, I'd stand in a circle of graduate students chatting about things of which I knew nothing, only to run to the library later to look up what they had been talking about. By the end of the year, I was thinking I'd made a terrible mistake in imagining I could teach theology. I should have been selling used cars (or something else useful) instead of trying hopelessly to disguise my incompetence as a graduate student. I'd reached bottom. My wife's love was all that sustained me. Knowing the burden I was to her at the time, I thought even of taking my life. My father had shown me how, after all.

But something happened at the end of that first year that changed everything. I had a dream. I've not been prone to dramatic religious experiences in my life. Yet I cannot discount the power of what came to me in the dream that night. I was teaching a class of graduate students gathered around a small seminar table. We were caught up in a discussion of Luther's Galatians commentary, exulting in his insistence that a person's worth isn't linked to her performance. Worth is determined by God alone.[22]

Amid the shared enthusiasm of the class, I became aware of someone standing in the corner of the room. It was Jim Morgan, the best teacher I'd ever had. He had taught me theology at Fuller Seminary the year before I came to Princeton. It was because of him that I'd gone on for doctoral study. I had loved his passion for theology, his commitment to social justice, his courageous sharing of himself in class. As a scholar and teacher he was everything I wanted to be.

During my final year at seminary Jim was diagnosed with incurable cancer. I took every course he offered that year. The best way to learn theology is to sit at the feet of someone who knows he is dying and wants to share what he loves most in the time he has left. Jim died nine months later, during my first year at Princeton. Yet I swear that he came back to me in my dream.

As the class I was teaching ended and the students left, Jim walked over from the corner of the room to sit at the table across from me. He looked at me with the eyes of a proud father (or older brother) and said, "Belden, I love you . . . and I want you to know that I couldn't have taught that class any better if I'd been here myself." I was overwhelmed in that moment by a euphoric sense of being affirmed. I was loved by a teacher who had died and come back for me, by a father who had left when I was thirteen but was still there for me, by a God who I now knew had indeed called me to teach. I woke up, shouting the word *"Abba, Abba . . .* Daddy" over and over again. If I'd stayed asleep, I suspect I'd have spoken in tongues for the first time in my life.

The next fall I went back for a second year of classes at Princeton Seminary. Nothing was any easier. The difference was that I stopped pretending, now allowing my vulnerability to show. In a long seminar one afternoon, we were wrestling with the complexities of Augustine's hermeneutics—reporting on German and French articles we'd been assigned. I walked out of class afterward with Bob Mathewson. Bob was the student who had known "Reinie" personally and had been over to Paul and Hannah's for dinner. I took a risk and told him I hadn't understood half of what was going on in the class. To my amazement, Bob replied that he hadn't either! I learned that he had been struggling with a bleeding ulcer during his first year of doctoral study. He'd been as anxious and intimidated as I was.

We started eating lunch together, dropping our need to hide the failure we both felt. We shared our frustrations, bitched about teachers, and began building a small community of celebrated imperfection. It got us through the program. Instead of hiding our flaws, our flaws became gifts connecting us in our deepest humanity.

The Gift of Imperfection

In the work I do now with men, through men's rites of passage and follow-up programs sponsored by the Illuman organization and Men as Learners and Elders, we find that the wounds in our lives can be the source of our greatest gifts. "We grow spiritually much more by doing it wrong than by doing it right," says Richard Rohr.[23] The only way to make progress is by making mistakes . . . over and over again. The seemingly perfect man isn't perfect at all. He's just better than others at hiding his shadow.

From a Zen perspective, one might say that growth is a matter of learning truly to make mistakes "perfectly"—that is, to bring such an attentiveness to what we do that we act with an immediate mindfulness of what we are doing. Paradoxically, when that happens, we aren't able to do it in the same way as before. Full, conscious awareness of a behavior will change the way we behave.[24] It points us to a new responsibility, a freedom to choose whether or not to be the person we know ourselves to be.

But this doesn't happen apart from a contemplative practice of some sort and the ongoing support of a community. In the men's circles of which I'm a part we bring our various histories of addiction, physical and sexual abuse, marital affairs, and failures with children. We're carried back through these failures to the mystery of being loved unaccountably. To our amazement we find that the place where we screw up the most is the place where God loves us the most. *Nothing* is closer to the heart of the gospel than this.

The disciple of a Sufi master once came to his teacher, saying, "Master, I've done terrible things in my life. I know Allah can never forgive me. What can I do?" "Ah, my son," answered the master, "Don't you see? All of us are connected to God by a piece of rope, one that is the same length for every one of us. When we sin, alas, we cut the rope that connects us to the Holy One. But when we repent, God is eager to tie the pieces together again. Every time you tie a knot in a rope, of course, it gets shorter. Hence, those with more knots in their rope are that much closer to God. So trust, my son, in the forgiveness of Allah, the Merciful and Compassionate One. He *loves* to tie knots!"

This isn't the celebration of failure, but the gift of the freedom to make mistakes. The difference is crucial. For years I belonged to a tiny circle of would-be writers in St. Louis. We called ourselves the Irving R. Feldman writing group. We had the good sense to realize that the greatest obstacle to our work was our fear of failure. It kept us from taking chances. So we had a single rule for continued membership in the group. We had to receive at least two letters of non-acceptance every year. It wasn't necessary to get anything published. But we did have to keep submitting pieces and risking rejection.

We named the group after a character in Herb Gardner's "A Thousand Clowns." According to Murray Burns, the zany protagonist of the play, Irving R. Feldman was the proprietor of the best kosher deli in his Manhattan neighborhood. Burns made a point of observing the man's birthday each year as a national holiday—using as the highest measure of success one's ability to make a really fine pastrami sandwich.[25] In adopting his name we wanted to honor that same alternative set of values.

As I think back on my failure to climb Mt. Whitney, I find comfort in the fact that John Muir didn't make it on his first try either. On the morning of October 15, 1873, he started out for the peak, leaving his horse to graze in a meadow in one of the lower canyons. After hiking all day, he couldn't find wood to build a fire so he continued climbing into the night, taking bearings by the stars. "By midnight," he wrote in his journal, "I was among the summit needles [though still shy of the top]. There I had to dance all night to keep from freezing, and was feeble and starving next morning." He finally had to turn back. But a week later Muir returned to scale the peak by a direct route from the east side.[26] It was the first time anyone had made that ascent.

We don't always succeed. But sometimes failure proves to be a better gift. Failure points us back to the true measure of our worth, to something grounded in nothing that we do, but only in what we are. The cloud-covered majesty of Mt. Whitney, the mountain I didn't climb, will always remind me of that.

Dying: *Mudlick Mountain Trail and* The Cloud of Unknowing

Ironic, but one of the most intimate acts of our body is death.
So beautiful appeared my death—knowing who then i would kiss,
I died a thousand times before I died.
"Die before you die," said the Prophet Muhammad.
Have wings that feared ever touched the Sun?
I was born when all I once feared—I could love.

RABIA AL-ADAWIYYA (717–801)[1]

Hopefully there will come a time when I have no words,
when I can honor and hold that kind of stillness that I so
need, crave, and desire in the natural world . . . One day
this landscape will take the language out of me.

TERRY TEMPEST WILLIAMS[2]

EVERETT RUESS DISAPPEARED in the redrock canyons of southeast Utah in November 1934. The twenty-year-old artist, poet, and vagabond had left the town of Escalante a few days earlier, setting out with his two burros along the Hole-in-the-Rock Road toward the Colorado River. He was no stranger to wilderness, despite his youth. He had wandered the West for years. But he was never seen again. Searchers found his two burros by his campsite in a remote gulch, his footprints leading nowhere in particular, and a word recently scratched on a sandstone wall: "Nemo . . . 1934." No one.[3]

How could the desert have swallowed him alive without leaving a trace? Was he killed by rustlers? Had he run away with Navajo Indians? What could erase him so quickly and completely from the desert landscape? The previous year he had written his brother about the irresistible joy of wild country, saying, "I'll never stop wandering. And when the time comes to die, I'll find the wildest, loneliest, most desolate spot there is."[4] Apparently that's what happened. There was no hint of suicide, no sign of violence. The mystery has never been solved.

The story's grip on the imagination is more than that of a cautionary tale, warning of the dangers of backcountry travel. You stand a better chance, anyway, of being killed on city streets than on the far reaches of the Colorado Plateau. Wilderness wandering is no more inherently life-threatening than driving home on the freeway every night. What makes wild terrain seem so menacing (and yet captivating) is the deceptively comforting character of our technological society. It gives us the illusion of being in control of our environment. Wilderness, by contrast, lies beyond the reach of our managerial skills. It challenges the ego. Its threat of death is more psychological and spiritual than physical. Unfrequented canyons broach the possibility of our dying to what we've known in the past, losing rational control, encountering a wonderment beyond understanding.

Everett Ruess perceived this potential of "dying before one dies" as something to be welcomed. He reveled in the wild beauty of the canyons because of the "large measure of self-forgetfulness" it afforded.[5] It took him out of himself into a mystery he couldn't comprehend, stripping him of words. His story stands as a commentary on the disappearance of the self in the practice of wilderness spirituality. It says as much about the teachings of the mystics as it does about the hazards of hiking in wild terrain.

The spiritual life involves risk. There's no way around it. The paradox of biblical religion is that God cannot be understood, much less managed. Coming to terms with ultimate mystery is always dangerous. But to our amazement, encountering the Holy can also mean being strangely and unaccountably loved. Poets and mystics agree that there's no greater risk than being loved—with God the most decisive risk of all, Pascal would add. To our unsettling delight, we encounter the ultimate in what is irrevocably wild and irresistibly loving. The language that people customarily use in describing wilderness experience strikingly resembles the language of mystics trying to "speak the unspeakable." Both sorts of encounter are rooted in a relentless desire for what disrupts (and delights) human consciousness.

Mary Austin, author of *The Land of Little Rain* (1903), lived in mining towns along the San Joaquin Valley at the end of the nineteenth century. She was intrigued by this double edge of the desert landscape. The desert's juxtaposition of wildness and love, fury and passion was tantalizing: "It would come leaping out at me . . . [like] coyotes hot in the chase." As a naturalist and poet, she discovered in the Mojave Desert what she "utterly desired"—what could "eat you up" and "love you to death." She also acknowledged:

> There was something else there . . . a lurking, evasive Something, wistful, cruel, ardent; something that rustled and ran, that hung half-remotely, insistent on being noticed, fled from pursuit, and when you turned from it, leaped suddenly and fastened on your vitals. This is no mere figure of speech, but the true movement of experience.[6]

Her language is curiously akin to Francis Thompson's chilling yet ecstatic account of being pursued by "The Hound of Heaven."[7] Discovering an unexpected joy at the moment of being overtaken in the chase was an allurement that neither could resist. Such an experience stretches the soul to the breaking point, as if the soul might find its highest joy in being broken.

The Descent into Hell: Dying Before One Dies

The myth of the hero's journey includes a necessary descent into the underworld, the labyrinth, the dark cave of death. Any possibility of new life lies on the other side of that threshold. Inanna, in the ancient Sumerian tale, passes through the seven gates of hell where for three days and three nights her corpse hangs on a hook before she is finally revived and released. Odysseus is trapped in a cave by the one-eyed man-eating Cyclops on his hazardous return to Ithaca. Frodo Baggins crosses the mountains of Mordor where he falls into Shelob's lair and is wrapped in spider silk, left for death. Bill Wilson lies in a New York hospital bed in 1934, having reached rock bottom in his years-long struggle with alcohol.

These are instances of the "soul initiation" that Bill Plotkin identifies in the life-changing movement from adolescent egocentricity to adult soulfulness. We see it in Jonah's experience in the belly of the whale, the "necessary fall" that Richard Rohr says we all pass through in growing toward maturity. Rilke speaks of it as a tree-whipping storm raging across your life. "The wind sucks the world from your senses like withered leaves." An "immense loneliness begins."[8] As you tread the spiritual path, you may negotiate multiple times of such withering in your life. Each new stage is preceded by the death of the previous one. In my own life, my father's suicide, my painful first year of doctoral study, and the recent approach of retirement have all been upheavals of this sort.

These occasions for "dying" in our lives begin with an attraction to a hostile yet compelling beauty. We're pulled, despite ourselves, into its life-altering mystery. Inanna craves the Great Below from her seat in the Great Above. Odysseus is seductively drawn by the death-bringing melody of the Sirens. Rilke "sings" the rising storm as he stands beside an open window. Frodo delights in the very ring that threatens to destroy him.

We know in our viscera that a necessary but deadly attraction lies on the path toward wholeness. We're drawn to what has to die in us as well as what wants to be born. Inherently we sense that the uncaring majesty of wilderness has the potential of breaking us open to love. Each passage to a new self begins with an allurement that threatens to kill, even as it ignites a new fire within.

The spirituality I speak of in this book is rooted in an experience of the ego being dismantled through exposure to a wild and reckless beauty. The soul exults in the intimacy that this dying-to-the-self affords. A beauty that "so coolly disdains to destroy us," despite its indifference (maybe even *because* of its indifference), evokes a deeper yearning for engagement. We know, like William James, that something "More" is calling us. Our desire is a response to what first desired us. The soul hungers for the "evasive Something" that Mary Austin found so compelling, even as the ego resists it. For the grasping self, God is a disconcerting threat. For the soul, God is a fierce lover and friend.

What we aren't able to comprehend, we nonetheless can love, says the anonymous author of *The Cloud of Unknowing*. Wilderness suggests that we can only *ever* be loved by what we don't understand. In our anxiety to be safe, we flee from all things wild, clinging to what we're able to explain. This keeps us, temporarily, from death. It also keeps us from love.

Relinquishing our claim to autonomy is part of any experience of transcendence. "Unless a grain of wheat falls into the earth and dies," said Jesus, "it remains alone; but if it dies, it bears much fruit" (John 12:24). Letting go of what we aren't able to handle is the goal of most spiritual disciplines. Welcoming the "little deaths" that release our clutching control on life, we move beyond the ego's exercise of power to an unanticipated awe, to the possibility of love. The French appropriately speak of the experience of orgasm as *la petite mort*. The most sublime moment of union with the beloved involves a prerequisite dying to self-sufficiency.

This interplay between the wilderness experience of losing control and the sublime experience of being loved forms the crux of my two most important spiritual practices: wilderness backpacking and contemplative prayer.

Each offers the possibility of leaving behind the restless activity of my life, getting out of my head, entering the presence of a mystery I'm unable to comprehend.

It isn't that the wilderness "loves" me or that silence reaches out to embrace me. In fact, they both repel and attract me at the same time. I hunger for the wild beauty and jarring solitude of a mountain trail. I'm drawn to the deep, unsettling silence in the backcountry of the mind. Yet I resist both— the very things I love—because I know they require my loosening my grip on the security of language and culture. In yielding to the unpredictability of the trail or the hush of meditation my scaffolding is knocked out from under me, as Henri Nouwen would say.[9]

We avoid those experiences in our lives when the ego has to take another hit. Yet if we stay at the discipline, we find ourselves exchanging a loss of imagined security for a breathtaking freedom. The "dying" you encounter in that moment is but "a stripping away of all that is not you," says Eckhart Tolle. "The secret of life," in fact, "is to 'die before you die'—and find that there is no death."[10] You discover that the soul has delighted all along in what the ego fears most. It exults in trails that haven't yet been mapped.

The importance of disabling the ego (and finding adequate techniques for doing so) is basic to the teachings of all the great religions. Their various forms of meditative practice aim at defeating the small self, the interfering mind. In the Sufi tradition, the goal of spiritual exercise—whether the repetition of the divine names or the dancing of the whirling dervishes—is *fanā*, the annihilation of the false self. The believer dies to her compulsive ego so that her soul can rest in the hands of Allah. In Hinduism, the Lord Shiva's task is to obliterate the autonomous self, freeing the believer from old habits and attachments, carrying her through death into new life. Shiva the Destroyer dances with multiple arms outstretched—one hand holding a devouring flame, the other a dancing drum; one raised in threat, the other lowered in a welcoming gesture of love. There's no way around it. The condition for intimacy with the Holy is the demise of the frantic, acquisitive ego.[11]

A Desert Father once confronted his confrere, Abba Poemen, who had taken personal offense at the words of another brother. "Poemen, are you still alive?" the monk asked him. "I thought you were already dead. Go, sit in your cell, and remind your heart that you have been in the grave for a year."[12] These old desert codgers had lived long enough in a bleak, empty landscape to have sufficient practice in dying to the easily disturbed, anxious self. They knew its death to be the route to freedom . . . and to the unaccountable wonder of being loved.

Death Lodge on the Mudlick Trail

A couple of years ago my dog Desert and I headed up Mudlick Mountain Trail in Sam Baker State Park in southern Missouri. I went with the intention of releasing my grip on the life of a university professor, an identity that had absorbed me for more than thirty years. My dog went for the sheer love of the trail. It was a late April day with new hickory leaves uncurling as we hiked the ridge overlooking Big Creek. The creek flows along the foot of Mudlick Mountain, an ancient knob on the Ozark Plateau. Its name derives from a dark igneous rock (mudlick dellenite) rising to the surface here—some of the oldest exposed rock in North America.

It was time to deal with the necessary closure that was looming in my life. Only a few years away from retirement, I sensed I was being called more deeply into the practice of the wild. I'd delighted in my years at a Jesuit university. I'd loved my students and the saints I'd studied in the history of spirituality. But it was time to relinquish my attachment to being a scholar, giving up the need for achievement and recognition. I was more than ready to surrender my role in helping to make Saint Louis University the "Best Catholic University in America." As much as I respected the Ignatian tradition, I didn't care much about being the "best" of anything anymore. I longed instead for the candor, spontaneity, and unrehearsed speech of wilderness.

I'd been reading Bill Plotkin on the importance of observing a ritual process in marking the transition to a new stage in one's life. He speaks, for instance, of a death lodge as "a symbolic and/or literal place, separate from the ongoing life of the community, to which the wanderer retires to say goodbye to what her life has been."[13] A death lodge is a place for acknowledging that a chapter in one's life is closing, with a new one beginning to open. In my case, it was the productive scholar—the loyal soldier—who had to be honored and dismissed so that the contemplative elder might enter into his own.

I went up Mudlick Trail that weekend with the intention of undertaking a death lodge, signifying the change that was coming in my life. Desert and I reached the ridge on Friday afternoon, arriving at the first of three Adirondack shelters built there by the Civilian Conservation Corps in the 1930s. These are rustic three-sided stone structures with fireplaces, similar to the cobblestone houses built from local stone throughout the Ozarks. Sleeping in them is like burrowing underground, surrounded by native rock. Nestled on the edge of the mountain's oak-hickory forest, they look out onto distant hills beyond.

We decided to spend the night there. While we sat on an outcropping of rock near the shelter as evening approached, a trio of turkey vultures buzzed us several times, passing just over our heads. Their red faces and yellow beaks contrasted starkly with their black wings tipped with white. Out of curiosity, I suppose, they were interrupting their own "dark work," as Mary Oliver calls it—their task of "settling with hunched wings" over the last dead thing they had found. They do this grisly work with such grace and even "thankfulness" that it becomes almost sublime. They give to death the fitting closure of ceremony and efficiency.[14]

That night I built a fire in the shelter's stone hearth, warding off the cold as we watched light dance on the ceiling logs overhead. Desert was getting old and welcomed the prospect of sleeping by a warm fire. This stray, half-breed German shepherd had wandered into my life some twelve years earlier. There had always been a wild streak about her. She demanded her own space and chose selectively whom she would love. In our years of hiking together, she had taught me a lot about boundaries, the letting go of what can't be held, and the nature of a fierce, unyielding love.

The next morning I got down to the business at hand—releasing my attachment to the letters behind my name, the "Ph.D." in which I'd taken pride for so long. My hope was to trade the mind of the scholar for the heart of a vagabond poet. I'd always walked the edge between the two but yearned now for a deeper plunge into the other side. In my backpack I'd brought along the last few pages of a scholarly book I'd been writing. I read these to the dog and the hickory trees, offered thanks for the work I'd been given, and then burned the pages in the fireplace.

Writing and teaching had given me joy through the years, but the life of the mind subtly dilutes the wildness of God, often substituting knowledge for love. It was time to disassociate myself from the academician's easy confidence in speaking of holy things, from the author's longing for distinction and the teacher's hunger for the adulation of his students.

The problem isn't the writing or the teaching itself. It's the need to be *known* as a writer and teacher. That's what the academy cultivates: a professorial aura of presumed intelligence, offering the *appearance* if not the substance of quality. I was attracted now to something wilder and riskier than that. Hence, the need for a ritual in releasing the long-held fretfulness that I'd never been a "real scholar" anyway.

I'd brought along a razor and shaving cream, planning to shave my head as a gesture of welcoming baldness, old age, and freedom from pretension of any sort. I wanted to give up the need for impression management, choosing to identify instead with cancer patients who bear in their body a mark of their struggle against a contrary growth. Ezekiel had taken a razor to his head, I remembered, burning a third of his hair, throwing another third to the wind, and striking the last third with a sword. He turned his back on all the cares of an angst-filled world, inexorably moving into exile. I, too, had to relinquish a personal (and societal) need for approval, for maintaining appearances on any level. The wilderness demanded more of me than that.

The Cloud of Unknowing *and Contemplative Prayer*

Having devoted so much of my life to knowing, I needed lessons now in *unknowing*. Consequently, I was drawn back to a classic in the history of Western spirituality—a book written about what *can't* be known by a fourteenth-century English scholar/monk who never even bothered to sign his name.

The Cloud of Unknowing is a handbook on the practice of contemplative prayer. It teaches a pattern of praying that surrenders the use of words altogether, giving up the control that language affords. Its goal is a quiet, undistracted resting in the heart of Mystery, without the person praying calling any attention to herself—in other words, a form of prayer that feels like a practice in dying. Its jettisoning of speech (and the power that words provide) allows entry into a void—and an intimacy—not unlike what one discovers in the vast silence of fierce landscapes.

The language of this anonymous writer in medieval Britain suggests the northeast Midland dialect used by Chaucer. He may have been a Carthusian monk at one of the abbeys in the deserted marshland of the fens north of Cambridge and Ely. This was a low wetland of sedge and reeds where dense fog arose every morning. It was prized by the monks for its solitude. There the unknown author of *The Cloud of Unknowing* instructed a young novice on the exercise of wordless, thoughtless contemplation. He encouraged emptying the mind so that the heart could learn to love.

Two themes are central in this guidebook on the practice of prayer. The first is the importance of going beyond mere head-knowledge into the deepest desire of the heart. The second is the need for a discipline (a deliberate method) for silencing the mind—letting go of words and opening the soul to what it longs for most. As indispensable as words may be, they often get in the way of what is most important.

Intellect alone won't get you where you want to go, says the writer from the fog-bound marshes of Norfolk. None of the essentials in your life are subject to rational proof. I can't "prove" my wife's love, for example, any more than I can verify the existence of God. But I can relish both, entering into a trust that secures the bond in each case. The English monk said that a veil of intellectual darkness, a Cloud of Unknowing, inevitably separates us from any definite knowledge of ultimate Mystery. We can't grasp the Divine in the same way we know other things. While God can't be thought, however, God *can* be loved. We can pierce the impenetrable cloud separating us from the Holy by the arrows of love, by the longing of the human heart. "Love knocks and enters," said Hugh of St. Victor in twelfth-century France, "but knowledge stands without." [15]

The writer of this medieval manual on prayer was especially wary of bookish intellectuals. He warned his pupil of "the curiosity which comes from the subtle speculation and learning such as theologians have." It "makes them want to be known not as humble clerics and masters of divinity, but as proud scholars." [16] He argued that no one can grasp the nature of his own conscious being, much less the hidden mysteries of the Divine. An utter simplicity is required of those who enter the presence of Mystery. You approach God in the vulnerability of your naked self, standing before a reality you cannot know, or even name. You "lift up your sick self, as you are, to the gracious God, as he is, without any speculation or special probing into any of the qualities that belong to your own being or to God's." [17] Yet by embracing this emptiness, he says, you're surprised by an inexplicable love.

You travel, as if through wilderness, with an openness to what is seen and not seen. "It is enough for you that you feel moved in love by something," says the *Cloud* author, "though you do not know what it is." [18] The experience is akin to falling in love with an Ozark landscape of budding spring leaves, winged scavengers, and Precambrian rock. You realize you don't understand any of it. But you love it nonetheless. You begin to recognize, in fact, that love is a way of knowing in its own right, with its own modes of verification. Love awakens the certainty of one's desire, if not the irrefutability of one's understanding. When all is said and done, says the author of the *Cloud*, it is our longing that most deeply defines us. "It is not what you are nor what you have been that God looks at with his merciful eyes, but what you desire to be." [19]

If this focused desire has any hope of attaining its goal, however, it must relinquish everything that is less than what it yearns for. The fourteenth-century teacher of prayer urged his novice to place a "cloud of forgetfulness" between himself and the potential distractions that arise around and within him. This intentional cloud distances the person praying from a world of divided attention. Symbolically, it situates him on the dark slopes of Mt. Sinai, separated from the boisterous crowd below by a "cloud of forgetting" and from the overpowering Mystery above by a "cloud of unknowing." [20]

As a cloistered monk, the *Cloud* author was adamant in insisting that one detach oneself entirely from life in the world, from "all the creatures that have ever been made." In his view, one has to renounce every object of sense and intellect in coming to prayer. [21] I'm not convinced myself that this is always necessary, even in the monastic life. It sounds too Neo-Platonic and other-worldly to me. In my experience, wilderness itself is able to occasion the forgetfulness of self and petty distractions that the medieval monk sought most to achieve. Far from being just another worldly distraction, wilderness bears a monastic quality of its own. It has an uncanny power to check the ego and quiet the soul.

Vultures flying over Mudlick Mountain haven't the least regard for the things that preoccupy me most. Their utter lack of interest in what I think important reduces me to the nakedness that the life of the spirit requires. Nature's stark indifference is as healing as it is distressing. Standing in the shadows of an old-growth forest, I don't dwell on what "God" is or what "I" am or what the short-leaf pine tree is (in all the intricacies of its being). I'm simply present to the fact *that* Mystery is, *that* I am, *that* the pine tree stands there in its naked, nameless presence. That alone is enough. More than enough. It's what continues to draw me to all things wild.

None of this is about achieving an esoteric, higher state of consciousness. The presence of God isn't something to attain anyway, says the *Cloud* author. You already are totally within it . . . just by living, by breathing. You don't achieve it; you only consent to it. Contemplative practice merely brings this given reality into focused awareness. [22] And even then, you can't presume that your ego has caused anything to happen. In the "non-experience" of contemplative prayer, says Thomas Merton, *nothing* happens . . . because there is no subject for it to happen to. "Here the subject . . . seems to have vanished. You are not you." You've ceased to exist as a separate, grasping, "experiencing" ego. [23]

When I sit for an hour or more on the ridge of Mudlick Mountain—thinking nothing, giving language a rest for a change—I begin to understand what these monks are talking about. I come to realize, with Merton, that "the grace of contemplation is most secure and most efficacious when it is no longer sought, or cherished, or desired. It is in a sense most pure when it is barely known." [24] When I'm in an Ozark wilderness, I'm not a self-styled "contemplative" gifted with quasi-monastic sensitivities. I'm just another old codger in the woods. Nor is God an ethereal Being, hiding magically in the shadow of every rock and tree. To be honest, God and I don't pay much attention to each other down there, at least so far as definitions and identities are concerned. We just are.

That's the trick. You have to move beyond the interference of language and thought in order to be present to the stillness of the moment, the power of the now. The *Cloud* author says you need a method for interrupting the mind's craving for analysis, the ego's incessant hunger for experience. He doesn't speak of wilderness as an aid in doing this, but suggests another technique for calling the mind to a stop in the exercise of prayer. He says the intellect snatches at distractions like a "greedy greyhound." Hence, you have to give the mind (the salivating dog) something to do—like reciting a single word over and over again. Let the greyhound of the mind gnaw on that word, like a bone, quieting itself while the heart is set free to claim its desire with a naked intent of love.

The monk of the fens recommends using a simple word like "love" or "God" as a quieting mantra. In repeating the word, you allow it to still the mind until you can leave even the word itself behind in the absence of distractions. You are left, at last, in the unadorned presence of the moment, resting in a silence without word or thought. If this feels like a dying, it's a death that the soul craves—being alone with what it loves.

This is a practice of prayer that began with the Desert Christians, was developed by the monks of Mt. Athos in the Middle Ages, and comes down to us through the teachings of this fourteenth-century English master. More recently, monastic teachers from John Main to Thomas Keating have refined the practice of "centering prayer" (as it is also known), extending it to the laity as well.[25]

The Dog, the Mountain, the Cloud

It is a paradox that coming to life in the power of the moment demands a prerequisite dying to so many other things. I've returned to Mudlick Mountain to remind myself of that. Two years have passed since Desert and I were here last. I'm within a year of full retirement now, exploring more deeply my entry into wilderness. I still don't know what lies ahead for me in a life beyond the university, but I continue my practice of contemplative prayer.

Sadly, I'm also here to remember an old friend. Desert died three weeks ago, my long-time companion in wilderness. Old age and the growth of a tumor on her back leg finally caught up with her. I held her in my arms on our dining room floor as the vet gave her a shot of sodium pentobarbital and she went to sleep for the last time. Surrounded by her family, she took her final breath in a moment of calm stillness, this dog who had been a contemplative master for me. We all wept.

Desert died, fittingly, during the writing of this chapter on dying. As I lean against the wall of the Adirondack shelter once again, I realize how much Desert had taught me about dying (and living) throughout her life. She initially came to us as a gift I wasn't ready to receive. She wandered as a stray pup onto the playground of the inner-city school where my wife taught. Patricia brought her home, to my dismay. I'd wanted to be deliberate in selecting the next dog we got, choosing something better than a mangy mutt from off the street. But our son named her Desert (because of her sandy coat) and she stayed. For months I refused to accept the dog. As a result, she didn't adjust well. Abused as a pup, she took it out on others, snapping at children. Patricia eventually spoke of maybe having to put her down.

That's when everything changed for me. The dog didn't deserve to die. I began to wonder, in fact, if she had been brought to us to teach me something I hadn't wanted to learn. Something about surrendering expectations and appearances, extending and receiving forgiveness, being clear as to what one loves and what one has to walk away from. So I took her with me on a backpacking trip. In the tent that night I apologized for having rejected her, saying I wanted to be open to what she had to teach me. We connected . . . and nothing was the same after that. We entered into a bond I've never had with another animal. Her rough-edged simplicity and freely given love were profoundly healing for me. She taught me a great deal about releasing the cares of the scholar for the love of the trail.

I held her in my arms on the morning she died, but Desert was on her own as she took her last trip into high country. She was heading into a wild terrain with stunning vistas like neither of us had seen before. She'd been preparing for the trip through the years on each of our journeys together . . . learning to be comfortable with silence and solitude, traveling light, practicing mindfulness, trusting that a second and third wind would come as needed. She was ready.

None of us know how we will face our own death. I'd like to think that when I come to the entrance of that final wilderness myself, I'll pass through as gracefully as she did. I don't want to be a blubbering coward, lingering at the trailhead in fear of what may lie ahead. I want to pause with the pack on my shoulder, asking for an invitation to enter (as we often did together at the start of a trail). When I hear the stirring of the wind or a bird's song in the distance, I'll take that as a sign to head on up toward the pass and the high mountain lakes beyond. There won't be a need for words then anymore. I'll have run out of language altogether.

Everett Ruess wrote a letter home six months before he died. He struggled to find words to express the mystery of what he had experienced in the Utah wilderness:

> Often I am tortured to think that what I so deeply feel must always remain, for the most, unshared, uncommunicated. Yet, at least I have felt, have heard and seen and known, beauty that is inconceivable, that no words and no creative medium are able to convey . . . I still try to give some faint but tangible suggestion of what has burned without destroying me.[26]

His inability to find the words he needed wasn't a shortcoming. It was a gift. The landscape took the language out of him. All he longed for was to move a little further up and further in, embracing the wild expanse of wilderness that had won his heart. What do any of us long for, in negotiating our own passage through death, than to find ourselves—at last—with a new ability to love?

Fourth Leg: Delight (Returning Home with Gifts)

Once the hero has trod the dark path or descended into the belly of the whale, says Joseph Campbell, his journey concludes with his bringing the runes of wisdom or the Golden Fleece "back into the kingdom of humanity." There the boon will redound to "the renewing of the community, the nation, the planet or the ten thousand worlds." [1] Persephone returns from the underworld to bring spring again to the earth. Odysseus comes back from the battlefields of Troy to restore love and order to Ithaca. St. Anthony the Great—after surviving the onslaughts of demons in the tombs of the Egyptian desert—reenters the company of others, teaching those who come to him at his desert hermitage. On returning from the desert, Jesus begins turning water into wine. The goal of wilderness spirituality is always to return to the familiar world of others, coming back home with gifts from the wild.

The pattern of this spirituality, as I've argued, begins with (1) *departure* from the world of restless activity, with venturing out onto the trail and being disillusioned enough to identify the deepest longing of our quest. Then comes (2) the need to adopt a *discipline*—learning to accept solitude, to travel light, and to practice the mindfulness required to negotiate the trail. Inevitably along the way the wanderer also makes (3) a *descent* into darkness and despair. Lost in wilderness, we wrestle with fear, failure, and an ultimate dying to everything that is unimportant. Yet in the end, there is reemergence into life and (4) *delight*. Having endured the desert ordeal, the traveler returns with a new gift of discernment, a richer sense of community, a hunger for justice, and the hilarity of holy folly (no longer having to take ourselves so seriously). These are the gold the adventurer brings back from the wild places of the psyche.

Discernment: Taum Sauk Mountain and Jelaluddin Rumi

*We often vacillate between a trust in the sure guidance of
Love that is God's will within us, and the feverish pursuit
of God's will as though it were something outside us that
we are left on our own to discover.*

ROSE MARY DOUGHERTY[2]

*Now is the time to understand
That all your ideas of right and wrong
Were just a child's training wheels
To be laid aside
When you can finally live
With veracity
And love.*

HĀFEZ[3]

FOUR HUNDRED MILLION years ago, Taum Sauk Mountain was a high ridge on a solitary island in a vast Paleozoic sea surrounded by coral reefs. Geologists describe it as a landscape of lofty volcanoes. It was one of the few parts of present-day North America that were never submerged under a primordial sea. At 1,772 feet above sea level, Taum Sauk Mountain has been worn down through the ages but is still the highest point in Missouri. It lies on the crest of a mountain chain several times older than the Appalachians.

The Taum Sauk section of the Ozark Trail is one of the most beautiful stretches in the Ozarks. The twelve-and-a-half-mile tract that runs from the blue pools and massive boulders of Johnson's Shut-Ins State Park to the top of Taum Sauk Mountain is studded with waterfalls, thick woodlands, rocky glades, and beaver ponds. It is a good place for reflecting on primeval things, gaining a long-range perspective on one's life, discerning what has gone and what may yet need to come. This is one of the boons of wilderness hiking.

Turning onto route CC off Highway 21 in Iron County on a Friday afternoon, I've made it to the top of the mountain a few hours before dark. My plan is to hike down the trail below Mina Sauk Falls, spending the night in the woods near Devil's Tollgate and moving on toward Johnson's Shut-ins the next day. I've come to an intriguing place. In wet weather, the water cascades 132 feet down rock ledges, forming the highest waterfall in the state. Below the falls the trail passes through an eight-foot-wide opening in a thirty-foot-deep section of magma that was part of an ancient volcanic caldera. Hardened now into fine-grained rhyolite, the geological oddity is dubbed the Devil's Tollgate. A pioneer wagon road once passed between its stone walls, making a convenient site for bandits to hide. The locals claim that Jesse James hid out on the mountain after robbing the Ironton Train in 1874. Until the State Park System built a road to its top in the 1950s, Taum Sauk Mountain was a remote and isolated place.

For many years stories were told of a Piankeshaw Indian chief, Sauk-Ton-Qua, whose daughter, Mina Sauk, fell in love with the captured chief of a hostile Osage tribe. When her father caused her captive lover to be thrown from the top of the mountain, she jumped after him, taking her life as well. Lightning then struck the mountain, the story goes, causing water to gush from the top of the falls down into the gorge below. The blood of the two lovers can still be seen in reddish flowers that bloom there in the spring, called Indian pinks.[4]

At this time of year, in the fall, the mountain is ablaze with red maples and yellowing pawpaw trees, their fruit long ago eaten by the birds. Elegant cedar waxwings forage in the woods while formations of Canada geese soar overhead. The chiggers are less active now than at the height of summer, but they remain a trial for any Ozark hiker. People in these parts joke about attending a funeral held for the five chiggers that died over an especially cold winter. They are a hardy breed, these tiny, six-legged mites that hide in tall weeds and feed on the ankles of innocent passersby. Lined up end to end, seventy-five of them can fit on the width of my thumb.[5]

I've come to Taum Sauk Mountain to let go of another busy semester, as well as to think about directions my life might take after finally leaving the university. The top of the highest mountain in the area seems like an appropriate site for seeking divine guidance. But it's just like me to expect stunning revelations out in the wilds. Only after getting past the inevitable disappointment of not experiencing one of Hildegard of Bingen's ecstatic visions do I usually find what I'm seeking in the simplest things. They offer the unassuming clarity I need most.

Discernment and the Passion of a Sufi Mystic

Discernment is the spiritual task of sifting through what is illusory in our lives to discover what is authentic. It's the process of making decisions that are compatible with who we are. One of the gifts I bring back from wilderness trips is the clarity of purpose that's apparent in everything I meet there. Things in the natural world know inherently how to be what they are. Discernment is naturally embedded in them as instinct. Only we humans struggle to figure out who we are and what we should be doing. As poet David Whyte observes, we are the one species able to resist our own flowering.[6]

Perhaps a place like Taum Sauk Mountain can point me again to my own most natural way of being and doing, as I choose what path to take at this juncture in my life. Some people talk of discerning God's "leading" in their lives. Quakers, for instance, speak of attending to "nudges" that arise in the interiority of the soul, coming from the inner light of the Spirit. I'm curious as to whether this ancient Ozark landscape might bring out insights that are already percolating inside me.

In the Evangelical setting where I grew up, determining God's will for your life was a major concern. Discernment meant listening for God's voice coming from outside yourself, telling you precisely what to do—usually through the reading of Scripture. People closed their eyes with their thumbs pressed to the pages of their Scofield Bibles, opening to a random page for explicit guidance. When I did that, I usually turned to a passage about so-and-so begetting so-and-so, which wasn't terribly helpful. We were taught to think of the Bible as a rulebook offering specific instructions for any given situation. We weren't allowed to consult a Ouija board, but the King James text could function in a similar way.

I've learned through the years that discernment usually comes from within rather than from without. It isn't a magical divining process by which a skillful biblical dowser can pinpoint God's will with precision. The point isn't to be told exactly what to *do* anyway. It's more being open to the quiet, inner perception that emerges as a result of extended time on the trail or a sustained exposure to the biblical text. It's a matter of settling into what we know ourselves most deeply to *be*. Traditionally, the "discernment of spirits" is a process for sorting out the deepest desires of the heart from the superficial yearnings that distract us. It requires our getting in touch with our truest self, being free to listen and act from our heart's desire. Wilderness hiking helps with that.

I'm fascinated by the shift in consciousness that occurs in the course of a long day's hike. It often takes me several hours on the trail to become present to myself. Initially I'm searching for birds and trees I can name, natural wonders I can describe with compelling artistry—like a Loren Eiseley or an Annie Dillard. Yet the weariness of the trail gradually quiets this foolishness as my body submits to its rhythmic pace. My left brain finds the routine boring, but my body loves it. Instead of pinpointing isolated phenomena with tunnel vision, my gaze widens, taking in the surroundings with a sweeping, peripheral awareness. I'm no longer simply observing. I belong. My limbs exult in the methodical, trancelike pattern of repetitive movement. Only then do important things begin to surface.

I've brought along an intriguing companion on this trip, the thirteenth-century Persian poet Jelaluddin Rumi. One couldn't ask for a more down-to-earth, exuberant, God-intoxicated hiking partner. Conversations with him under the stars at night can be a drunken revel, peppered with earthy imagery and raucous laughter. He talks of God in relation to chickpeas cooking on an open fire, the moon reflected on a pond's surface, the scent of willow trees, or the longing of Potiphar's wife for Joseph's striking beauty. For Rumi, the encounter with the holy is always anchored in earthy human experience. Knowing the Great Mystery—discerning the will of Allah—is, for him, more like falling in love than like receiving instruction from a written text.

Rumi was born in the year 1207, in a small village in what is now Afghanistan. He traveled west with his family as a child, settling in the town of Konya in central Turkey. There his father became head of an important religious school where he was regarded as the "sultan of the Scholars." Rumi was groomed to take his place. Thoroughly trained in the rules and regulations of Islamic religious law (*shari'a*), he remained deeply committed to his faith throughout his life.[7]

One cannot understand Rumi's work apart from the Quran and the teachings of the prophet. Like other saints in this book, he has to be read within a specific social, religious, and geographical context. We can't reduce any of these spiritual writers to a generic mysticism, stripped of the particular background that has shaped them.[8] In each case, they push the edges of their tradition only by being profoundly steeped in it.

While Rumi began his life as a meticulous scholar, he suddenly morphed into a playful theologian, multiplying images and transcending the literal meaning of texts. The change occurred one autumn day in 1244, when he met a traveling teacher and gadfly by the name of Shams-i-Tabriz. This charismatic *sheikh* or spiritual master became a lightning-rod for the young scholar, awakening in him a sense of his deepest purpose in life. Meeting Shams, Rumi fell head over heels in love with God.

There are rare occasions, it seems, when you may meet an extraordinary human being who mirrors a capacity for something you've never recognized in yourself. This carrier of divine energy can be flawed personally in all sorts of ways, but he or she sparks a fire in the dry tinder of a hungry heart. The fire may not burst into full flame, however, until the teacher departs. Rumi wrote his finest poetry only after Shams's death, as longing was stirred by the remembrance of his teacher. Often the master has to leave for the apprentice to incorporate his truth.

The heart of Rumi's teaching lies in the Sufi concept of *tawhid* (or "oneness"). This is a longing for mystical union with the Beloved, with the divine lover from whom one has been separated. In the opening lines of his most famous work, the *Masnavi* (his "flute songs"), Rumi portrays the soul as a reed cut from the damp reed-bed of God's own heart. It yearns to return to its source, finding a transient joy in becoming a reed flute through which the divine breath of love's fire passes.[9] Like a drunken fool, Rumi is smitten by love. He can think of nothing else.

The core of discernment for him, therefore, isn't a question of "What should I do?" or "What is expected of me?" It is rather "What do I love? What arises now most naturally from my heart?" For this thirteenth-century Persian poet, religion isn't primarily what you think, or even the actions you perform. It is what you *desire*. "Out beyond ideas of wrongdoing and rightdoing there is a field," he promises. "I'll meet you there."[10] In a sunlit field strewn with love, like wildflowers, the heart wanders, intoxicated. The Sufi master warns that the mind alone won't get you there, any more than concentrated effort. Yearning is what connects you with the divine. Love is a camel that can't be squeezed into the chicken coop of the intellect.[11] Nor will keeping the rules guarantee a relationship with God.

The poet of Konya tells a story of Moses passing an uneducated shepherd along a dusty road. Moses, the stern lawgiver, overhears the man speaking to God as if to a child, saying, "I want to fix your shoes, comb your hair, and wash your clothes. I want to kiss your little hands and feet when it's time for you to go to bed." Moses shouts out indignantly, "What is this blasphemous familiarity? You don't talk about shoes and socks with God!" His harsh words send the repentant shepherd off into the desert, sighing as he goes.

But then God himself rebukes Moses, saying, "Don't scold a Lover like that. I don't want your proper words. I want burning. Burn up your thinking and all your forms of expression." Chagrined, Moses runs after the shepherd and catching up with him, exclaims, "I was wrong. God has revealed to me that there are no rules for worship. Say whatever your loving tells you to." But the shepherd replies, "Ah, Moses. I've gone now even beyond that. The Divine Nature and my human nature have become one. I haven't words at all anymore." The shepherd, in his simplicity, has pierced through the veil of speaking and doing, joined with the holy through the immediacy of the heart.[12]

To borrow another of Rumi's metaphors, the shepherd has been "cooked" and softened—roasted over a fire so as to be transformed at last into the shape of love. This radical change can be excruciating. The chickpea screams when the cook throws it into the boiling water: "Why are you doing this to me?" But when he understands that the cooking is meant to give him flavor, vitality, and an altogether new life, the bean stops resisting and welcomes the process of conversion. "Boil me some more," he cries. "Hit me with the skimming spoon. I can't do this by myself." [13]

Discipline is necessary to transition from the raw to the cooked. Only over time is the lover transformed into the image of the beloved. At first, he stands knocking on the door of the one he desires. "Who is it?" the voice inside replies. "It is *I*," he responds. "Go away," she retorts. "This is no place for people who are raw and crude." Scorned and rejected, he wanders away in despair, spending a year in the fire of separation, being cooked and burnt. Slowly he matures in the sustained absence of what his heart desires. At last he returns to knock at the door once again. "Who is there?" asks the beloved, as before. This time the lover answers, "It is *you*." "Ah, come in then," she replies, "now that you and I are one. There is no room in this house for two 'I's." [14]

Love is a school of fire, Rumi teaches. You embrace its mystery only in losing yourself, in finally *becoming* what you love. In the process, you discover that what you had thought to be entirely *outside* had been within you all along. In a similar analogy, Rumi affirms that every lover is pregnant—like Mary—with Jesus. Only in celebrating this mystery, carrying the pregnancy to term, and accepting the transformative pain that gives birth to Christ can her joy be made complete.[15] The poet keeps falling back on multiple figures of speech, struggling to convey what he isn't able to put into words. He knows, like Carl Jung, that people are transformed by images far more than by concepts. He reaches for poetry, storytelling, even song and dance in a crazed attempt to express the inexpressible.

To this day, his disciples commemorate his "wedding night," the night of his death on December 17, 1273, as the occasion of his final ecstatic encounter with the hope of his longing. On that night every year, in music and dance, they reclaim the power of a medieval poet who has never stopped singing.

Nature's Simplicity: Returning to the Reed-Bed of Love

Discerning the heart of the Beloved isn't a game of hide and seek, guessing at God's will—as if the secret of what God wants were wholly outside of us. Rumi says that every time we cry out in yearning for insight, murmuring, "Allah, Allah," God is already there in our speaking. Indeed, our yearning is itself the reply. Heart speaking to heart is the deepest way lovers converse. "Not only do the thirsty seek water; the water also seeks the thirsty." [16] The whole world pulses with a reciprocity of desire. We look beyond ourselves for what we imagine to be hidden in the other, only to find a mirror of our own longing.

"Whithersoever you turn there is the Face of God," the Quran proclaims. [17] Rumi spoke of creation as God's first prophet, a window revealing God as the "hidden treasure" within all things. "The world is like a reed pipe and God blows in its every hole." [18] The poet admired an earlier Sufi mystic, Bayazid al-Bistami, who declared, "I never saw anything without seeing God in it." [19]

This ability to discover the holy in everything is a gift of discernment that emerges from one's encounter with an extraordinary human being, a revelatory text, or a vivid experience of nature. Ignatius of Loyola was another saint who spoke of "finding God in all things." He suggested a pattern of meditative prayer that began with reflecting on natural phenomena like the elements and plant life, moving through the rest of creation to discern God's image in the human soul. He marveled at himself as a dwelling place of the Most High, even as Rumi reminded the lovers of God: "*You* are the Kaaba. Walk around *yourself* in wonder." [20]

For the Muslim mystic the will of God isn't an obscure enigma to be discovered by intellectual probing or miraculous disclosure. It is rather the business of determining which of your desires are too small. This is a wisdom acquired in the intimate way that lovers know best. When the heart is cooked, passing through the fire of abandonment to love, it acquires a knowing of its own. But this won't surface until the ego submits to the annihilation of its independent identity. It has to shed the distractions that keep it from knowing the truth about itself. Consequently, says Rumi, you won't *be* what you *are* until you stop pursuing an identity in anything other than God. The source (and love) of your life rests in that mystery alone.

Other things in nature have no difficulty in being what they are. They've never been uprooted from the reed-bed of God's nature. They don't have to work at being themselves. The young wood thrush doesn't worry that it may not learn how to sing. The leopard frog carries no grief over its loss of identity as a tadpole. The sedimentary rock doesn't fight the heat of the sun gradually transforming it into soil. Each of them stands on the threshold of change, without having to ask what they ought to do next. They simply are what they are. "What makes you think you need a ladder if you're already on the roof?" asks Rumi.[21] When you are grounded in the reed-bed of reality, knowing what to be and to do comes naturally.

Things in nature are optimal teachers to help us discern how to be ourselves. They point us back to the reed-bed of a common connectedness. We've been separated from the source of our identity and have to fall in love with it all over again. We need to give ourselves to the wellspring of our passion, says Rumi—delighting in its beauty and accepting the discipline that love requires. We recognize what we *are* most deeply only as we relinquish what we *aren't*.

When we give ourselves to love, says Rumi, we will know innately what to do. We will "let the beauty we love be what we do." [22] Our *doing* will arise naturally out of our *being*. The lover doesn't have to consult a rule book or keep a record of the deeds she performs. Her nature is to be present to the other, open to love. Rumi learned this from his teacher Shams. Witnessing this exceptional man's remarkable fullness of life, he could declare, "The meaning of the Book of God is not the text; it is the person who guides. *He* is the Book of God, he is its verses, he is Scripture." [23] The innermost truth of the text resides in a life that exhibits its power.

One finds rare teachers who embody this quality of being in every culture and faith tradition. They know intimately who they are in relation to what they love. The Lakota healer nods to the stranger who appears unexpectedly at Pine Ridge. "I've been waiting for you," he says. The Hassidic rebbe passionately tells a story that opens the Red Sea once again on a Shabbas night in Brooklyn. In a dusty Mexican town, a curandera gathers herbs and holy water for a ritual that restores wholeness to a grieving family. In each instance, the teacher knows instinctively what to say or do without the need of written instructions or outside authorities. His or her truth has been wholly internalized.

The Desert Fathers were like this. Living close to the land, they drew on the natural, if irregular, patterns of windstorm and flood, the slow growth of acacia trees and raven flight. They had an uncanny ability to read clouds and souls alike, were skilled in the discernment necessary for subsistence farming as well as spiritual direction. Adapting themselves to the desert's unpredictability, they weren't bound by rigid regulations. They readily made exceptions, urging young monks to attend most carefully to the leading of the heart. In story after story, says one observer, we see "the *abbas* and *ammas* of the desert invoke rules only to break them in the name of discernment and love." [24]

In the very first entry of one of the collections of the *Sayings of the Desert Fathers* a brother asks Abba Anthony, "What rules shall I keep to please God?" A few sayings later, Anthony replies, "Whatever you find that your soul wills in following God's will, do it, and keep your heart." [25] He turns the seeker, in other words, back onto the discrimination of his own deepest insight. He affirms that a heart formed by a life of prayer will know instinctively what needs to be done.

In the subsequent history of spirituality, more thoroughgoing instructions for the practice of spiritual discernment would emerge. Ignatius of Loyola's suggestions for decision making proved especially helpful. He offered guidelines for discerning the spirits in three different situations. The first has to do with those times when you have a deep *gut*-level sense of what is right. If your motivation is good and peace abides, then this can be a clear and easy decision. The second has to do with situations in which the choice isn't clear and you're caught between conflicting feelings. The *heart* work of testing your deepest desires will be important here. The third relates to circumstances when the choice isn't clear, but you're able to sift through the options with a degree of objectivity. This involves the *head* work of listing the pros and cons, thinking through what seems to be the most reasonable decision to make.

All three are important, yet Ignatius kept coming back to the longing of the heart as the surest sign of God's leading. "What do you desire?" he continually asked of the people he led in his *Spiritual Exercises*. [26] He knew that the inner witness of the Spirit was a decisive factor in discerning the will of God for one's life. But you attain that freedom, he warned, only after passing through the earlier steps described in this book. It is the fruit of risk and disillusionment; the consequence of a discipline of solitude, simplicity, and mindfulness; the result of a journey through fear, failure, and the death of the false self. It won't likely happen without the assistance of a spiritual guide or soul friend. That's why the *saints* are so vital. One doesn't accomplish it all on one's own.

Many of these teachers say that the natural world itself functions as a guide, inviting the soul back to its depths. The ancient oracle at Delphi, the

Druids' practice of talking across species, and the Native American tradition of a vision quest are examples of seeking discernment through nature's wisdom. In the Christian tradition, Irish monks looked to oak trees for spiritual guidance. Hildegard of Bingen wrote of the healing properties of plants, animals, and stones. Even the Puritans celebrated the instructive role of creation, underlining a passage from Job 12:7–9: "Ask the animals (the birds, the fish, and the earth itself) and they will teach you." They perceived the entire world as alive and full of God's glory, urging attention to its voice in discerning the will of God for one's life.

Seeing in the Dark: The Way of the Heart

On my second night on the trail, I've camped beside a beaver pond that interrupts the flow of Taum Sauk Creek in a quiet hollow near Proffitt Mountain. I took the path to Johnson's Shut-ins and back today; and I'm tired. Tomorrow I'll head on to the car at the trailhead on Taum Sauk Mountain. In December 2005, the 55-acre Taum Sauk Reservoir atop this adjoining mountain gave way, sending a billion gallons of water rushing down a slope not far from here. Amazingly, no one was killed, though the Union Electric Company had to answer a lot of hard questions about the failure of its pumped storage hydroelectric project. A three-mile stretch of rubble, stripped of trees and soil, still scars the land.

As the day turns slowly into night, I sit beside a cluster of red sumac berries. A covey of quails flies out from plume-heavy stalks of Indian grass. The last of the honeybees are making their way home at dusk. None of these creatures struggle to know what they ought to do. The bees follow a natural pattern of discernment by pheromones. They trust their sense of smell to tell them what they should do next.

Last spring a caterpillar wove the empty cocoon I see dangling from a milkweed plant near my campsite. It didn't have to fret about triggering the imaginal cells of the monarch butterfly within its larva. It simply yielded to what it was meant, by nature, to become. Everything here makes choices spontaneously, following the rules of its being, not stewing over what it should or shouldn't be.

Beavers have been repairing their dam nearby, laying in a supply of wood for the winter. They've gnawed through most of the smaller trees in the vicinity—willows, maples, and cottonwoods. Beavers are the "engineers of the forest," a keystone species in a landscape like this. They create wetlands, raise groundwater levels, filter out sediments and pollutants from the creek, and

provide habitat for other animals and birds. Their biology, the instinctive impulse of their being, is what drives them in their work. Their teeth never stop
growing—they have to chew on trees constantly to keep their front incisors
from getting too long. Their upper and lower teeth are self-sharpening, constantly grinding against each other like knives on an emery board. These animals do what they do as a matter of being what they are. That's how it is with
everything here.

As I think of decisions I have to make in my life now, I realize that I,
too, am simply asked to become what I already am. By nature and by choice,
I'm a lover of wilderness, a teacher and student drawn to the mystery of the
sacred, a weaver of stories helping to lead men's rites of passage in places out
on the edge. At this time in my life, I'm graduating into a still deeper practice
of those very things, embracing a broader kinship of knowing and loving.
Wilderness draws me out of the dry, intellectual security of the university.
It sharpens my hunger for a beauty that I cannot master. Here I fall in love
again with a God more wondrous than I have words to express.

The elders in a society, says Bill Plotkin, traditionally speak for the wider
concerns of the earth, calling others to a deeper respect for life. They have
internalized (and outgrown) the institutions that once defined them, citizens
now of a larger community. They don't belong anymore to the academy or
the workplace, nor exclusively to the nation or church that previously framed
their identity. Their life isn't about accomplishment or belonging. Nor is it
about playing small. Too much is at stake for that now.

Joanna Macy, one of the great elders of our time, says that the human
species finds itself—spiritually, ecologically, and culturally—on the cusp of
a Great Turning. We're experiencing a vast shift in consciousness from an
industrial-growth civilization to a life-sustaining society. We are learning, by
painful necessity, how to live in (and with) the rest of the world, without
destroying it.[27] For my part, that means witnessing to a wilderness gospel that
is prophetic, challenging what we've long assumed to be true. It summons me
to a discipline that serves the ends of love. It points to a Cosmic Christ who
lures the world toward the celebration of its inherent dignity and beauty. In
leaving the university, I'm opening myself to a more catholic and universal
way of thinking, embracing an untamed world and the God it discloses to
me. This is who I am, after all. And that invites me to what I have to do.

On the final day of the trip, I'm making my way back to the car on Taum
Sauk Mountain. I've been hiking all afternoon, moving again into the weary,
hypnotic pace that proves so strangely healing. I feel as if I could walk like this
forever. Yet I notice that night is gathering more quickly than I'd expected.

I have another mile or more of trail to cover and my flashlight batteries have quit. Dusk is rapidly turning to dark and there won't be a moon tonight.

I resist the temptation to panic, giving myself instead to the pattern of repetitive movement that I've been practicing these last few hours. I yield to the darkening shadows, my eyes sweeping rhythmically from side to side. My feet sense the peculiar texture of the packed earth on the trail. My ears become attuned to the crackle of leaves that signals any movement off the path. I find, to my amazement, that I'm able to "discern" (without seeing) the trail before me in a way that I wouldn't have thought possible. I'm seeing in the dark, trusting a wider exercise of the senses than I knew myself capable of.

Perception takes many forms, says Ken Carey, a naturalist who enjoys hiking the Ozarks at night. "Objects possess an inner glow that one can learn to sense if able to suspend the natural preference for lumens," he argues. It's like Kirlian photography. Tibetan Buddhist teachers speak of the *Lung-Gom-Pa*—highly trained trance walkers whose consciousness is no longer guided exclusively by the eye or brain. Practiced in meditation and yoga breathing (*pranayama*), they move effortlessly over difficult terrain, walking for hours, even in the dark of night. Their "feet seem to be endowed with an instinct of their own, avoiding invisible obstacles and finding footholds, which [apparently] only a clairvoyant consciousness could have detected." [28]

I can't explain this, but it resonates with my experience. It's also a good metaphor for the discernment process. I don't have to "see" clearly what God's will is for the rest of my life. I only have to be open to love, making myself available to wilderness, letting it point me back to what is already inside. There I'll know inherently what I'm finally to do. "Do not look for God," exclaimed Rumi. "Look for the one looking for God. But why look at all? He is not lost. He is right here. Closer than your own breath." [29] Simply close your eyes and breathe. Whatever comes will be as wild as it is good.

In the dark of night, I reach the top of the mountain at last and sit for a while in silence before moving on to the car. I realize that in these last few hours I've participated in a mystery similar to the one described by the eighth-century Chinese poet Li Po. One night this wandering Taoist bard sat alone on Jing Ting Mountain overlooking the Shuiyang River below. There he penned these words:

The birds have vanished into the sky,
and now the last cloud drains away.

We sit together, the mountain and me,
until only the mountain remains.[30]

In that moment of gathered emptiness, the poet loses himself, while also becoming more fully himself than ever before. Discernment is for him no longer a need. The drunken immediacy of love has triumphed. Only the mountain remains. He knows now that the true work of his life has been cut out for him.

13

Community: Lower Rock Creek and Teilhard de Chardin

When we try to pick out anything by itself, we find it hitched to everything else in the universe.

JOHN MUIR[1]

The natural world is the larger sacred community to which we belong. To be alienated from this community is to become destitute in all that makes us human. To damage this community is to diminish our own existence.

THOMAS BERRY[2]

I'M UP FOR vigils, but the monks are still asleep. They were noisy last night at compline. The peepers were nearly as loud as the bullfrogs. The whole choir chanted like mad as stars came out over the creek. When I first set up camp along this quiet Ozark stream, I hadn't realized I'd entered a cloister full of exuberant frogs cheered by yesterday's rain. Their enthusiastic interpretation of the Psalms made me think of the deep-throated chanting of Tibetan Buddhist monks. The sound echoed off the steep rock walls where Cathedral Canyon narrows at this point. Its acoustical effect seemed to take their performance to new heights of liturgical excellence.

The night sounds of a Missouri forest are often exhilarating. A humid summer evening offers a riot of jazz improv, as raucous as last night's monkish choir. The jam begins with the soft background rhythm of grasshoppers rubbing their legs against their wings, punctuated by the loud clicking of cicadas. Green tree frogs then add a nasal *quank, quank, quank* to the high-pitched call of the peepers and the rasping, vibrating *preep* of chorus frogs. Think of a fingernail running over the teeth of a comb. Then, just as things are warming up, the bullfrogs—Missouri's state amphibians—launch into the deep *jug-o-rum* that resonates from their great puffed cheeks. It's Louis Armstrong on a late-night riff in a crowded New Orleans bar.

Lower Rock Creek runs through a narrow gorge cut into the rock of the St. Francois Mountains. Some people call it Cathedral Canyon, others Dark Hollow. It has no official name. It's not on most maps. But it's one of my favorite, most secluded places in the Ozarks. Driving down in the rain yesterday I was happy to find the road into the trailhead in worse shape than ever, the trail itself almost overgrown. The blackberry bushes are full, spider webs undisturbed. Not many guests seek out the solitude of this cloistral setting. It's just another forgotten Missouri hollow. Who would expect a community of crazed contemplatives chanting their evening office at the close of a summer day in a place like this?

There are 4,145 species of frogs and toads in the world. Twenty-six of them are found in Missouri. They form a wildly celebrative part of a highly varied community. Living in two very different ecological domains through their lives, they combine aquatic and terrestrial worlds. They teach me kinship with the interlocking character of nature that is so abundantly evident here in wilderness. Consequently, an appreciation of community is yet another one of the gifts I bring back with me from time alone on the trail.

The Connecting Web of Community and Solitude

The community I encounter along this creek is exceedingly diverse, full of disparate energies that feed each other. An Ozark riparian ecosystem brings together frogs and water snakes, sycamore trees and scouring rush, water striders and algae-strewn rocks. Each contributes to a larger interactive network, the whole being more than a sum of its parts. Yet each piece retains its integrity. This isn't a community that absorbs its members into an undifferentiated sameness. Nor, when I'm here, do I "become one with" a larger whole, dissolving into a soupy mix of the earthy and the divine. Everything remains itself while participating in a vast web of interconnectedness. My own solitude—the very "difference" I bring—is essential to the unity I share.

Backpacking as a spiritual practice walks a fine line between the communal and the individual, between the woodsman's knowledge of the land and the seeker's openness to mystery. The one doesn't have to rule out the other. Solo backpacking doesn't necessarily lend itself to a self-absorbed or narcissistic individualism. It can do that, of course, but when you assume it as a spiritual discipline, you discover the paradox that solitude doesn't exclude community at all. Aloneness at its best is firmly grounded in relationship.

Merton wrote of his experience in the hermitage at Gethsemani: "It is in deep solitude that I find the gentleness with which I can truly love my brothers. The more solitary I am the more affection I have for them. . . . Solitude and silence teach me to love my brothers for what they are, not for what they say." [3] Only by being alone do we recognize the ties that bind us to everything else. Wilderness can teach this as readily as a monastery.

Desmond Tutu describes the power of community in terms of the African notion of *ubuntu*. *Ubuntu* is the acceptance of others as parts of the sum total of all us. It affirms that "*I am* because *we are*." One is never a human being in isolation. My connection to others is what defines my very existence: I am what we are together. No one is an island. [4]

This doesn't deny the value of the individual. Indeed, it presupposes it. I'm freely able to offer back to the community only what I've accepted as my own individual gift. "I can't be for *us* what I'm not also for *myself*." Hence, communal and personal identity—the role I share as part of a fellowship and the acknowledgment of my unique worth before God—are inseparable.

I'm reminded of this by the red-topped British soldier lichens that pop up along Lower Rock Creek each spring. Lichens are the product of a distinctive symbiotic relationship, as I learned in Boy Scouts years ago, when we had to memorize a ditty about Angie Algae and Freddy Fungi "taking a lichen" to each other. We learned how these two separate species set up housekeeping together. Freddy builds the house, using threadlike fibers that provide support, and Angie does the cooking—providing food through photosynthesis. The alga and fungus thus form a "composite organism," contributing to the unity they share by remaining what they are in themselves. True community is always like that.

Unfortunately, given our Jurassic Park model of evolutionary warfare, we imagine the world as filled with solitary creatures pitted against each other in antagonistic rivalry. Where survival-of-the-fittest is the rule, we know there can't be community. Yet survival-of-the-most-collaborative is what carries the day more often in the natural world. Naturalist Paul Gruchow argues that "instances of cooperation in nature surely equal those of competition. For every predator-prey story there is a lichen story." [5] In the day-to-day operation of communities in nature, mutual interdependence is far more prevalent than rugged individualism.

This mutuality, however, doesn't exclude the reality of conflict, competition, and even the taking of life within a given interdependent system. The shared exchange of eating and being eaten is fundamental to the life of the biome. Consequently, "politeness" has never been a quality of the wild.

"There are many ways of avoiding seeing nature, but surely seeing it as nice is one of them," Gruchow observes.[6] Authentic communities are necessarily boisterous, edgy, full of exuberant and insistent life.

Frogs along the creek snap up and eat blowflies that circle over the water. Red-shouldered hawks, in turn, snatch unwary frogs as food for their young. Maggots later hatch in the decaying bodies of dead hawks, producing flies once again. Nature's hoop thus turns in an endless round of recycled energies. It takes no delight in senseless bloodletting or violence for its own sake. Yet it honors the mystery of the giving and taking of life that all bionetworks require.

In nature, individual communities are nested, like Russian wooden dolls, within successively larger contexts. Each contributes to the sustenance of the other. The frog and lichen populations in this Missouri gorge are part of an interlaced ecosystem within the larger Eastern Ozark bioregion. This, in turn, forms a unit within the wider Mississippi Basin at the heart of a still more encompassing North American continental system. Each of the continents, furthermore, drifts in relation to the others within the vast self-stabilizing system that we call planet earth. Life is invariably a function of communities within communities, systems within systems.

Joanna Macy explores this interactive nature of community through the insights of living systems theory.[7] Her goal, as a Buddhist teacher and environmental activist, is to foster what she calls the Work that Reconnects. She seeks to revitalize our human appreciation of the intricate web that unifies the various parts of our planetary biosphere. Life scientists no longer seek to reduce the world to its individual components, isolating the basic building blocks of the universe. Instead they look at how the parts are organized into wholes and how these wholes operate as interrelated, balanced systems.

The world acts as if it were alive. An elegant system of interconnecting cycles regulates its energy exchange with the sun, global circulations of water and air, soil-building mechanisms, and patterns for recycling materials. Lower Rock Creek exemplifies this collaborative way of traveling light, leaving no trace, making evident the interlocking web of nature. It reincorporates waste at every stage of its production.

What may be discarded in one part of the system becomes food or habitat in another. Termites and slugs feed on the remains of dead trees and plants. Microscopic decomposers break down dead leaves to enrich the marshland along the creek. Dung beetles happily make their homes in cow manure on the farms nearby. Mockingbirds spread the seeds of flowering dogwoods in their droppings, fertilizing them in the process. Deer scat puts nitrogen back into the topsoil. Earthworms ingest dirt and excrete it again as an earth-enhancing compound, processing a hundred times their weight in a single day. From nature's point of view, when shit happens it's a glorious thing, recycling life at every turn. Meister Eckhart spoke with biological as well as spiritual insight when he said that "relation is the essence of everything that exists." [8]

The universe I encounter at Lower Rock Creek is, in short, holographic. The genius of the whole is mirrored in each of its parts. I hear a cluster of frogs croaking on a wet summer evening, and I'm aware of the whole world singing in four-part harmony.

Teilhard's Notion of a Conscious World Community

The saint who most awakens me to this elaborate pattern of relationship is a French Jesuit paleontologist named Pierre Teilhard de Chardin (1881–1955). He was a mystical thinker far ahead of his time, as well as a victim of the church's fear of change in the early twentieth century. Two of his books—*The Divine Milieu* (his most accessible work) and *The Heart of Matter* (the final volume of his collected essays)—are small paperbacks that fit easily into the outside pocket of one's knapsack.

Teilhard grew up in a Catholic family amid the rocky, heavily forested province of Auvergne in southern France. At the age of seven he discovered an iron plow hitch in the corner of his yard and was fascinated by its massive witness to the primeval power of matter. Fossils and rocks intrigued him for the rest of his life. At the age of eighteen he entered the Jesuit novitiate, going on to earn a doctorate in paleontology at the Sorbonne in Paris. During World War I he served as a stretcher-bearer with French troops at the bloody battles of the Marne, Ypres, and Verdun. Paradoxically, it was the horror of war that initially gave rise to his mystical vision of the world.

In the early 1920s he taught geology at the Institut Catholique in Paris, where he wrote enthusiastically of evolution, the emergence of human consciousness, and the need for the church's dialogue with science. As a scientist and theologian, however, he proved too intellectually adventurous for the church and too mystically religious for his academic colleagues. Church authorities criticized him for raising questions about the doctrine of original sin. Others accused him of pantheism, as rejecting the notion of a personal God. Though he was never charged with heresy, in 1925 the hierarchy asked him to repudiate his views. None of his theological writings could be published in his lifetime. Ironically, the church's silencing of this brilliant

Catholic proponent of evolution occurred on the same week as the Scopes "Monkey Trial" in Dayton, Tennessee.

Over the next twenty years Teilhard spent most of his time in China, traveling also in India and Java. He took part in geological expeditions and played a major role in the discovery of "Peking Man" (*Homo erectus*). In 1948, he moved to the United States, where he carried out research, living with the Jesuits at St. Ignatius parish in Manhattan. He died on Easter Sunday, 1955.

Four themes from his thought stand out for me: his sense of the world as a spiritual reality, his view of evolution as moving toward the emergence of consciousness, his insistence on the cosmic significance of Christ, and his unfaltering zest for life.

The World as Divine Milieu

Teilhard scorned the idea that matter and spirit are wholly separate realities. He refused to think of the tangible world as any less significant in the spiritual life than the world of pure thought. In his mind, they form two dimensions of a single cosmic reality seeking a common synthesis. "The world, this palpable world, which we are wont to treat with boredom and disrespect," he said, "is in truth a holy place, and we did not know it. *Venite, adoremus.*" [9]

He argued that Christianity is in danger of losing itself if it doesn't acknowledge this reality. "Unless it receives a new blood transfusion from matter, Christian spirituality may well lose its vigor and become lost in the clouds," he warned.[10] The biblical doctrine of creation and the Christian belief in the incarnation require a vigorous celebration of the natural world. You can't embrace the life of the Spirit apart from a rowdy world where hedgehogs give birth, oak trees are struck by lightning, and human beings get lost on forest trails. *This* world, fraught with all its earthy unpredictabilities, is the divine milieu. "Never say, 'Matter is accursed, matter is evil': for there has come one who said . . . 'This is my body.'" [11]

God enters into a world of bodily risk and physical beauty, said Teilhard, so as to draw it into a community more fully conscious of its wholeness. "Matter . . . contains the spur or allurement to be our accomplice towards heightened being." The French Jesuit who took such joy in digging up fossils spoke of wanting to "love Christ passionately . . . in the very act of loving the universe." He wasn't suggesting anything new in the history of the church. Augustine had declared long before that "God is poured forth in all things and God is Himself everywhere, wholly." Teilhard simply situated this enthralling mystery within the unfolding process of evolution.[12]

I imagine him taking delight in the startling splash of color that erupts in the flight of an Eastern bluebird along Lower Rock Creek. With its azure brilliance, the Missouri state bird "carries the sky on its back," as Thoreau once observed. Every feature of an Ozark woodland has the capacity to entice, even that which also frightens. Take the shocking beauty of a Missouri red milksnake. Its red and white segments are bordered in black, causing people sometimes to mistake it for the highly venomous coral snake. Yet it's harmless. The red markings on coral snakes are adjoined by rings of yellow, not black. That's why hikers recall the old saw: "Red on yellow kill a fellow; red on black friend of Jack."

The lesson is that beauty in wilderness is never wholly divorced from danger. Everything in the natural world has a facility for touching us with mystery. "By means of all created things, without exception," says Teilhard, "the divine assails us, penetrates us, and molds us. We imagined it as distant and inaccessible, when in fact we live steeped in its burning layers." As a faithful son of Ignatius Loyola, he insisted that "nothing is profane for those who know how to see." [13]

Convergent Evolution

Teilhard also affirmed that, from an evolutionary perspective, all of life is being drawn into the realization of its latent spiritual dimension. Even a swallowtail butterfly yearns for a greater, more sentient fullness of being. Teilhard spoke of a "within" dimension of every created being—an inchoate self-awareness, an echoing response to the Creator—that varies in degree according to the complexity of the organism. [14]

The movement of evolution, he explained, is toward a maximum level of complexity and consciousness. It involves the development of what he called the "earth's thinking layer" or "noosphere," a quality of awareness that arises from within the larger emergent community of the biosphere. Everything in the universe, each segment of the world, is being pulled together into an increasingly alert and responsive whole. It longs for a livelier capacity for more interactive relationship. The divine power of love is what entices it toward this center, says Teilhard. Allurement operates within the course of evolution as a transfiguring force, awakening matter to its luminous character as a spiritual reality. "Love alone is capable of uniting living beings in such a way as to complete and fulfill them, for it alone takes them and joins them by what is deepest in themselves." [15]

This may be better theology than it is science. I'm not in a position to judge. But it resonates with what I know about Lower Rock Creek. The rural community I encounter there is more than the efficient operation of a well-ordered ecosystem. It sings. It shares a common life and sustains itself through mutual woes. I find examples of cooperation—even signs of a shared consciousness—that contribute to the integrity of the whole. The place simply won't let me dismiss as fanciful Teilhard's insistence that consciousness is a cosmic and not merely human reality.[16]

Squirrels and field mice along Lower Rock Creek assist in the distribution of tree growth, hiding far more acorns and pine seeds than they ever dig up again. Turkey vultures circle the high bluffs, watching these busy farmers, keeping their population within sustainable numbers and cutting down on the diseases they carry. Windstorms and the creek's work in undercutting tree roots help regulate the balance of shade and sun needed by smaller plants and shrubs. Bobcats pass through the canyon stealthily at night, looking for rabbits. They move in a zigzag pattern, stopping regularly to study their surroundings like a night watchman making sure everything is in order.

The place gives off an energy I associate with other downhome communities like Wendell Berry's Port William, Kentucky, or William Faulkner's Yoknapatawpha County. It has its own cast of lively characters, maintains a rhythmic pace set by the seasons of the year, and honors a history written on the canyon walls by the creek's irregular flow. I'm more at home in this community than anywhere else I go in the Ozarks.

This is a place where I've fished the body of a dead coyote out of the creek, burying it under a pile of rocks up the ridge. I've told a story to a handful of small trees around a campfire here, finding healing when my mother was dying.[17] I recently scattered the ashes of a dog who lived for nothing so much as to hike in this canyon, lying beside me at the end of a day, listening to water falling over rocks. I've delighted in bringing students on class trips to its quiet seclusion, many of them sleeping in wilderness for the first time in their lives.

I'm a part of this backwoods community. Like family, it can scold me at times for a failure to pay attention or for being in too much of a hurry. But I share in its living and its dying. I'm a member of its *sangha*, as it were. If there is an evolutionary movement toward convergent kinship at work here, they have to count me in.

The Cosmic Significance of Christ

Teilhard goes on to identify the Cosmic Christ as the unifying principle of this converging earth community, indeed of the entire universe. Christ is the

Omega Point to which all things are drawn. People from other traditions might speak of the earth's Buddha nature, the way of the Tao, or the living impulse of Gaia. But for Teilhard, the ultimate lure pulling evolution toward its goal is the creation-centered reality of the risen Lord.

As he read the New Testament writings of Paul and John, he was captivated by the "astonishingly cosmic character" of the Body of Christ. These biblical writers depict the resurrected Jesus as having been present from the beginning of creation. In him all things hold together and toward him all things converge (John 1:1–2, Colossians 1:15–17). From this perspective, one needs to trace the initial manifestation of the incarnation back 13.7 billion years to the advent of scintillating matter in what scientists call the Big Bang. Throughout the history of evolution, God has been waiting for us in things— in the very stardust from which everything in the universe derives.

The center and goal toward which the cosmos turns is revealed most perfectly in the humanity of Jesus. This, Teilhard said, is "God's chosen instrument for unifying the scattered cluster of all the fibers that make up the universe." This is the cosmic Lord toward which the world moves in anticipating its ultimate completion.[18]

Teilhard's sacramental theology led him to extol creation as "a living host." He viewed the earth as an extension of the Body of Christ. On the Feast of the Transfiguration in 1923, he dared to celebrate Mass amid the vast emptiness of Mongolia's Ordos Desert. Lacking any of the resources he required, he simply prayed, "Since once again, Lord . . . I have neither bread, nor wine, nor altar, I will make the whole earth my altar and on it will offer you all the labours and sufferings of the world." There on the steppes of Asia he took dirt in his hands and offered a "Mass on the world." Treating the whole of the cosmos as a consecrated host, he participated in "a real though attenuated divinizing of the entire universe." [19]

This isn't heresy. It's sound Orthodox theology, recalling the imagery of the great icons of the transfiguration in the ancient Eastern church. In these paintings, not only is *Jesus* bathed in brilliant light, but his three disciples *and* the bright green grass, trees, and shrubs of Mt. Tabor as well! *Everything* is transfigured in the promise of its final glorification. Teilhard asserted this incorporation of creation into the fullness of God's glory without falling into a muddled pantheism. He responded to those who accused him of "worshipping nature" by urging that "God, who cannot in any way blend or be mingled with the creation which he sustains and animates and binds together, is nonetheless present in the birth, the growth, and the consummation of all things." [20]

Everything moves toward that hope. As evening falls along the banks of Lower Rock Creek, I discover even here—in the banjo-like twang of green tree frogs—the heralds of a creation pining for its long-awaited glory. Tree frogs are the original bluegrass performers in these southern Missouri hills. On a warm summer night they can't resist strumming a jazzed-up *Te Deum* . . . with all the finger-picking magic of Earl Scruggs or Bill Monroe.

A Spirituality of Wonderment

A final theme that delights me in Teilhard's thinking is his zest for life, his sense of intoxicating wonder. This is what allowed him to see the world as ever more animated and alive. He avowed that a passion for life is the mainspring of evolution. The development of the human spirit aims inexorably toward an ever-greater capacity for wonder. In all the scientific and spiritual investigations he undertook, Teilhard pursued a journey from what he called "simple life to 'Life Squared,'" from the commonplace to the visionary.[21]

His restless exuberance led him to explore the most inaccessible parts of the earth in search of the mystery of human origins. He took part in geological expeditions to the Abyssinian bush and the Gobi Desert, to the Salt Range Valley of Kashmir and the birthplace of *Australopithecus* in the prehistoric caves of South Africa.[22] You find a similar passion for life in the friendships he kept, especially his long-term relationship with the American sculptor and artist, Lucile Swan. He once spoke of her as "the very expression of my life." Their love for each other, though platonic, had an enormous impact on him, as seen in their recently published letters.[23] Teilhard's intense vitality in every sphere of life led him to scorn the "dead prose" he found in most religious writing. He grumbled that it regurgitates "truths already digested a hundred times and with no living essence."[24]

As one might expect, he defended his critique of the hierarchy by speaking, in good Jesuit fashion, of the need to recover a vigorous theological imagination at the heart of the church. In a 1951 letter to the superior general of the Society of Jesus, he explained, "What might have been taken in my attitude during the last thirty years for obstinacy or disrespect, is simply the result of my absolute inability to contain my own feeling of wonderment."[25] He was motivated in everything he did by irrepressible awe in the face of nature's mystery.

I'm startled, again and again, by the marvels of a place like Lower Rock Creek. Though a neophyte in all things scientific, I'm astounded here by the ability of water striders to walk the surface of pools along the brook. They catch air pockets in the waxy hairs on their feet and skate effortlessly over the water on their bubbles. It's a process called hydrofuge. These insects have three pairs of legs: two short front ones for grasping and eating, two middle ones for oaring across the water, and two rear ones for steering.

On a hot summer night along the creek, I'm just as taken by the mystery of cricket chirping. As male crickets work at attracting mates, the rate of their wing-clicking increases in direct proportion to the rise in temperature. A principle called Dolbear's Law calculates that you can tell just how warm it is by counting the number of cricket calls within a fifteen-second time span, then adding the number forty. Wonder in this place is as mathematical as it is divine.[26]

Community and Responsibility

Perhaps the measure of any community's vitality is its ability to surprise. I'm endlessly dumbfounded by the allure of the places and the remarkable lives of the saints that I write about in these pages. All of the habitats and wisdom elders I describe are members of communities to which I want to be faithful. It may sound strange to suggest that solo backpacking generates a communal identity, but I share in the life energy of these places. I'm an appreciative novice under the tutelage of extraordinary teachers. I share a responsibility to (and for) them. In some inexplicable way, we belong to each other.

The saints I travel with are more than companions on the trail. When I'm backpacking, I listen to their silences, their laughter, their readiness to jolt me out of my distractions. Back home I ask them for their prayers, for help in understanding and interpreting them aright. We even work together at letting the wilderness take us places where neither of us might have gone before in our thinking. Ours is a vigorous, intimate discourse. We wrangle back and forth; they humble me by the depth of their passion. I sense the weight of my responsibility to them, but I love them as well. The "communion of saints" is far more than a line in the creed for me. These endearing trail-weathered mavericks are my teachers—giant sequoias that fill me with awe.

With places and spiritual guides like these in your life, you have to be accountable. You have to speak out when the community is at risk. It concerns me that Lower Rock Creek still hasn't been designated as a state wilderness area, despite efforts to that end. The 12,000 acres of this site are owned by the Forest Service, the LAD Foundation, and a few private property owners. Recently the Forest Service has been planning salvage logging operations and road building in the area. Mining companies are pushing to drill exploratory holes throughout Mark Twain National Forest. These pose a serious threat to the region due to the porous nature of its karst terrain, making the land more susceptible to ground pollution.

The greatest danger to the wider ecosystem, however, is the damaging effect of rural development projects and unrestricted recreational use. Agribusiness initiatives, ATV trails, and vacation homes continue to encroach on Missouri's wilderness areas. Even low-impact hikers like myself contribute to the problem. Endangered species—such as the Ozark Hellbender salamander—are in jeopardy. These are the largest salamanders in the world, growing to a length of two feet. Fewer than six hundred of them remain in the wild today. They are a small but important part of a larger community in peril.

I'm ambivalent about even identifying an off-the-map place like Lower Rock Creek. Do I put it further at risk by calling attention to it? Yet I'm obliged to speak on its behalf, despite the possibility of doing it harm. Being part of its community demands as much. Stephen Jay Gould argued that people will fight to save only what they've first learned to love.[27] We bear a responsibility for all that we cherish.

There's something miraculous about being accepted into a community you might have thought impossible to enter. It's an experience that approaches the transcendent, especially when boundaries between species are crossed. Around a campfire years ago I heard a story about a woodsman with expertise in tracking and survival skills (was it Tom Brown? I don't remember).

As he was wandering one weekend through a familiar wilderness area, he noticed three white-tail deer making their way through the same pine forest. He decided to follow along.

They knew he was behind them, but he posed no threat. He wasn't in a hurry. Nor did he exhibit the steely interest characteristic of a hunter. The deer gradually came to accept his presence, even looking back at times to check that he was still with them. Ungulates like white-tail deer take their time moving across a terrain. At dawn and dusk, they'll browse on shrubs, looking for water. During the day and late at night they'll bed down in dense brush. The well-trained woodsman followed a similar pattern, grazing on plants, berries, and nuts as he wandered, taking naps when the others did.

He noticed that whenever the deer lay down to rest, they kept their feet beneath them for quick escape, positioning themselves in a triangular pattern. From three different vantage points, each animal was able to survey a third of the surrounding terrain. They were "standing point" like soldiers on guard duty, watching for predators. The man kept his distance, respecting their wariness. Over several days a companionable relationship began to develop.

On their third night of nomadic rambling, the man found a place to bed down for a few hours, knowing the deer were foraging somewhere nearby. To his astonishment, as the others slowly settled in around him, he saw that they arranged themselves this time in a *square* pattern, relative to where he lay. The deer stood point as before, but now they included *him* in their formation, trusting him to keep watch on his assigned quadrant. He was overwhelmed by this uncanny act of inclusion into the company of "another." Never had he felt so *accepted*—by the universe, as it were—as he was that night in a remote pine forest.

Teilhard de Chardin would have delighted in such a story . . . as would Lower Rock Creek, for that matter. Ultimately everything in creation reaches beyond itself to another. Such is the impulse of evolution. Survival demands teamwork. "Driven by the forces of love," said the French scholar, "the fragments of the world seek each other so that the world may come into being." [28] When that happens, community is born, responsibilities are shared, and absolute wonder arises out of the traversing of frontiers we'd once thought impassable. We join together as fragments of a greater whole, standing in awe at the immense and holy company that constitutes our common life.

Justice: The Meramec River at Times Beach and Mohandas Gàndhi

Sentiment without action is the ruin of the soul.

ED ABBEY[1]

To live, we must daily break the body and shed the blood of creation. When we do it knowingly, lovingly, skillfully, reverently, it is a sacrament. When we do it ignorantly, greedily, destructively, it is a desecration.

WENDELL BERRY[2]

THE SPRING-FED MERAMEC River wanders for 218 miles through six Missouri counties before it flows into the Mississippi eighteen miles south of St. Louis. It cuts across the northeastern corner of the Ozark Plateau, carving out bluffs of white dolomite limestone along its way. The stream passes by Onondaga Cave, Meramec State Park, and Meramec Caverns, becoming a lazy river fed by smaller tributaries and floated by weekend adventurers. Overhanging sycamores and cottonwoods crowd its banks. Springs and caves invite floaters to tie up their canoes and explore. Mussel beds are plentiful, as are crappie, rainbow trout, and channel cat. The name "Meramec," in fact, comes from an Algonquin word meaning "ugly fish" or "catfish."

I've put the kayak into the water at the river's Allenton access south of I-44 near Eureka, Missouri. Paddling eight miles downstream, I've stopped for the night just past the old Route 66 bridge near Times Beach. Today Times Beach is a ghost town, but it's still remembered as the site of the worst environmental disaster in Missouri history. In the early 1970s, the country's largest civilian exposure to dioxin (TCDD) occurred here along the banks of the Meramec. Waste oil containing the toxic chemical used in making Agent Orange was spread on the town streets in order to keep down the dust. The Environmental Protection Agency ended up buying out the entire town and incinerating everything. All that's left of Times Beach today is what locals refer to as the "town mound," a long raised embankment of incinerated dirt covered with grass.

Since 1999, the site has been turned into Route 66 State Park, commemorating the Mother Road of public highways, begun in 1926. Historic Route 66 was the first of America's cross-country highways, extending from Chicago to Los Angeles. It crossed the Meramec River at this point. Known as "The Main Street of America," the road symbolized the nation's fascination with the automobile and the movement west. "Get your kicks on Route Sixty-Six" crooned Nat King Cole in his R & B classic of the 1940s. Today the old concrete bridge over the river goes nowhere. Route 66 is closed, replaced by Interstate Highway 44 nearby. A town that was once a town and a road that was once a road have both known better days.

Environmental Pollution and the Times Beach Affair

"There are no unsacred places," says Wendell Berry. "There are only sacred places and desecrated places."[3] Times Beach is one of the latter, of which there are many in Missouri. Hiking through the lead belt south of St. Louis in Jefferson and Madison Counties, I've learned more than I want to know about the extent of lead pollution left by the Doe Run Plant at Herculaneum along the Mississippi. To get to the Cave Springs Trail going down to the Missouri River at Weldon Spring, I pass a huge nuclear waste site left by the U.S. Army and the Mallinckrodt Company. Looking for a polluted stream known as Dead Creek in East St. Louis, I walk by numerous toxic waste sites left by Monsanto and other chemical companies. Under the rusted steel trestle of the McKinley Bridge, ground pollution levels of PCBs, lead, and dioxin have threatened the health of children for years.

Hiking the trails of the Ozarks and learning to love its wilderness terrain makes me appreciate the community of all those who share the land. Compassion gives rise, in turn, to a vigorous demand for justice. As Alice Walker says, "Activism is my rent for living on this planet."[4] If she's right, then a lot of us are way behind on our payments.

Righteous anger is an appropriate response to the environmental degradation caused by chemical, mineral, and agribusiness operations in this area of the Midwest. Companies here have a long history of polluting the earth and endangering the poor. They've given us streams running with toxic waste, lead poisoning in rural communities, and abnormal rates of childhood asthma just across the river from where I work. Where the earth hurts most, says Leonardo Boff, the poor hurt with it.

Another liberation theologian, Gustavo Gutierrez, quotes the prophet Job as lamenting: "If my land cries for vengeance against me and its furrows weep in concert, if I have eaten its produce without giving back to the land, or caused the death of field-workers, then let brambles grow instead of wheat, rank weeds instead of barley" (Job 31:38–40).[5] *Eco*-logical justice necessarily attends to the needs of all those who share the same house (*oikos*). People here in the American heartland have been befouling their home for years.

I recognize my own complicity in not being more involved, and honor the prophetic outrage of those who act on behalf of the earth and the people who suffer with it. They allow a holy anger to pass through them, without being warped by it. Sue Hubbell observes that "Shitfire!" is an effective and frequently used Ozark expletive. The expression can be "extraordinarily relieving and satisfying," she says, "if correctly pronounced."[6] I find it particularly helpful in speaking of the trashing of the land and its inhabitants at the now-defunct town of Times Beach.

Times Beach was founded back in the mid-1920s as a summer resort. After the Great Depression it deteriorated into an area of low-income housing. Two thousand people lived there in 1971, when a waste hauler by the name of Russell Bliss was paid to spread oil on its dirt streets. He mixed motor oil with chemical waste acquired from the Northeastern Pharmaceutical and Chemical Company, a nearby producer of Agent Orange during the Vietnam War. The dioxin content in the oil was many times stronger than the defoliant sprayed over the jungles near Da Nang and the Mekong Delta. The dirt roads of Times Beach turned an eerie purple after being sprayed. Neighborhood dogs, songbirds, and horses quickly began to die.

The Centers for Disease Control confirmed that dioxin was the cause of the deaths, yet it took years for the EPA to make an inquiry. Only when the residents of Times Beach hired a local laboratory to conduct private testing did the federal agency proceed with tests of its own. On December 3, 1982, an EPA crew arrived, wearing silver-white moon suits, gas masks, and protective boots. They gathered soil samples as townspeople watched nervously from their windows. Two days later the Meramec River overflowed its banks and a raging 500-year flood forced all of the town residents from their homes. This raised greater concerns about the spread of dioxin throughout the area.

Alarming levels of PCBs as well as dioxin were eventually found in the soil there, yet curiously no efforts were made to trace the source of this even more toxic chemical substance. In the 1970s, the sole producer of PCBs in the United States was the Monsanto Corporation, with its headquarters in nearby St. Louis. Russell Bliss later testified under oath that Monsanto had been his principal supplier of industrial wastes. Yet contracts that he signed have since disappeared. Soil sample records originally made by the EPA have also gone missing.[7]

In the early 1980s, the EPA was accused of consorting with the chemical companies it was supposed to be monitoring. Prominent EPA administrators were members of the boards of directors of Monsanto and Solutia, for example. But as the agency resolved the case, Russell Bliss and the Northeastern Pharmaceutical and Chemical Company were the only ones held accountable for the Times Beach debacle. Other companies that may have been involved got off unscathed.

After bobbling Love Canal, the EPA needed a "poster child" to show its effectiveness in handling environmental disasters. Times Beach provided such a case, assigning a quick and partial blame while allowing other—even more serious—polluters and contamination sites to go unheeded. The EPA spent nearly $150 million on the buyout and cleanup of Times Beach. The irony is that recent researchers now suggest it may have been an overreaction. The dioxin threat might not have been as severe as first thought.

However you read the story, the "resolution" of the Times Beach affair raises worrisome questions about the systems we have in place for identifying and dealing with hazardous waste sites. Other cases of environmental pollution in the wider Ozark region remain overlooked—from toxic waste sites in East St. Louis to the Big River Mine Tailings/St. Joe Minerals Corporation in Desloge. One observer contends that Times Beach was but "the tip of a hazardous waste iceberg in Missouri."[8]

The Call for Justice: Radical Environmentalism and Nonviolent Direct Action

How do we go about the work of seeking environmental justice and initiating change? The history of organized environmental action in the United States goes back at least to the founding of the Sierra Club in 1892. Two years earlier John Muir had succeeded in gaining congressional approval for the creation of Yosemite National Park. Subsequently he recognized the need for an organization that would educate and enlist the public in the support of continued wilderness preservation.

By 1912, Muir was bringing all his persuasive skills to bear on an effort to preserve Hetch Hetchy Valley, a stunningly beautiful section of Sierra wilderness not far from Yosemite. The City of San Francisco at the time was trying to dam up the valley and turn it into a reservoir. "Dam Hetch Hetchy!" Muir roared. "As well dam for water-tanks the people's cathedrals and churches!" But he lost his battle to protect what he called "one of Nature's rarest and most precious mountain temples." Despite his attack on the "temple destroyers" and "devotees of ravaging commercialism," the dam was built and the valley flooded.[9]

Muir was devastated. He had hiked many times along the Tuolumne River on the floor of that vast glacial basin; it had awakened his passion for beauty, his love of God. Its desecration struck him as blasphemous. Once you've sensed the power of the divine in nature's wild and dazzling face, he asked, how do you serve what you've learned to love? How far do you go in the struggle to preserve pristine wilderness? Others after him have continued to ask these questions, offering very different answers. Ed Abbey, with characteristic rage, would urge people to harass the bastards who dare to cut down old-growth forests. Julia "Butterfly" Hill preferred to love and befriend the trees themselves. In the late 1990s, she lived for 738 days in a thousand-year-old California redwood named Luna.

There's something to be said for both approaches. Which one you choose, however, depends on how you configure the shape of justice itself. Abbey's perspective would define justice as the equitable retribution of wrongs. Its goal is to make sure that lawbreakers (whether the law of the land or the "higher" law of moral values) don't go unpunished. Hill's approach, on the other hand, argues that the restoration of community is more important than simply righting wrongs. For justice to be sustainable, it has to be grounded in a fierce caring that affirms the dignity of everyone involved. The goal of restorative justice is the maintenance of a well-knit, cooperating circle of life. As a rule, even in the natural world, animals don't seek vengeance. Nor do they take more than they need. Lions and gazelle know that they share a world where, ultimately, everything belongs.

One can discern both conceptions of justice running through the history of American environmentalism. Martin Luther King's success in the civil rights movement prompted a number of activists to appropriate Gandhi's principles of nonviolent direct action in addressing ecological issues. Greenpeace was founded in 1970, drawing on the Quaker notion of "bearing witness"—protesting injustice by placing observers in places where it is happening. Their first action involved sailing into a nuclear blast zone near the

Alaskan island of Amchitka, picketing an atomic test site. Greenpeace advocates went on to protest the killing of gray seal pups, unregulated whale hunting, and the dumping of nuclear waste in the oceans' depths.[10] They sought to awaken public awareness by sharing the vulnerability of those who suffer within the larger earth community.

About the same time, in the state of Acre in the Brazilian rainforest a rubber tapper named Chico Mendes began organizing indigenous workers to resist deforestation and land-grabbing by wealthy ranchers and agribusiness companies. He, too, employed Gandhi's nonviolent techniques in defending the rubber trees and their tappers. Mendes is remembered today as "the Gandhi of the Amazon." Dorothy Stang, a Notre Dame de Namur sister, did similar work in the Amazon basin, helping the poor while confronting illegal loggers. Due to their stubborn commitment to nonviolent change, both Stang and Mendes were eventually assassinated by angry ranchers.[11] The success of their work may have been marginal in the short term, but their witness as eco-martyrs has been profound.

By the late 1970s, however, people on the radical edge of the environmental movement began to question the effectiveness of a nonviolent approach. Paul Watson left Greenpeace in 1977 to form the Sea Shepherd Conservation Society, a group that resorted to direct action in the ramming and sinking of whaling ships. He argued that a shepherd has a duty to protect his flock, even by violent means if necessary. Justice, as he saw it, requires a forceful exercise of retribution.

Ed Abbey's tongue-in-cheek novel, *The Monkey Wrench Gang*, appeared in 1975, offering additional support for this radical perspective. It told the story of a motley crew of ecological-minded misfits led by a Green Beret Vietnam vet named George Hayduke, loosely modeled after Abbey's friend Doug Peacock. Roving the canyons of Utah and Arizona, they responded to industrial development and ecological destruction by torching billboards, pulling up survey stakes, and pouring Karo syrup in the gas tanks of bulldozers. Ultimately, their goal was to blow up the Glen Canyon Dam. As Hayduke asked his fellow monkeywrenchers, "What's more American than violence?" [12]

Dave Foreman followed a like-minded pattern in organizing the radical activist group Earth First! in 1980. They pledged themselves to "no compromise in defense of Mother Earth," employing dramatic civil disobedience campaigns that sometimes included eco-sabotage. Activists have toppled power line towers at nuclear power plants and resorted to arson at a ski resort in Arizona's San Francisco Mountains. Foreman perceived himself as acting on the earth's behalf, arguing that "Any creature will fight back when threatened." He ridiculed Gandhian "ideas of stepping out of the violent cycle [as being] presumptuous and anthropocentric, setting human beings apart from the semi-violent natural world." The eco-warrior, he maintained, stands in solidarity with the earth's own ferocity.[13]

Gandhi's Linking of Spirituality and Politics

Abbey's sendup of American industrial development is appealing in its belligerent defense of wilderness. He rouses the ire of wilderness lovers like myself. Yet Julia Butterfly Hill's self-sacrifice in protecting a single redwood tree provides an alternative that is just as courageous and maybe more efficacious in the long run. In December 1997, this twenty-four-year-old daughter of an itinerant preacher began sitting in the top of a 200-foot coastal redwood in northern California. She was protesting the clear-cutting of these ancient giants by the Pacific Lumber Company, convinced that turning primeval trees into patio furniture was immoral (not to mention the mudslides from vegetation-stripped slopes that were destroying nearby homes).[14]

The spiritual practices that sustained her in this work were prayer and fasting, following the examples of Gandhi and Cesar Chavez. Her commitment to the larger community of life eventually earned her the grudging respect of some of the loggers and even the president of Pacific Lumber himself. Her achievement was rooted in the conviction that justice has to embrace everyone: the well-being of the trees, the livelihood of local people whose homes were threatened by mudslides, the loggers and their families, and the long-term viability of the lumber business as well. Justice, she knew, is the fruit of interdependence. It thrives naturally in systems where each participant is granted respect.

The twentieth-century roots of her thinking go back to an unimposing Indian activist named Mohandas K. Gandhi (1869–1948). "Bapu" Gandhi, revered by many as the "father of India," was a man five feet three inches tall who never weighed more than a hundred pounds. He was born in the coastal town of Porbandar on the Gujarat Peninsula, some 400 miles north of present-day Mumbai. During his formative years as a lawyer and political activist in South Africa, he developed a program of nonviolent action that proved remarkably effective. One of its best examples is the celebrated Salt March of 1930, organized by Gandhi to center world attention on the injustice of British rule in India.

The action highlighted Indian poverty and high taxes, yet (like all of Gandhi's work) it involved sensitivity to environmental concerns as well.

His respect for life was based on the widest possible conception of community. In the spring of 1930, he was seeking a way of exposing the unfairness of the British tax system. He chose to focus on the salt tax. Annually, it amounted to as much as half a week's wages for an Indian laborer. But more importantly, it symbolized the plight of the poor. Salt, for the wealthy, is a spice flavoring one's food. For workers sweating in the tropical sun it's a deterrent against dehydration.

Gandhi decided to challenge the British monopoly on the making and selling of salt, initiating a 240-mile march to the sea. Starting from his ashram in Ahmedabad on March 12, he arrived twenty-four days later at the seaside village of Dandi. There, in the presence of news correspondents from around the world, he took water from an ocean that belongs to all creatures, boiled it to make salt, ate the salt to relieve his suffering, and thereby broke the law of the British Empire. The irony was lost on no one.

As a practitioner of "soul force" (*satyagraha*), Gandhi had from the beginning recognized the importance of symbolically connecting his work to the ethos of the land. His very first action in India, in 1917, had been to support tenant farmers in their resistance to the oppression of British indigo planters. The colonial landowners had put all their financial resources into monocropping, turning the peasants into sharecroppers in the process. Gandhi drew a direct correlation between the dignity of farmworkers and a life lived in natural harmony with the land.

On his march to the sea, he and his fellow protesters slept each night in the open, to emphasize their solidarity with the earth. If it were up to him, Gandhi said, he would dispense with roofs altogether. Then he could "gaze out at the starry heavens overhead" without interruption. Even walls, he claimed, "seem to confine me, to restrict me, to restrict my liberty, to wean me from Nature."[15]

As they walked toward the coast at Dandi, growing numbers of villagers lined the roads, rotating their *charkhas* or small spinning wheels as Gandhi passed. The spinning wheel had become another symbol associating Indian dignity with the earth's natural gifts. Gandhi urged the spinning of cotton and wearing of homespun clothes as tangible ways of protesting the British monopoly on textile production. The spinning wheel symbolized self-sufficiency and independence, as well as the quiet discipline of prayer and meditation essential for successful nonviolent action.

In all these ways, Gandhi resolutely refused to compartmentalize spiritual and earthy concerns, as if the world of human aspirations could be separated from a larger ecology of life. Religion, for him, was never otherworldly, disconnected from the needs (and dignity) of the poor. "There are people in the world so hungry, that God cannot appear to them except in the form of bread," he argued. Building on the truths of the *Bhagavad Gita*, he insisted that religious language be grounded in a "grammar of action." "Those who say religion has nothing to do with politics do not know what religion is." [16]

The central tenet in Gandhi's thinking was the inherent worth of the individual in every sphere of common life. This was for him a religious conviction, expressing itself in four spiritual principles that underlay his entire program for nonviolent direct action. In summarizing these principles, my concern is to show how they served the ends of a justice that honors community. As I float the Meramec River along the banks of a town that has now vanished, I wonder how things might have been different had Gandhi's principles, spelled out below, been taken into account here.

Gandhi on Restorative Justice

1. <u>A profound appreciation for all living beings</u>. Coming from a home that held religious pluralism and respect for others in high regard, Gandhi valued life wherever he saw it. His mother was a follower of the Pranami cult within Hinduism, deeply influenced by Islam. Jainism was another formative source of his ethical outlook. Its central tenet of *ahimsa* taught a reverence for life that pledges non-injury to every living thing. Mahavira, its sixth-century BCE founder, refrained from harming anyone, even using a broom to sweep aside insects as he walked. Gandhi wrote in his autobiography that "A votary of *ahimsa* remains true to his faith if the spring of all his actions is compassion, if he shuns to the best of his ability the destruction of the tiniest creature." He knew that in any system of life everything counts. *Ahimsa* sustains the sacredness and interdependence of all the participants within a given network of relationships. [17]

2. <u>A community's need to bring suffering to consciousness</u>. Gandhi knew that continual awareness of this common bond is necessary. Any injury to another must be raised to the consciousness of all those involved. It cannot be dismissed as simply "the way things are." An unjust system that sanctions injury to anyone is inherently dehumanizing to all parties. It dissolves the binding glue of a shared humanity, the very dignity of life itself. Gandhi grasped this for himself in 1893, when he was thrown off a train in South Africa because of the color of his skin. He sat through the night in a Maritzburg train station, realizing that he could no longer participate in a system that allowed others to harm themselves by degrading him.

3. <u>Risking oneself in the work of restoring community</u>. He went on to argue that the vulnerability of those who are injured can be a powerful moral force in the transformation of society. Calling attention to one's suffering under the rigors of an unjust law is a first step toward justice. When people break such a law and freely accept punishment for doing so, they bear in their bodies a corporal witness to what is fundamentally wrong. Julia Hill did this when she decided to "put my body where my beliefs are."[18] Taking suffering on herself, as opposed to turning it back on her opponent, she invited all parties in the dispute to participate in a larger communal reality. Gandhi is often quoted as having summarized his program by saying: "First they ignore you, then they laugh at you, then they fight you, then you [both] win." As idealistic as such an approach may sound, its effectiveness in the late twentieth century has been undeniable.[19]

4. <u>The need for a spiritual discipline in sustaining community</u>. None of this works without a cadre of highly trained and committed people. Contemplative practice is prerequisite to restoring the wells of compassion and resisting the temptation to react in violence. Gandhi's exercise of prayer and fasting within a tightly knit community became the lifeblood of his movement. By the time he died in 1948 at the age of seventy-eight, he had spent six years in Indian prisons and almost another year in the jails of South Africa. He welcomed the opportunity this provided for meditation and work with his hands. When he left South Africa in 1914, he gave Gen. Jan Christiaan Smuts a pair of leather sandals he had made for him in the prison to which the general had confined him. Years later Smuts returned the sandals, saying that while he had often worn them he had never felt "worthy to stand in the shoes of so great a man."[20] Gandhi hadn't simply won a victory. He had won Smuts over, inviting him into a shared relationship where each affirmed the dignity of the other. The justice they achieved together ensured the integrity of the entire community. Restorative justice doesn't distinguish between the worth of victims and offenders. Its first concern isn't to punish wrongdoers, but to preserve the safety and dignity of all. Had Gandhi lived another fifty years, he would have marveled at the work of the Truth and Reconciliation Commission that did so much to heal the wounds of apartheid in South Africa. When South Africans anticipated a wave of violent retribution in the 1990s, the work of Desmond Tutu and others provided the means for restoring community.[21]

Wilderness and Restoration

With Gandhi in mind, I walk the overgrown streets of Times Beach, thinking of the community that once flourished here. On mornings like this, barefoot children used to follow these dirt roads down to the river, along with old men carrying cane poles and pouches of Apple Jack. They dumped trash in the woods like everyone else, but their respect for the river and its life ran deep. They fell victim to a chemical-industrial world that swept them away, leaving only scorched earth behind.

How might things have ended differently had the chemical companies been more responsible in their handling of toxic waste, had the EPA been more thorough in its investigation, had a respect for life in general been more fully observed in this place? Who knows? "Justice is like a train that is nearly always late," mused Russian poet Yevgeny Yevtushenko. It obviously came too late for the town of Times Beach.[22]

But life is insistent. Despite the loss of its people, the deceit of agro-chemical conglomerates, and the inadequacy of government agencies, something of the original simplicity of the Times Beach site is gradually returning. I wander past oak, hickory, and white pines along the old waterfront. The sun catches the orange-rust color of maple leaves. Winterberry holly bushes, once planted in a row, are thick now with red berries. The town's past spreads before me like morning fog.

The river looks cleaner than it has in years. The deer are back in droves. Families bring their children to the playgrounds and picnic tables of the new state park without any awareness of what once happened here. There's a danger in that forgetfulness. But there is hope, too, in the collective memory of the earth and those who insist on telling its stories.

Backpacking as spiritual practice is connective. It does more than nurture my aesthetic appreciation of landscape. It makes me ethically responsible to a wider community. It awakens a hunger for justice. The best soulcraft practices do that. Dorothee Sölle argues persuasively that mysticism and resistance naturally go together. She probes the work of Gandhi and others to show how an antiauthoritarian mystical element in each of the great religions stirs the impulse to political action.[23]

Take the Desert Christians. Their compassion for the poor was as renowned as their attainments in the life of the spirit. The monks thought of the wilderness as the birthplace of justice. They knew that it bred a respect for life, an interdependence with one's neighbors (both near and far), and a fearless prophetic voice. We misunderstand these ascetics if we regard them as misanthropic, isolated loners. They didn't renounce their ties to the rest of the world in coming to the desert. They honored them as never before.

Each community of monks in the monastic settlement at Arsinoë west of the Nile regularly contributed four hundred bushels of grain a year for distribution to the poor. According to one ancient text, they dispatched "whole ship-loads of wheat and clothing to Alexandria for the poor . . . It was rare for anyone in need to be found living near the monasteries." The monks didn't separate the spiritual discipline of prayer from the corporal works of mercy. "Nowhere have I seen love flourish so greatly," wrote St. Jerome, "nowhere such quick compassion, such eager hospitality." [24]

On my own spiritual retreats into wilderness, I too am answerable to a world of which the parts are necessarily related to the whole. I'm accountable for how I participate in the larger earth community that Times Beach represents. I can't afford romantic visions of myself as a lone cowboy, a backcountry rambler simply "passing through" with no responsibility to the communities that welcome him.

Looking through these trees toward the river, I long to reaffirm my place in the family of things. My poverty is that I've not often attended to the most important of all Lakota prayers: *Mitakuye Oyasin.* The Sioux medicine man intones these words as he enters the sweat lodge to pray: "All my relations," he cries. Everything . . . *everything* . . . is connected.

I'm obliged on this early October morning to acknowledge all of my relations here. The deer, the oak trees, the burnt earth and displaced people, the interstate highway system, the waste hauler with his deadly spray, the chemical corporations, and the agencies that oversee them. I'm tied to each of them more intimately than I'd like to think. I am the pain they inflict and the anger they carry. Call me by all my true names. [25]

The task we share is that of becoming a community more fully aware of itself. Only when we honor the interconnectivity that binds us will we discover a justice born of compassion. Until then, I can choose to belong to all the others . . . or not to belong at all. In words attributed to Gandhi, I have to *be* the change I want to see in the world. [26]

15

Holy Folly: Aravaipa Canyon and Thomas Merton

Modern investigators of miraculous history have solemnly admitted that a characteristic of the great saints is their power of "levitation." They might go further; a characteristic of the great saints is their power of levity. Angels can fly because they can take themselves lightly.

G. K. CHESTERTON[1]

Who said Zen? Wash out your mouth if you said Zen. If you see a meditation going by, shoot it.

THOMAS MERTON[2]

THE TRIP DIDN'T make sense at the time. Most backpacking trips don't. There are always more pressing things to do. We didn't have the time or the money, but went anyway. Sometimes you just gotta drive to the end of a long dirt road in the middle of the desert and keep walking. When Aravaipa Canyon lies at the end of that road, you know you won't be disappointed.

Mike and I had come to southeastern Arizona to hike the twelve-mile length of the Aravaipa Canyon Wilderness Area. "Laughing Waters" is the name the Apaches gave to the site. The Aravaipa band of the Western Apache lived here in the nineteenth century. They did well at first—hunting deer in the side canyons; gathering saguaro fruit, mesquite beans, and pinyon nuts; catching native fish that thrived in the creek. But by the 1870s, drought drove them out. When they sought relief at Camp Grant a few miles away a Tucson mob organized a massacre that left them decimated. The government relocated the remainder of the tribe in the White Mountain Reservation to the north. These canyon walls, reaching a thousand feet high in places, hold memories of children playing under reddish-brown hoodoos and dark stories etched in the desert varnish of the rock.

Today the Bureau of Land Management regulates entry into the canyon, limiting permits to thirty hikers a day at the western entrance. For much of the way you slog through ankle- to knee-deep water, stopping at every bend to marvel at what rises before you. Towering red cliffs, stands of green willows and cottonwoods, jimson weed and desert marigolds, cactuses of every sort. This is a place where humans are outnumbered by bighorn sheep, where poisonous centipedes hide in thick grass, and serpentine side-canyons darken ominously in the late afternoon sun. I've loved it since I first set eyes on it.

At the start of this book I mentioned a night I'd spent alone in the desert near here a few years earlier. What I experienced that night would finally make sense on this subsequent trip into the canyon proper. Wisdom, says David Whyte, grows more from wistful memory than flashes of insight. More often than not, the fool's journey takes him back home to discover what he'd been looking for all along:

> One day you realized that what you had wanted
> had already happened long ago and in the dwelling place
> you had lived in before you began
> and that every step along the way, you had carried
> the heart and the mind and the promise
> that first set you off and drew you on and that you were
> more marvelous in your simple wish to find a way
> than the gilded roofs of any destination you could reach . . .³

Mike had come along on this trip to help me celebrate (or was it also to lament?) my approaching retirement. With a single semester left to teach, I needed to make peace with a career that was ending. It was time to transition into something new, at least to assure myself that I could still shoulder a pack. I was letting go of what I had loved for years—the joy of teaching, the excitement of research, the honor of serving a tradition. As a scholar about to be unchained from his iron loop in the basement floor of the university library, I had mixed feelings about my pending release. The imprisonment had been self-chosen, often even rewarding. But I was tired of spending so much time indoors. I was weary of faculty meetings, of having to pretend to know more than I did, of my worth being measured by a rank and tenure committee. As a self-styled scholar-in-recovery, I knew what I was recovering *from*, but not yet what I was recovering *to*.

I took comfort in the craziness of Cheryl Strayed—a woman who, when facing a major transition in her life (a mother's death and a recent divorce), decided to hike the Pacific Crest Trail—alone and without any prior experience of backpacking. She launched out into a world that was two feet wide and 2,663 miles long, lacking the knowhow and inner resources for even beginning. She trusted, absurdly, that the wilderness would teach her what was necessary. That's the kind of folly I'm tempted to call holy.[4]

I knew that like her, I needed Coyote, the Apache trickster. He's an ambiguous character, both evil and good, possessing the power to help as well as to harm. To follow Coyote's path is to disrupt the order of things, to shake words loose from their meanings, to play the fool. For years I'd devoted my life to writing, to the interpretation of texts and the power of language to shape new worlds. I'd looked to Hermes, the trickster deity from Olympus whose job was to foster communication between humans and the gods. He encouraged the work of hermeneutics, the studied interpretation of holy books. But he was also the patron of thieves. Having stolen his brother Apollo's cattle, he delighted in confusing, tricking, and seducing readers into alternative understandings of texts. I hoped that some of his trickery might lie ahead on the trail.

My friend Mike came with his own desires, wanting more than anything else to see a mountain lion. Lions were so plentiful in Arizona that year that twenty tags had been sold to hunters. The surge in the cougar population explained why we weren't hearing many coyotes at night. The lions were thinning their ranks. So Mike's yearning to spot a lion warred with my desire to meet coyote. As it worked out, neither of us exactly found the animal we were seeking.

Yet we found more than enough to delight us: sleeping under starlight beside tall cottonwood trees near the creek; watching the moon rise over the rim of Horse Camp Canyon as Jupiter set on its opposite rim; weaving our way up a winding side creek into the haunting mystery of Hell Hole Canyon. There, in that strange, unnerving place, we stopped to light sage and offer tobacco. We hoped for an entry into its mystery, thinking a bit of ritual might prompt the Holy to reveal itself in some grand and fitting way.

Instead at that moment we were overtaken by five chatty men from a Phoenix Bible church. We hadn't seen anyone on the trail in three days, and suddenly the divine appeared in a manner we hadn't expected. We'd been caught doing something suspiciously pagan, obviously in need of being saved from our spiritual degradation. Wouldn't you know? Mike had come looking for lions and he got Christians instead. And damned if Coyote hadn't arrived for me in a form I should have anticipated from the start . . . a barrage of religious talk breaking the silence in the depths of a desert canyon.

The Archetype of the Holy Fool

The holy fool does that to you. He or she invites you to laugh at yourself and the silly pretensions that crowd your life. The gift of the fool may be the most telling of all the benefits that derive from backpacking as a spiritual practice. There's no end to the stories you can tell of dumb mistakes you've made on the trail. Self-effacement is easy, even for gearheads and hard-core hikers.

The Christian tradition of the sacred fool extends from the apostle Paul's exhortation to be "fools for Christ's sake" to Erasmus's *In Praise of Folly*, from the medieval Feast of Fools to colorful saints like Isaac Zatvornik in eleventh-century Russia and Philip Neri in sixteenth-century Italy. You see it in Cervantes's *Don Quixote* and Dostoyevsky's *The Idiot*. The fool laughs at what others take seriously and takes seriously what others laugh at. He models a pattern of cultural resistance, challenging dominant structures of religious, political, and intellectual power. The fool knows that the path of any meaningful life is invariably paved with surprise.

Fra Mariano Fetti was a Dominican brother who served as archjester at the court of Pope Leo X in the early sixteenth century. His title was *capo di mati*, chief of fools. He would jump onto supper tables, slapping cardinals and bishops, organizing food fights, and chasing wild chickens through the papal court. His buffoonery had a purpose. He understood that at the highest reaches of ecclesiastical authority there's a great danger of people taking themselves too seriously. The mendicant orders unflaggingly called people to radical simplicity. A thirteenth-century Franciscan, Jacopone da Todi, attended chapter meetings crawling on all fours, the saddle of an ass on his back and a bridle and bit in his mouth. He knew, like G. K. Chesterton, that "seriousness is not a virtue."[5]

One finds celebrated fools in every cultural tradition—from the "wise men" of the village of Gotham in Nottinghamshire to the "first schlemiel" in the town of Chelm in Poland, from the fools of Schilda in Germany to Mulla Nasrudin in Muslim folklore. The Russian *yurodivya* walked the streets in rags. Raven was a trickster-fool in tales of the Pacific Northwest. The image of the Zen Clown attracted Thomas Merton to Buddhism. He delighted in monastery fools like Han-shan, doubled over with uncontrollable laughter, or the dancing, pot-bellied Pu-tai, often pictured with a frog on his head.

The most venerated Zen masters howled with laughter at the idea that people thought them holy. They gave titles to each other, such as "Great Bag of Rice" or "Snowflake on a Hot Oven." They drew pictures of themselves with fat stomachs and scowling faces, dressed in tattered clothes, playing in the dirt with children. Merton himself howled at the image of Tan-hsia, a ninth-century master usually pictured as warming his bare backside at a fire he'd made from a wooden image of the Buddha. America's favorite monk, tucked away in the Kentucky hills, found in the office of the Zen fool a deadly weapon against pious illusions.

The holy fool's vocation is to upset people's confidence in words, their efforts to control reality, their restriction of the holy to predetermined categories. He or she sees through the forged personas we project in trying to foster a reputation. Erasmus, in sixteenth-century Europe, mocked his fellow "foolosophers." He laughed at long-winded lecturers, sanctimonious cardinals, and self-congratulating theology professors like himself. The latter, he observed, add Greek phrases to their Latin orations when they aren't even necessary "so that those who understand the words will be all the more pleased with themselves, and those who do not understand will admire the more in proportion to their ignorance." [6]

For the fool, self-mockery is a route to freedom. Laughing at oneself may be the surest sign of growth in the life of the spirit. By contrast, warned C. S. Lewis, self-approving solemnity is one of Screwtape's finest snares.[7] The Desert Fathers were prime examples of this freedom, persistently minimizing their reputation as spiritual guides. They laughed at a vision of Abba Moses, the venerable ascetic, sitting in a boat with the angels eating honey cakes. They revered Abba Macarius who, when falsely accused of fathering a child, made no protest but simply chuckled, "Macarius, you've found yourself a wife. You just have to work harder to feed her now." They held Abba John the Dwarf in high regard, a fool who planted a dead stick in the ground and watered it every day. They abhorred spiritual notoriety. "Don't live in a famous place or close to a man with a great name," cautioned Abba Zeno. Better to be a fool that no one ever notices.[8]

Mark it down as a principle: in the tradition of holy folly, progress in the spiritual life is seldom what you expect. It brings an increase in foolishness, not sanctity; laughter at one's failures, not gravity at one's self-importance. Befuddled, you end up discovering the holy in the last place you anticipated.

Merton as Zen Clown

Thomas Merton (1915–1968) was a highly improbable monk. His checkered history as roué and honky-tonk pianist should have told the Trappists that this guy wasn't typical monastic material. Born in France to parents who were wandering artists, he got a girl pregnant at an English prep school, drank heavily as a student activist at Columbia, and showed more promise as a writer for *The New Yorker* than as a cloistered monk. He admitted that his first experience of sex was with a Viennese whore he'd picked up in Hyde Park.

Yet at the age of twenty-six the new convert entered a Cistercian monastery in the backwoods of Kentucky, bringing the earthiness, creativity, and relentless search for truth that were naturally his. Each of these flourished in his life at the Abbey of Our Lady of Gethsemani. He loved the silence, the repetition of the Psalms, the simplicity of rural life, even the hand signals used to communicate in the cloister. There he learned to lose himself in the adoration of a mystery he couldn't name. In his assigned roles as abbey forester and fire watcher he spent more and more time among the scrub pines that cover the knobs of central Kentucky. The woods outside drove him to prayer as much as the daily office within the cloister.

Merton's autobiography, written shortly after he entered the monastery, quickly turned him into a cult figure.[9] He became an idealized monastic hero. In the years that followed, he worked hard at dispelling the image. "Due to a book I wrote thirty years ago," he mused in the 1960s, "I have myself become a sort of stereotype of the world-denying contemplative—the man who spurned New York, spat on Chicago, and tromped on Louisville, heading for the woods with Thoreau in one pocket, St. John of the Cross in another, and holding the Bible open at the apocalypse." [10]

Merton always surprised people. When Jim Forest of the Catholic Worker movement hitchhiked to Gethsemani to meet him in the early 1960s, he was asked to wait in the silence of the Abbey chapel. He soon heard tumultuous laughter nearby. On investigating, he found Merton talking with a friend in the guest room, laughing uproariously, lying on the floor with his feet kicking in the air, black and white robes askew, clutching his belly like a fat Friar Tuck. Forest had come to meet America's most acclaimed monk and found a crazy fool instead.[11]

It's not that the much-admired author of *The Seven Storey Mountain* adopted a substitute persona as some free-wheeling Bohemian ascetic. He simply understood the monastic life as necessarily grounded in a deep humility and ordinariness. At the hermitage he wore overalls and a straw hat, dismissing himself as just another "old bat" living in the Kentucky hollows. "What I wear is pants. What I do is live. How I pray is breathe." [12]

As novice master in the monastery, he thought it important to model this freedom from monastic pretentiousness. One of his charges later recalled, "The first time I saw him he was bouncing down the cloister making all the signs we weren't supposed to make, and which he bawled us out for making. We were all going into the church and he was going in the opposite direction which I supposed was a part of the joke. He never wanted you to take him too seriously." [13]

Ironically, Merton came more fully to realize his vocation by practicing it less earnestly. It was the levity he brought to his monastic experience that revealed to others its greatest appeal. He urged people to view the monk as the only person in American society free to do nothing and not feel guilty about it. The monk is a sort of "outlaw," he argued, a genuine prophet in the rat-race craziness of American life.[14] He invites those outside the cloister to a similar kind of eccentricity.

Merton had found in Zen Buddhism not only a confirmation of the importance of the holy fool, but also a critique of the overly intellectualized and frenetic mindset of Western culture. He found Zen liberating in its "quest for direct and pure experience," set free from "verbal formulas and linguistic preconceptions." [15] It called people away from descriptions of life to life itself, from labels and titles to immediate experience of the given moment, from harried distractions to studied mindfulness.

Merton once met a Zen novice who had just finished his first year in the monastery. He asked him what he had learned, half expecting to hear about encounters with enlightenment, exciting discoveries of the spirit, even altered states of consciousness. But the novice replied that the most important thing he had learned during his beginning year in the religious life was how to open and close doors. He had concentrated on being present to what he was doing in any single instant—not hurrying from one place to another, slamming doors behind him. That's where he had to start, and perhaps also end, in his monastic practice. Merton was delighted with the answer.

His interest in Zen expressed itself in many of his writings, including *Zen and the Birds of Appetite*, *Mystics and Zen Masters*, and scattered references in *Conjectures of a Guilty Bystander* and the *Asian Journal*. In 1964, on one of his rare trips outside the monastery, Merton traveled to Columbia University to meet D. T. Suzuki, the famous Japanese interpreter of Zen to the West. They had corresponded, but this was their first meeting. Immediately, each discovered in the other the simplicity they valued most in their own traditions. Merton said he felt that in this ninety-four-year-old man he had met the "true Man of No Title" of whom Zen masters speak. Suzuki said that he had found no one in the West who understood Zen better than Merton.

They celebrated a tea ceremony in Butler Hall before departing. Merton was taken by Suzuki's natural ease and un-self-consciousness in performing the ritual. "It was at once as if nothing at all had happened and as if the roof had flown off the building. But in reality nothing had happened. A very old deaf Zen man with bushy eyebrows had drunk a cup of tea, as though with the complete wakefulness of a child and yet as though at the same time declaring with utter finality: 'This is not important!'" [16] That's what Merton most appreciated about Zen—its never standing on ceremony, yet discerning the heart of reality in every simple action.

The Zen critique of verbiage allowed him also to laugh at the quantity of words he produced as one of the most prolific writers in the history of the monastic life. Zen uses language against itself, undermining the conceptual framework to which the ego desperately clings. In our Western, Cartesian tradition, we talk (or write) incessantly about reality, so as to avoid (it seems) being present to it. We gather endless amounts of information, seeking out external authorities to quote so as to appear impressively knowledgeable. But we shun the interiority of our own experience and become increasingly disconnected from the living, breathing earth.

Merton was fascinated by the parallels between Zen meditation and the Christian practice of contemplation. For him, the latter was something thoroughly ordinary—what he experienced on the front porch of his hermitage. Listening at times to the sounds of the forest, he heard them coming together in a single note of *consonantia* (harmony), as "heat, fragrant pine, quiet wind, and bird song" blended into a "central tonic note that is unheard and unuttered." He described this kind of contemplation as a "seeing straight into the nature of things as they are," recognizing that "everything that is, is holy." [17]

He urged that contemplation of the natural world should lead to a more immediate encounter with God through contemplative prayer. Its "preference for the desert, for emptiness," for a poverty of words and images, takes you outside of yourself—beyond all thought, into the stillness of the soul. Here the contemplative begins to realize that "His presence is present in my own presence." [18] What you had glimpsed by "knowing" in the macrocosm of the world is mirrored by a deeper "unknowing" in the microcosm of the soul. To your astonishment, you find the God of majestic wilderness, the God of love-starved saints, right there in the mystery of your own being.

"In prayer we discover what we already have," Merton explained. "You start where you are and you deepen what you already have, and you realize that you are already there. We already have everything, but we don't know it and we don't experience it. Everything has been given to us in Christ. All we need is to experience what we already possess." [19]

There were days when he would watch the morning mist drifting through the pines around his cabin, its mystery taking him beyond himself. On other days, he recognized the same mist as intimately one with his own breathing. He understood how inner and outer landscapes reflect each other. Mystical encounters entail a radical strangeness as well as a deep familiarity. God is unlike anything we've ever experienced, yet closer than the next breath we take. "There is an infinite metaphysical gulf between the 'I' of the Almighty and our own inner 'I,'" Merton observed. "Yet paradoxically, our inmost 'I' exists in God and God dwells in it." [20] The bramble-filled thicket behind his snug and familiar hermitage helped him appreciate the tension between these two realities.

One Windy Night in Aravaipa

The most important truth one learns from wilderness is that the holy is "utterly within you and utterly beyond you at the very same time." [21] Backcountry, in its wild and unmanageable "otherness," takes you outside yourself *and* most deeply into yourself, only to find there a still more compelling wilderness. Threatening terrain is disconcerting. You realize that what fills you with dread *out there* is but an echo of an even greater awe *within*. "Every angel is terrifying," says Rilke, not least the one you glimpse in the mystery of your own being. [22] Something terrifyingly holy whispers inside, calling you back to a truth you've held back from claiming.

Four years ago, when I first came to the area around Aravaipa Canyon, I spent a night alone in the dry arroyo. That's where my body felt a deep resonance with the land, moving through the cavernous interior of the earth's body, knowing intrinsically that I belonged there. I had come as part of a men's gathering with Richard Rohr. He had sent us into the desert for an overnight solo, urging us to listen to the teachers we might find. He mentioned in passing that on Native American vision quests it isn't uncommon for one to receive a new name.

I made my way down the winding arroyo, finding a place to spread my tarp under an old cottonwood tree. A broken limb hung from its trunk; yellow-green leaves rustled in the wind. By nightfall, the wind had become an incessant, disturbing presence. A desert wind can be primeval, even cruel. Early Norwegian settlers on the northern plains were driven insane by the relentless wind, finding nothing they could hide behind.[23]

A storm was brewing in the distance. Lightning flashes reflected off the canyon rim. It hadn't been a good idea to camp under a hanging dead limb in a dry creek bed. So I climbed onto a ledge of salmon-pink sandstone, lying there on the rock. Buffeted by the wind, I studied the section of sky I could see between high canyon walls. After a while I felt an urge to tell a story, as if the stars and whirling cottonwood leaves were asking for relief from the monotony of the wind. I told them story after story that night—narratives that I'd used in teaching, tales I hadn't remembered in years, stories I'd never been able to tell without notes. They came from the depths of a memory I didn't know I had. Tales weaving themselves through the windblown intensity of the night.

Then, in the darkness before dawn, I heard it. A voice carried on the wind that seemed to speak inside my body. I didn't *think* it. I simply received it, with an undeniable certainty. Four words addressed to me: "Speaks with the Wind." Nothing more. But I knew in that moment that I had been called . . . I had been *named*.

All my life I'd been telling stories of wounded parents and dashed dreams, tales of winding trails and desert-worn saints. I'd been searching in the wilderness for a lost father, for spiritual guides who could answer questions I didn't even know how to ask. I'd sought words to convey the dread and adoration that overwhelmed me in wilderness places. I'd been smitten and loved by a God-beyond-names, left as a teacher lacking language for what he most wanted to teach.

But now the earth was calling forth a voice within me—one that could speak in, with, and for the places I had learned to love and the saints who had taught me there. It wasn't about me. But it required me. It's the height of foolishness to imagine an old white man—a bookish, academic type—being named by the desert: fancying himself another Kevin Costner in "Dances with Wolves," adopting an Apache name. I'm still tempted to dismiss the whole thing as nothing more than a romantic fantasy on a windy night. Let's be realistic. An appropriate name for someone like me wouldn't be "Speaks with the Wind." Coyote would prefer something more like "He Who Passes Wind When He Speaks."

Yet I can't get away from what happened that night. An authentic experience of being named comes with a touch of folly. "You've gotta be kidding," you respond. It's the last thing you would have thought true of yourself. The hardest thing we ever do is to claim what is said of us by the voice within. We can't explain it, and yet we can't deny it either. To do so would invite the even greater danger of not living into what our names require of us.

So what do I make of this? I'm intrigued by the connection I sensed that night between the turbulence in the canyon and the freedom with which I told stories. I felt a visceral connection between the fierce desert wind and the breath it evoked from my body. Boundaries between inside and outside dissolved, wind speaking to wind.

The haunting power of wind is ingrained in the wisdom of every culture. Indigenous people consider winds to be sacred, giving them names like Aeolus, Zephyros, Vayu, Mamatele. Winds bear messages from the gods. They bring a change in weather, sometimes even a change in fortune. In primal cultures, people who do not reverence the power of wind and breath are treated with suspicion. Native Hawaiians have applied the term *haole* (pronounced HOW-lee) to white-skinned foreigners since the arrival of Captain Cook in 1778. The word literally means *"without* breath, wind or spirit." It refers to the colorless, paste-white absence of spirit seen in those lacking a respect for the land and the dignity of its people.[24] To be without breath is to be cut off from the earth's animating life.

To be sensitive to air filling one's lungs and wind singing in eucalyptus trees is to be open to the life and language of the spirit. As humans, we communicate by forcing breath across our vocal chords, giving it timbre in the cavern of the mouth, shaping words by the interrupting movement of lips and teeth. In similar fashion, the earth creates wind by the rotation of its body, sending high- and low-pressure fronts across an intercepting landscape of mountains, forests, and desert canyons. The speech in either case is a movement of life-giving breath.

In the Genesis account of creation, life begins with the wind passing over the face of the waters *and* with spirit being breathed into living beings. The two are inseparable—exterior and interior operations of a single reality. The Hebrew writers used the same word to speak of breath, spirit, and wind: *ruach*, a guttural sound mimicking what it names. Nor is it a coincidence that the most revered name for God in Hebrew usage is one that shouldn't be pronounced, only breathed. There are no sibilants in the name Yahweh. The word is sounded by unobstructed breath alone: *Yahhhh—wehhhh*, an effortless flow of breathing in and breathing out.

This mystical dimension of wind and breath is what struck me that night in the canyon near Aravaipa. For air-breathing vertebrates like ourselves, respiration is an automatic, involuntary movement, sustaining life without our having to "think" it. This is why the Desert Fathers and Mothers were among the first to make use of short "breath prayers" in fulfilling the biblical injunction to "pray without ceasing."

Their custom was to sit outside their cells, weaving palm fronds as the desert wind beat against their faces, breathing (in and out) prayers of a single word or phrase. This was the origin of the "Jesus Prayer," the repetition of a few words to still the mind and center the heart. The persistent desert wind reminded the monks of the God Moses had met in the burning bush, a God utterly beyond them. Yet the quiet passage of breath through their bodies assured them that this same God dwelt intimately within.[25]

The Ultimate Folly: The Holy Within

The name "Speaks with the Wind" comes as an invitation to what is disturbingly new and yet deeply familiar. How do I understand myself as storyteller and fool—acknowledging this calling as a fitting completion to an academic career, the proper fulfillment of any theologian's work? A new name suggests a new way of conveying the truth of one's life. The elders within a culture are those responsible for remembering its stories. They have to trust in what they desire even more than in what they know. Their finest words are borne on a night wind in the desolate places of their lives.

Speaking with the wind is akin to speaking in tongues—a desert gift less concerned with being understood than with giving vent to the inexpressibly wild. Its longing is to discover love in the last place you might have thought to look. This mystical insight recurs repeatedly in the saints discussed in this book. John of the Cross speaks of the dark night as an absence-filled yearning for God. The *Cloud* author writes of a divine mystery ultimately beyond knowing, yet not beyond loving. Teilhard exalts a Cosmic Christ who entices the universe by love's alluring power. Rumi sings of love as a school of fire where the distinction between Lover and Beloved vanishes. They all speak the unsayable language of fools. Lacking adequate words, they're left only with stories . . . full of wind and fire.

They realize that what they'd sought in the mind-numbing terror and heart-rending stillness of the wild (*out there*, in the realms of mystery) had been within them all along. "My deepest me is God," shouts Catherine of Genoa, running through the streets of her fourteenth-century town. "The mystery of Christ is within you," Paul proclaims in Colossians 1:27. "*Tat tvam asi*: You are *that*! You *are* what you seek!" the Upanishads boldly declare.[26]

You are the temple of the Holy Spirit, they insist. You are the dwelling place of the most High God. You are loved beyond measure by what you can't even begin to understand. The wilderness you've sought throughout your journey has been within you from the start.

Walking with Mike back to the trailhead on our final morning in Aravaipa Canyon, I lagged behind, feeling the weight of my pack. I was carrying memories of my previous experience in the area, understanding it more clearly now. With a sense of déjà vu, I recalled one of the stories that had come to me that night four years earlier in the nearby canyon—an eighteenth-century Hasidic tale about a holy fool.

In a time hidden in memory, or so the story goes, there was a Jew by the name of Isaac son of Yekel—a poor man who lived in the town of Krakow, Poland. He had a wife and several children, but never enough food to put on the table. One night he had a dream. In his dream, he saw the distant city of Prague with the Vltava River flowing through it. He noticed a bridge crossing the river and a treasure buried under the far end of the bridge.

On waking, Isaac told his wife about his crazy dream. She agreed it was crazy. "But it was so real!" he insisted. "Every detail so vivid!" In fact, the next night he had the *same* dream. And the *next* night as well. Every night, for two weeks running, he had the same dream of the far-off city of Prague, the river passing through it, the bridge over the river, and a treasure buried beneath the bridge.

Finally he resolved to drive this *dybbuk* (this evil spirit) from his mind, deciding to walk all the way to Prague to prove it right or wrong. He took a few crusts of bread and, by begging along the road, managed to travel the 250 miles to the outskirts of the city. To his amazement, he recognized everything from his dream. Seeing the Vltava River, he walked along its bank until he spotted the bridge in the distance. He began then to run, stooping under one end of the bridge to look at last for the treasure. But a soldier suddenly grabbed him by the back of the neck and hauled him away to prison.

There an officer interrogated him, asking what he had been doing prowling around under that bridge. Not knowing what else to say, Isaac blurted out the truth, saying he'd been looking for a treasure he had seen in his dream. The officer burst into mocking laughter, shouting, "You stupid fool. Don't you realize you can't believe what you see in your dreams? Why I *myself* have had a dream every night for the last two weeks about a Jew named Isaac son of Yekel who has a treasure buried under the pot-bellied stove in the hovel where he lives . . . in a place called Krakow! But wouldn't it be ridiculous for me to go all the way to Krakow (wherever the hell that is), to look for a Jew named

Isaac son of Yekel? There may be a hundred of them there by that name, or none at all. Only a *fool* would look for a treasure that doesn't even exist!" Still laughing, the officer gave him a swift kick and threw him out.

Isaac son of Yekel walked all the way back home to his little shack in Krakow. There he pushed aside the pot-bellied stove in his kitchen, pried up the floor boards, and found a great treasure. Isaac son of Yekel lived to a ripe old age as a wealthy man. My favorite part of the story, however, is that one of the rabbis later observed, "Isn't it interesting: The treasure was at home all along, but the knowledge of it was in Prague." [27]

This is the ultimate twist of folly: to realize that what you have sought everywhere else in your life has been at home all along. From the beginning, the mystery was yours, bearing you along on its restless energy. What you sought *out there*—on steep wilderness paths, in the feverish lives of the saints, under a bridge in the far-off city of Prague—had been closer than you ever imagined. Having longed for a God of wild beauty, you discover the Lover to have been there all the while . . . in the longing itself.

The saints speak of this as holy foolishness. They boldly invite me to declare that *I* am the saint I've been seeking all along. I am the spiritual guide I've longed for, the father and mother who had never quite been there for me. The love I've sought so desperately *outside* of myself has been, from the outset, as close as my own breath.

This "self" isn't the compulsive ego or *false* self. It isn't the fragile identity that I've tried so hard to shore up in my own life. It's my *true* self, what has passed through brokenness to love, what discovers the gift within the wound, what speaks with the wind. It flourishes within the ragged community of those who know wilderness.

But I wouldn't have grasped this apart from the risks of backcountry wandering. It's out *there*, in whatever wilderness we wander, that we encounter the trickster and rule-breaker—Coyote, the con-man who cons us out of the self-importance we'd worked so hard to build up. There we embrace the fool, releasing the baggage we've carried and finding a new, unexpected treasure. Like Jacob after his night alone in the desert of Haran, we hear ourselves saying at last: "You were here all along and I never knew it. How awesome is this place" (Genesis 28:16–17).

Fifth Leg: Reprise

So why do we do it?
What good is it?
Does it teach you anything?

TERRY RUSSELL[1]

Why do hikers like me risk being caught in a storm on a mountain trail, spending the next twelve hours under a wet plastic tarp, drinking lumpy, icy chocolate? Why do we willingly sleep on a cobblestone river bank? Or lace up our boots again, after putting moleskin over blisters that had formed on top of blisters? Why do we hike an extra two miles just to see the wild flowers at the crest of a sidetrail? Or eat granola bars for breakfast, lunch, and dinner after the rest of our food has been lost in the rapids?

Is it Love? Determination? Art? Music? Religion? All of the above, says wilderness wanderer Terry Russell. You welcome the little disasters of the trail because they give you hope in facing the bigger ones in your life. They teach you through the trial and error of your inherent foolishness. Aldo Leopold said it well: "The elemental simplicities of wilderness travel [are] thrills not only because of their novelty, but because they represent complete freedom to make mistakes."[2]

Backpacking as a spiritual practice is about making yourself vulnerable in order to be stretched into something new. It's the need to recognize your limits, to be taken to the end of yourself where resources are exhausted and you stumble in blind faith toward that which is more than you. In the beauty-mixed-with-terror of a backcountry wilderness, you begin to discover that for which the mystics had no language.

And you realize that if you can do it there you can do it at home as well . . . knowing that when you've run out of everything you have, what is left is enough. More than enough.

It's the pattern we've seen throughout this book: (1) Venturing out, only to be disillusioned and forced to ask what it is we really want most. (2) Assuming a discipline of being alone, traveling light, and practicing mindfulness. (3)

Accepting the descent into fear, failure, and even death. (4) Returning home, finally, with the unexpected gifts of insight, community, a fearless commitment to justice, and a laughable awareness that what we'd sought all along had been closer than we ever dreamed.

Epilogue

Reading is a form of magic.
DAVID ABRAM[3]

WE'VE CAUGHT THE ferry at Anacortes, standing by the rail as the vessel weaves its way through the San Juan Islands off the coast of Washington. Eagles soar overhead as dolphins dive and surface off the ship's bow. We dock briefly at Shaw Island, where a brown-robed Franciscan sister, wearing a phosphorescent safety vest, lowers the ramp for a few vehicles to exit. The next stop is Orcas Island. There on the dock we meet an unkempt man with dark brown hair. There's a touch of wildness behind his wide, generous smile. He has serpent rings on the third and fourth fingers of his left hand. His name is David Abram.

A friend and I had come to spend a weekend with this environmental philosopher, shaman, and sleight-of-hand magician who had two years earlier published *The Spell of the Sensuous*, an extraordinary book, drawing on his work among indigenous medicine people in Sri Lanka, Indonesia, and Nepal. David Abram is a forest imp and street performer, a trained phenomenologist and *agent provocateur*, an intellectual shape-shifter sliding easily between worlds alternately wild and literate. I'd been fascinated by connections he made in his work between wilderness, reading, and magic.

Abram argues that language itself is magical. It isn't the static transfer of an idea from one mind to another, using abstract signifiers that have no relation to the things they represent. In its origins, language imitates the animate sounds of the natural world. When we speak of the splashing, gushing, rushing, and trickling qualities of the word "water," we copy the sounds of a stream makes in falling over rocks. Language, at root, is a sensuous participation in mystery.

"Our commonplace practice of reading texts has its deepest ancestral source," says Abram, "in the indigenous hunter's careful reading of animal tracks pressed into the surface of the earth."[4] Reading the earth was our original ancestral training in the reading of anything. It involved all of our senses.

The three of us are sitting in a corner of the Olga Café, near the waterfront on Orcas Island's East Sound. We've come here for lunch, after walking around Mountain Lake in Moran State Park—exulting in huge cedars, soaring osprey, and the red-bark beauty of Pacific madrones. David reflects on how easy it is for humans to speak as if the rest of the animate world *weren't* a part of our conversation, as if the plant growing on the window ledge nearby were nothing more than wallpaper, as if we had nothing to say (in honor or appreciation) to the animals listed on the menu. We've forgotten that language is anchored in a vivid interaction with the living, breathing earth. Our lives have been stripped of magic.

The table has been cleared and David begins to play with a coin, rolling it over and under the fingers of his right hand. He speaks of the coin as if it were alive, wanting to stretch itself, to pass over boundaries it hasn't yet explored. But the coin needs to loosen itself up before it can change, he says. David runs it through its paces, inviting the coin and the three of us at the table into a desire to see it bend and fold and transform itself. The coin, he says, wants to find the precise spot on the tabletop where it can be tapped and sent through, effortlessly, to the table's underside. And, of course, it eventually does this, passing through the table top, then, to our delight, hiding itself in my friend's shirt pocket and emerging from behind my right ear.

David's success in sleight-of-hand magic depends upon our longing (as observers) for unexplained mystery. We naturally try to figure out how the trick is done, but we're fascinated by the transformation the coin undergoes. We, too, wish to be "loosened" enough to pass through boundaries with ease. We experience a primitive wonder in witnessing a seemingly dead object coming to life.

This magical awakening of desire is what also happens in the reading of a particularly seductive text, within a lively and evocative context. Take my trail-side reading of Francis of Assisi asking an almond tree (in midwinter) to speak to him of God. The tree suddenly bursts into bloom.[5] As I'm reading the tale aloud in a Wyoming wilderness, I sense the Douglas fir tree under which I'm sitting taking note. A crow cocks his head at me from a branch across the clearing. Clouds passing overhead seem to pause for a fraction of a second. Even the grass feels alive. Is it my imagination, or do they share in my desire to be transformed by what I read?

In *In Bed with the Word*, Daniel Coleman says that "Reading exercises and gives shape to the outward-reaching energy within us that is our spirituality. In this sense, reading is erotic and like all eros, it leaps with energy and passion; it compels your focus; it reaches out toward an Other." [6] This is the magical quality of reading in wilderness that has intrigued me from the very start.

Reading and backcountry wandering don't appear to have much in common. Poring over someone else's experience in wild terrain feels like a denial of the immediacy you seek in being there. To bring books (even books full of wisdom) into a wilderness setting seems like a contradiction. Reading can sometimes be an exercise in abstraction, reducing embodied realities to disembodied signs. It reduces the sudden whirl of a dust devil in a desert canyon to a handful of squiggles on a page. There's no question that the written word has distanced us from the world of nature.

But there remains an element of magic in the act of reading, something we too easily forget. Words on a page don't simply describe; they have a capacity to create. Written texts possess an unpredictable, loopy magic of their own, says Abram, "a capability for metamorphosis." [7] Their meanings shift, depending on the context in which we read and reread them. This is especially true with outdoor reading. Books haven't forgotten their intimate relation to trees, after all. They're still commonly made of paper. We speak of a book as having "leaves" and a small book as a "leaflet." An avid reader is a "bookworm," one who "branches out" into various areas of study. An idea "takes root" within us. [8] Some of us have wonderful childhood memories of reading a book in a tree we had climbed, the tree participating with us in the magic of the text.

Abram reminds us that the English word "spell" has a double meaning: to set down in order the letters of a word and to charm, fascinate, or bewitch. Reading a powerful text (whether the prophet Isaiah or the poet Rilke) in an evocative landscape (whether an Oregon coastline or a New Hampshire forest) can be a spell-binding experience. Your sensuous awareness is hooked, your imagination pulled into something new. You willingly enter a world of mystery, a world of sorcery, perhaps.

Lectio Divina, Lectio Terrestris

This was the nature of the spiritual reading of the medieval monks, their habit of *lectio divina*. I've tried in this book to combine their monastic way of meditating on the Scriptures (or the writings of the saints) with a highly sensory practice of reading particular places or landscapes. What they called *lectio divina* can be practiced alongside what we might call *lectio terrestris*, a richly interactive reading of the earth itself with the expectation of being changed by what we read.

Lectio divina was a fourfold pattern of "praying the Scriptures" formalized by a twelfth-century Carthusian monk named Guido II. He was prior of the Grande Chartreuse, a monastic community in the mountains of southeastern France.[9] The first step in the pattern of prayer he proposed was (1) *lectio* proper, the active, acoustical reading of a biblical text. The monk should read the words aloud, letting them reverberate throughout his body. The brothers viewed this as a "carnal activity," a sensuous hearing of the "voices of the pages" (*voces paginarum*). They saw the text as taking on an oral life of its own.[10] As early as the sixth century, the Rule of Saint Benedict urged the monks to be careful not to disturb each other when reading alone in their cells. Sounding the words aloud was thought crucial to their being received most deeply.

A similar kind of embodied attentiveness is necessary for reading the distinctive sounds and energies of a place. Giving the earth its voice, letting it resonate through the whole of one's being, is a process that can't be rushed. A tribal elder takes years to acquire the different "dialects of conifers," the ability to distinguish species of pine, spruce, or fir by simply listening to their needles rustling in the wind. Annie Dillard lies motionless for hours, waiting for a muskrat to take her breath away. In patient amazement, Barry Lopez watches a caribou herd that stretches from horizon to horizon on the arctic tundra.[11]

Lectio terrestris demands the exercise of all of our senses. Moving through a field, into a forest, even across our own backyard, we come with the expectation of finding a teacher. We have to give ourselves to the enigmatic "text" that opens itself before us. Arrow Mountain in the Wind River Range of Wyoming, for example, has often functioned as such a text in my experience. Overlooking Ring Lake Ranch and the Glacier Trail, it offers a stunning view of the Continental Divide to the west, the Absarokas to the north, and Crowheart Butte to the east. I've stood entranced at tree line (just above 10,500 feet), reading the harsh tale of endurance written into the gnarled whitebark pine trees that grow there. These are the highest-growing pines in the Rockies, whipped so fiercely by wind and sleet that they survive sometimes only as *krummholz*, twisted branches clinging to the ground.

Whitebark pines are the monarchs of the high country, able to withstand long winters and the worst possible conditions for survival. The oldest one in the United States—in the Sawtooth Mountains of central Idaho—is 1,275 years old. These are teachers of what it means to persevere. I sit amazed in their presence, content to "read" them for hours. They've trained me in a profound reverence for the wild.[12]

Guido, the French Carthusian, described the second step in his *lectio* process as (2) *meditatio*, the oral repetition and thoughtful pondering of a text so as to apply it to one's life. Again the pattern is thoroughly sensuous, engaging the body. The monks spoke of "ruminating" over a passage, like a cow "chewing" its cud, "masticating" the words. They pored over its multiple meanings, delving into its otherness, relating its distant world to their experience. Gradually they came to internalize the text, allowing it to define them in unexpected ways.

The task of *meditatio* requires focused attention and a disciplined effort to let the "other" speak in all of its differentness. You must not be quick to reduce its "meanings" to metaphors of your own experience. You have to listen to it on its own terms, prepared to be brought up short at times by the power of the text.

As I've learned more about whitebark pine trees—meditating on their distinctive role in the environment—I've been intrigued by the part they play as "nurse trees" in a subalpine terrain. They aren't the "rugged individualists" I might have imagined. They survive at altitudes where other trees cannot, helping to reduce soil erosion and delay snow melt into summer. Their large pine seeds are high in nutritious fats, providing a primary food source for red squirrels, Clark's nutcrackers, and even grizzly bears. Clark's nutcrackers depend entirely on whitebark pine seeds for food and, in turn, are important seed dispensers for the trees. They couldn't survive without each other. A single bird can hide up to 98,000 pine nuts in a given year, many of which are never recovered and germinate, growing new trees.

Whitebark pines are a keystone species within a fragile landscape where life depends on symbiotic relationships. Everything here is connected—the gray birds with black wings, the white-tipped grizzlies, and the weather-beaten bark of ancient trees. Leaning against the trunk of one of these old masters, I ponder the fact that none of us ever make it alone. Trees like these are Buddhist teachers, modeling the mystery of the "interdependent co-arising" of all things.[13] Nothing exists entirely in and of itself. Only together do we come into being.

The third step that Guido prescribed in his pattern of *lectio divina* is what he called (3) *oratio*, a spontaneous response of prayer evoked by the text. He asked, What desires arise out of your reading of the passage? What do you find yourself yearning for in response to what you read? The monks expected an increase in longing—greater empathy for others—to arise out of their reflection on the text. Prayer, in this respect, became a spawning ground for compassion . . . and for action.

Desire is the attracting, integrating force of the cosmos, said Teilhard. The more you attend to any single thing in the universe, the more you learn to love it. Over my years of hiking Arrow Mountain, I've come to know and love these whitebark pine trees. The first time I saw them, growing out of the scree near the saddle below the peak, I felt an aching recognition of the sublime. The harsh beauty of their wildly contorted limbs spoke to something deep within me.

But I'm alarmed by what I've seen happening in recent years. Many of these trees are dying. They've proved vulnerable to a blister rust (a fungal disease) introduced from Europe. And they are succumbing to bark beetles, which are moving to higher elevations as a result of climate change. Our human effect on the environment is causing the death of trees that have survived hundreds of years of harsh weather, lightning strike, avalanche, and fire.

In July 2011, the U.S. Fish and Wildlife Service placed whitebark pines on the threatened species list. This was the first time the federal government has declared a widespread tree species to be in danger of extinction. I can't imagine a world without the wise presence of these arboreal elders. Standing at the top of the world, they witness to the fierce tenacity of life. They stir my desire . . . and my determination to speak on their behalf.

Guido identified the fourth and last step of sacred reading as (4) *contemplatio*, entry at last into silence, moving beyond all interpretation, beyond all words. The early Desert Christians described this as resting in the heart of God, letting the mind descend into the heart. To read with a contemplative mind, they said, is to shut down one's inner dialogue, focusing (if anything) on one's breathing alone, allowing the text to penetrate to a level deeper than thought.

Something elusive, almost magical happens in this radical letting go of words. I remember sitting one afternoon beside a dead whitebark pine on Arrow Mountain, moving (in my "reading" of it) beyond attentiveness, reflection, and even desire. Simply *staying* with the tree, beneath its needle-less branches, sharing a deliberate and thoughtless silence. The tree had nothing to offer, and yet the "nothing" we shared at the time was profound. An undemanding presence may be the finest gift we ever give or receive.

Allowing this to happen isn't easy. Like most people, I'm a pathetic contemplative—not very practiced at "staying," distracted continually by intruding thoughts. My exercise of contemplative stillness is like a daily bath in a deep-felt inadequacy, my inner poverty. It seems a worthless exercise, accomplishing nothing. Yet my ability to be open to others is rooted in my capacity to "stick," to stay with being present to what I love.[14] Moreover, it teaches me not to plunge immediately into action, dashing down the mountain to do what I can to save the dying trees. One's most effective work can grow out of first learning to do nothing well.

The practice of *contemplatio* is an exercise in non-dual consciousness, a matter—in the end—of *becoming* what you read. If sleight-of-hand requires you to identify with the coin and its "longing" for transformation, contemplative prayer demands that you abandon fixed distinctions between subject and object. The magic of shared silence "gathers you up into the body of the present moment so thoroughly that all your *explanations* fall away."[15] Sitting at tree line above 10,000 feet, you slip out of awareness of yourself as a separate, individual consciousness.

The distance between you and the whitebark pine dissolves. You "disappear," as the Zen master might say.[16] You and the tree are joined in the immense solitude of the mountain. You need do nothing more than rest in knowing you're alive. The most effective action you ever undertake will come from that place. There you realize that you have finally *become* what you have read.

Caveat Lector: *Reading as Risk*

I don't want to minimize the unsettling connection between the life of the wild and the danger of the text. "If the book we are reading does not wake us, as with a fist hammering on our skull," urged Franz Kafka, "why then do we read it? . . . A book must be like an ice-axe to break the frozen sea within us."[17] Classic spiritual texts open us to an inner liminal terrain where change is demanded of us. Places in the wilds have a similar capacity for writing themselves into our flesh. "You can hear the needle scratching into us right now," says Craig Childs, hiking the remote canyons of Utah. It etches itself into your body:

> Every little detail down there, shapes and colors we've never seen before. They all leave this mark, this second landscape inside of us. You can hear it. Like a pencil scribbling something on paper. . . . Everything has something to say here. We need to be fluent.[18]

Yet we lack fluency in speaking and reading the languages of the *other*. That takes time . . . and a risk we're reluctant to embrace. It demands that we venture out into the wilderness places of our lives. It requires us to sit at the feet of teachers whose lives and practice have taken them farther into backcountry than we ourselves have dared to go.

Here at the end of my academic career, I realize at last how theology must always be done, how the tradition of the saints must ever be read: over against the howling of wind in the dark of night; on a wilderness crag where beauty and danger intertwine; amid the pain and mystery of a world that dances through tears. Johann Baptist Metz warns the reader of the biblical texts that their stories of discipleship can be deeply disturbing, fundamentally unsafe. "They invite us not to contemplate but to *follow* . . . We will not understand them," he admonishes, "if we do not admit the category of danger into our theology." [19]

This is an invitation as much as a challenge. You can't let the fear of danger keep you from plunging into the rugged high country where your soul comes to life. John Muir offered sound advice to the fearful traveler who dreads mountainous terrain. "Few places in this world are more dangerous than home," he countered. "Fear not, therefore, to try the mountain-passes. They will kill care, save you from deadly apathy, set you free, and call forth every faculty into vigorous, enthusiastic action." [20]

Besides, that's where the magic happens—out where trails become hard to follow. In that wild terrain you learn, like the magician's coin, to pass through boundaries with ease, to yield yourself to the sorcery of the text, to be transformed by what you read. You discover that this alive and breathing land is "not primarily a set of mechanisms waiting to be figured out . . . It is, rather, the very body of wonder—a shuddering field of intelligence in whose round life we participate." [21] Only then do you come face to face with a mystery that fills you with as much awe as it does love.

You sit leaning against a whitebark pine as the afternoon shadows make their way up the mountain. You enter the quietness of the day's abandonment of itself. The journal has been put aside. You listen to nothing beyond your own breathing. Words have left you. All that remains is a naked intent to love, as the *Cloud* author would say—an object-less form of prayer, sent out into the universe.

This reaching out of the spirit attracts the attention of all things wanting to be loved. In that moment, you are spotted from high above by a golden eagle. You tremble to realize, like John of the Cross, that you are about to be caught by what you have been hunting. In one of his poems, the Spanish mystic pictures himself as a spiraling falcon, flying "so high, so high" on the wings of love. He snatches on the wing the sparrow he imagines to be God. But overtaking his prey, he knows *himself* to be overtaken by Love. He becomes a victim of the divine ambush. *He* is the prey, the one captured and wounded. His cries out, "O sweet cautery, O delightful wound . . . in snaring me you have changed my death into life." [22]

There in the heart of wilderness—circling higher and higher on the thermals over the mountains of the Sierra Nevada—John experiences an intimacy he had never dreamed of. He falls in love with the mystery that overtakes him. He will never be the same. Neither will those of us who follow a similar path into the wild. We may not be able to put into words what we've come to love. But as we lean against the whitebark pine, our eyes follow the flight of the eagle above the ridge and we count ourselves happy to be alive. We recognize the wounds we carry as gifts. We acknowledge the wilderness we walk through as home. We honor the world we share with the others as filled with magic.

Returning Home Again

The process of reentry, of finally coming back home, isn't easy. Driving back from the silence of a three-day trip into wilderness, we reenter a world of noisy distractions. The shock is overwhelming. We struggle to remember the mind-numbing terror and heart-rending stillness of the wild. We forget what we learned out there . . . that life *everywhere* is life on the edge. All that can save us is a return to a daily practice of *lectio*—warding off inattentiveness and discerning once again the wonder that hides in everything.

After David Abram's time with indigenous people in Southeast Asia, he found it hard to readjust to American culture. He sought solace in places on the boundaries—Indian land, old-growth forests, and zoos. Practicing sleight-of-hand tricks in zoos, he found himself mesmerized and healed by the animals' responses. He says that a monkey, watching a silver dollar play across his knuckles and suddenly disappear, screamed in wide-eyed wonder and ran to pull the tails of others to come see this mystery. He says that a pair of cockatoos, perched overhead in the bird house, went crazy on seeing the coin vanish, as he opened his hand to reveal its absence. They shrieked and swirled in opposite circles around the rod they clutched in their claws—gymnasts on parallel bars run amuck.

As a trickster, David Abram affirms magic as a joy shared across species. It rattles all of our cages, suggesting unguessed-at possibilities. He wants us to imagine living in a world where extraordinary exchanges across species readily occur. Yet true magic is more than sleight-of-hand tricks. It isn't a power to be wielded so much as a wonder to which we yield. It demands a shifting of our perception, a way of reading the world differently, a new manner of living.

The highest magic—the most transformative—is love, of course. But beware: giving yourself to the restless energy of the saints, or to any of these teachers of the wild, will ultimately break your heart. Pondering their texts (participating in their lives), you will no longer be able to accept the world as you have known it. You'll welcome the joyous and dangerous possibility of falling in love all over again.

This was the experience of St. Bernard of Montjoux, a tenth-century Benedictine monk who deliberately chose a life posed on the edge of danger. He and his brothers founded a monastery and hospice in the rugged mountains of northern Italy, at the highest point on a pass in the Pennine Alps between Aosta and the Swiss canton of Valais. It was a place of treacherous avalanches and snow drifts sometimes forty feet deep. The monks used dogs to search for pilgrims caught on the trail. St. Bernard threw himself into this work, becoming the patron saint of alpinists, climbers, and backpackers—as well as the namesake of the huge, shaggy-haired dogs known to this day for their rescue work. A book on backpacking with the saints can't end without a tribute to him . . . recalling the risks he encouraged for the sake of love.

So where do I find myself? I'm back in St. Louis, trying to remember the silence and solitude of Arrow Mountain. Last week I cleaned out my office and turned in the key. It was unsettling to relinquish the "place" I'd occupied so long at the university. There's a deep mystery in being poised on the edge of something new in my life, asking how to maneuver the next part of the trail before me. I've reached an "angle of repose," as Wallace Stegner would say.[23]

This is a technical term used by geologists and engineers in calculating the slide of rubble down a mountain slope. It refers to the thirty-four-degree angle at which sand stops drifting down the leeward side of a sand dune. It's the angle of an antlion's sand trap, the angle at which dirt and pebbles stop rolling. Stegner used it as a metaphor for the point of repose at which people sometimes arrive in their lives, provided they've made enough mistakes and weathered sufficient storms.

At this angle of repose in my life, the truth sinks in that the lost father and spiritual guides I've been seeking have been here all along. The mystery I've sought on wilderness trails, the healing of the family secrets I've carried, the beauty I've pursued in what I've taught, the love that ties me to everything alive . . . it's all here.

Entering the unmapped terrain of retirement, I don't have to look anywhere else for what I seek. I don't have to "accomplish" anything further. The disparate particles of my life, clinging together in their downhill roll into the future, find what they desire at this holding point on the mountain's slope. All my backpacking trips through the years have been practice runs for the work that now begins. I'm summoned to an improved practice of adoration, marveling at the wonders of a world I still cannot fathom. Abraham Heschel had it right: Wonder is the wellspring of love . . . and love, in the end, is what drives us to a passion for all things wild and at risk.[24]

Appendix: The Meanings of Wilderness

ON THE MORNING of April 26, 2003, Aron Ralston started hiking into Blue John Canyon in the wilds of southern Utah. He had no idea what his body would be teaching him over the next 127 hours. As he climbed his way through narrow slot canyons, a falling chockstone suddenly pinned his right hand to the wall. He couldn't pull himself free. For six days he survived the desert's heat and cold, drinking his last liter of water as well as his own urine. Keeping his mind focused to ward off panic, he was able finally to escape— breaking the bones of his arm and cutting through his flesh with a dull knife.[1]

What sustained him was a spirit image that came to him in his fantasies, not unlike the ancient images painted by shamans on the Great Gallery in Horseshoe Canyon a few miles away. It was an image of a little boy whom he recognized as his own son. But the boy hadn't been born yet. Aron had yet even to meet his mother. But the premonition sustained him through his ordeal.

How do we name what held him up through his trial? Was it the *earth's* body, alive with colors, clutching him in its sandstone womb until he was ready for new birth? Was it his *own* body, forced to be more vividly attentive than ever before in his life? Was it "*God's* body," evident everywhere, yet so apparent in the image of a child reflected off canyon walls? Only the wilderness knows. That's why it fascinates us so completely.

Interpreting Wilderness in Western Thought

What, then, do we mean by this notion of "wilderness" and its spiritual significance? How does it function as a construct of the imagination, given the assorted "readings" of wilderness that populate the history of Western thought? In this appendix I want to acknowledge the cultural baggage that Americans like myself bring to the idea of wilderness. I want also to reflect on how people find wild terrain to be deeply healing and to explore more carefully the nature of outdoor reading in the history of Christianity.

What *is* it that I'm "entering" when I venture with my knapsack into wilderness? What is this cluster of complex notions and convictions that draws on 12,000 years of cultural experience as *Homo sapiens sapiens*? I go into wilderness as a human being who "knows that he knows," who reflects on his powers of reflection, who is able—by a strange alchemy of the mind—to transform reality into thought (and thought into reality). I create wilderness as a place of savagery or a potential garden of the New World. I come at times as an amateur anthropologist, at other times as a spiritual seeker or Joseph Campbell's hero setting forth on a mythic quest. Whatever combination of images I carry with me, I hit the trail with a great deal of cultural baggage.

Wilderness is far more than the U.S. government's definition of "a minimum of not less than 5,000 contiguous acres of roadless area."[2] Through the centuries, mythic interpretations of wild terrain have exerted an overwhelming impact on human thought and behavior, often in contradictory ways.

Wilderness has often been perceived as a threatening concept in the Western imagination, from ancient Greece and Rome through much of the history of Christian thought.[3] Some historians say that not until the rise of Romanticism, with early modern poets like Samuel Taylor Coleridge, did the notion of wilderness begin to assume a favorable, even captivating allure. Yet others have identified a "Christian wilderness tradition" that celebrates wild nature, extending from the Desert Fathers through Celtic monasticism to the Franciscan movement.[4] The truth is that the threat and allure of wilderness have *both* been a part of the Judeo-Christian reading of wild, uninhabited terrain. It simultaneously draws and repulses the human spirit. That's what makes it a powerful symbol.

From the biblical images of Israel's experience in the Sinai to Puritan conceptions of New England as a howling waste, from St. Anthony's celebration of the Egyptian desert to John Muir's ecstatic portrayal of Yosemite Valley, the mythic significance of wilderness has thrived in the Western religious imagination. It often bears a double meaning, evoking spiritual connections in seemingly opposite ways. Biblical writers and historical saints depict wilderness as a realm of temptation, threat, and death, the haunt of scorpions, demons, and wild beasts. Yet they also depict it as a place of refuge and romance, to which Yahweh draws his bride in a covenant of love. These negative and positive images stand side by side, pointing to the necessary connection between the dismantling of the ego and union with the divine.

Western Catholicism has emphasized the dark side of wilderness experience, painting the desert as a "trackless waste" where the wandering pilgrim engages in spiritual warfare. Eastern Orthodoxy, by contrast, perceives the desert as a place for inner illumination and a return to an Edenic paradise of union with God.⁵ Wilderness can serve as both threat and gift. It demands an emptying of the self, but for the sake of deepening the encounter with mystery. I rediscover the pattern on most of my trips into backcountry. It's easy there to make the necessary mistakes that stretch me beyond my limits.

There is also a tension between our appreciation of wild terrain for its own sake and our tendency to turn it into a symbol of something else. Naturalists meticulously analyze the details of a wilderness ecology while poets and philosophers reflect on its significance for the life of the spirit. The one looks at nature for what it *is*; the other asks what nature *means* in human experience.

The two occasionally come together, as in the work of Henry David Thoreau and John Muir. The best nature writers are perennially torn between the objective reporting of what they observe and the deeper question of how it moves them. The natural world suggests endless horizons of symbolic meaning, yet its stubborn realities challenge every metaphor we're tempted to make of it.

For religious writers in particular, there's the danger of reducing the world to a series of moral lessons or spiritual types. In their search for meaning, they reach for a reality *beyond* the thing in itself. They forget that it's enough for turkey vultures circling over an Ozark creek to be turkey vultures. They don't have to be symbols of death or evil. Naturalists, on the other hand, occupy themselves with observing, counting, and listing what is simply *there*. They dispassionately analyze the operation of the bionetworks within a given ecosystem, separating any personal connection or moral judgment from what they study. Yet they too inevitably bring a subjective element to their work.

Naturalists like Aldo Leopold are caught between the need for an accurate report of what they see (the threat of wolves in a Western landscape) and their own personal experience of it (witnessing the "fierce green fire" in the dying eyes of a wolf he had just shot). What makes their writing compelling is the intensity of their encounter with the natural world. Loren Eiseley's work is so poignant because he's as fine a poet as he is an anthropologist. Yet, strictly speaking, his personal engagement with the data compromises the "unbiased accuracy" of what he reports.⁶

In the end, it can't be one or the other—*either* scientific objectivity or creative imagination. Writing about the human experience of wilderness requires a deliberate dance between the two, rigorous attention to detail and fierce delight in beauty.

Wilderness as Image and Reality

When I write about my experience of wilderness, then, am I doing more than talking about my own inner world, substituting culturally determined images of wilderness for the actual terrain? Do I gloss over the hard, insistent "otherness" of backcountry by talking about *God* in relationship to it? Inevitably, I'm torn between the awareness that nature speaks to me in powerful images and that she also keeps her cards close to her chest, remaining mysterious and unavailable. Wilderness is a home I love, one to which I keep returning. Yet it doesn't love me back; it isn't solicitous of my well-being. Keeping these realities in tension is crucial if I'm to be honest in what I write. I can't package the natural world as a guaranteed source of spiritual solace. I have to let it be what it is.

That's why I delight in Ed Abbey's indictment of religious spiritualizations of landscape. As a ranger at Arches National Monument near Moab, Utah, he scorns the "pious Midwesterners who climb a mile and a half under the desert sun to view Delicate Arch and find only God." On a raft trip down the Colorado River through Glen Canyon he disdains those who readily glimpse the presence of the divine in its wild beauty. "God? . . . Who the hell is he?" he asks. Yet, ironically, Abbey himself engages in the very thing he derides in others.

At a bend in the canyon, he is overwhelmed by its grandeur, wondering, "Is this at last the *locus Dei*? There are enough cathedrals and temples and altars here for a Hindu pantheon of divinities."[7] The irony is intentional. As much as he wants to reject religion, he knows that the land has to speak with its own voice *and* that the human soul has to reach for the mystery within it. Both are true. Wilderness is a window onto the inner life, but it's also a check on turning the world into nothing but metaphor.

The more I wander into wilderness, the more I appreciate the wisdom of indigenous people like the Australian Aborigines or the Tukano people of the Amazon. They don't experience the dichotomy between the inner life of the soul and outer life of the world that I find so obvious. They don't objectify nature as a lifeless, inert reality. Nor do they reduce it to otherworldly, spiritual lessons. From a traditional Navajo or Japanese Shinto perspective, the human, the spiritual, and the natural are part of an unbroken continuum. They can't conceive of nature and human (even religious) experience as separate, freestanding ideas.

Yet this is foreign to us. Our culture of shimmering computer screens and wired reality multiplies facsimiles of wilderness without our ever having to live in it. We continually "represent" the world without being present to it. A surfeit of nature videos, coffee-table books full of exotic landscapes, and digital images of wilderness substitute a "virtual" nature for nature itself. We don't have to venture into the world beyond our screens.

From the safety of our cubicles, we idealize a pristine wilderness of peaceful serenity (available to the wealthy in carefully guarded five-star resorts) or we dwell on sensational images of wild animals tearing each other to bloody bits. We romanticize wilderness, on the one hand, and demonize it on the other. Bucolic images of "getaway" places soothing the soul vie with Weather Channel depictions of an outrageously violent world. Either way, wilderness becomes a mythic construct, removed from any actual, intimate, or ethical relationship to the land. Our immersion in the *image* inevitably makes possible our destruction of the *reality*.

"We are no longer able to think of ourselves as a species tossed about by larger forces," writes Bill McKibben, "now we are those larger forces."[8] We've separated ourselves from the very world that embodies us. For our "safety," we drive predators in the wilds to extinction. In our support of endless "development," we risk the loss of rainforests, tundra, coral reefs, and arctic glaciers.[9] Huge numbers of species vanish from our planet every year. Given the global impact of climate change, habitat destruction, technology, and agribusiness, we no longer have any areas of "pure wilderness." There *are* no more "natural" places, free of cultural influence, unaffected by human pollution. Everything is "second nature." The best we can do in speaking of wilderness is to define it as a place where "the natural aspects remain predominant over the built ones."[10] Talk about wilderness is increasingly an exercise in nostalgia.

In the end, we have to admit that the very idea of "wilderness" is elusive. It defies definition. The earth itself resists our speaking of it in the abstract, as if we weren't a part of its breathing reality. Ed Abbey asserts that "wilderness begins in the human mind."[11] It is a deeply held *value*, not merely an intellectual construct. Wilderness is a conviction that binds us to the earth, a commitment that acknowledges our indissoluble relationship to everything wild. For Abbey and others like him, it provokes intense love for the earth as well as rage at its abuse. Wilderness occasions the awe that Elijah encountered on Mt. Horeb, Plutarch on Mt. Ventoux, and Thoreau on Mt. Ktaadn. But it requires the conscious work of preservation as well. To defend wilderness is to insist on the continuity of human and more-than-human life, protecting the earth from a consumer culture that denies its role in the larger web of nature.

Wilderness and the Wildness of God

When I speak of wilderness as a place of divine–human encounter, certain theological and moral problems naturally arise. This book suggests, for example, that God is far "wilder" than most of our highly domesticated images of the divine. We think of God delighting in the safe and beautiful garden where Yahweh walked with Adam and Eve in the cool of the day (Genesis 3:8). But we're also told that God's own home lies in thick darkness, in a dark cloud atop a high mountain (I Kings 8:12). The "place" where people encounter God in their lives isn't always safe, providing a warm and loving reception. It's more often a wild, dangerous place—metaphorically, if not geographically. To meet God there can be as disturbing as it is comforting.

Part of what attracted the early monks to the desert, in fact, was its fierce indifference. It cared nothing about their reputation, their well-being, all the things they had given up in adopting an ascetic discipline. Having fled the accolades of a society built on status and prestige, they found the desert's indifference refreshing. Being ignored proved to be a gift. It allowed them to accept their being loved as a grace, not as something to be earned.

But what about *God's* apparent indifference? Not all things in wilderness end up being loved. Wild terrain is a harsh, uncaring place—where struggle for life is intense. How, then, do we reconcile the suffering of creatures with the notion of a benevolent Creator? If God works through the slow, grinding wheels of evolution, where competition among species is as prevalent as cooperation, how can we speak of a God who longs for relationship, a God of love? How do we affirm God's wildness and God's caring at the same time?[12]

There aren't any satisfactory philosophical answers to questions like these. They can't be resolved in the abstract, but only (if at all) from *within* the heart-rending wilderness where relationships are hardest to reconcile. I marvel and shudder at what I frequently encounter along Missouri woodland trails. Harmless rat snakes provide for their young by climbing trees in search of bird nests. There they eat the eggs, the baby birds, and the mother as well if they can. Antlion larvae (or "doodlebugs") dig cone-shaped pit traps in dry sand. Ants who wander into them aren't able to secure a foothold, inescapably sliding into the jaws of the waiting predator below. Butterworts are carnivorous plants that attract insects by their bright yellow-green leaves and purple flowers. The leaves, however, are coated with a sticky mucilage, like flypaper. When an insect is caught, the leaf slowly folds over it like a long tongue. All this fills me with a fascination mixed with horror, realizing that my own way of staying alive rests on similarly predatory behavior.

I balk at the violence that is endemic to the natural world. Yet I have to be realistic, too. An evolving creation—riddled with violence and death—appears to be "the only way in which God could give rise to the sort of beauty, diversity, sentience, and sophistication that the biosphere now contains."[13] It remains a spiritual as well as biological principle that anguish is a necessary part of one's growth toward fullness. Even God participates in this anguish, we're told, as the whole of creation groans in eager expectation of a fullness yet to come (Romans 8:22–24).

Creation isn't finished yet, theologians affirm. God continues to work through the evolutionary process to bring the world to a higher sense of connectedness and consciousness. Yet the anticipated renewal of the earth won't necessarily mean the final elimination of wildness and risk—at least I hope not. Such a world would occasion no awe. Its God would be too dull (too "nice") to evoke worship or respect.

So as a Christian who struggles to believe, I hold two seemingly opposite things in tension. I honor nature's bewildering power and beauty, mirroring a God of wild adventurousness. I affirm, at the same time, the New Testament disclosure that God enters into the suffering of every creature, knowing its pain as his own. The cross is God's promise of this. The Father/Mother God I love is both of these. God roars in exultation as sky-rending lightning strikes dead timber in the Montana Rockies. God also grieves at the loss of life that follows, whether that of firefighters from the U.S. Forest Service, mule deer, or field mice. An irresistible boisterousness and irrepressible love churn together in the heart of the divine being.

There are no easy answers to the problem of suffering. Job himself, when confronted with the whirlwind, was satisfied in the end not by "explanations," but by a call to relationship. He was driven to silence in the presence of a God that he learned was utterly at home in the wildness of the Judean hills, familiar with every natural and frightening detail, intimately related to all its inhabitants.[14]

The Healing Power of Wild Terrain

Another way of appreciating nature's ferocious edge is to consider the role that wilderness plays in human healing. Its power to astound is an integral part of its power to heal. The final appeal of backcountry isn't its panoramic grandeur or stylized beauty, but its unnerving way of astonishing us. Wilderness teaches what Abraham Heschel calls Radical Amazement. He views the wonder experienced by Hebrew prophets in the rugged terrain of Judea as a "form of thinking" in its own right, a kinesthetic encounter with mystery that surpasses every other kind of knowing. It makes the flesh crawl and the hair stand on end.[15]

We see the therapeutic value of wilderness today in the increasing number of Outward Bound programs for troubled teens, terminally ill patients, developmentally disabled children, and people with addictions. Exposure to wild terrain takes people out of their comfort zone, providing a catalyst for transformative experience. It awakens new delight in the world and fosters a shift from dependence to interdependence in one's relation to others. An expanded ecological sensitivity emerges as a byproduct of personal growth.[16]

Wild places do this for children and adults alike, for uneducated peasants and trained scientists, for deeply religious people and people wanting nothing to do with religion. Wandering in nature is what naturally draws us as children and what we go back to as broken adults.

Children under six, we are told, have one of the highest survival rates of those who are lost in wilderness. Small children going astray in the woods are more likely to be absorbed in wonder, more inclined to stop and rest when they need it, even to crawl into a hollow tree to go to sleep. They don't panic as adults frequently do, running faster and faster in what is usually the wrong direction, ending up exhausted, hungry, and cold.[17] When given the chance, children naturally delight in wilderness forts and treehouses. They run in packs, hunt frogs and lizards, play hide-and-seek in tall grass. Wild places feed their native propensity for amazement. Yet the outdoor experience of most kids today is limited to organized sports, led and supervised by adults. They suffer from "Nature-Deficit Disorder," says Richard Louv, a spiritually anemic condition of being deprived of wilderness. They long for the irrepressible and unregulated run of nature.[18]

If children yearn for unprotected wildness, wounded adults seek it even more. Doug Peacock was a Green Beret medic who returned from Vietnam after the 1968 Tet Offensive, numb and speechless, consumed by rage. He couldn't deal with the memory of helplessly watching Vietnamese babies die. He spent the next ten years in the Montana wilderness, living as close to grizzly bears as he could. Their wild ferocity became a mirror and release of his own torment. "A danger married to beauty" was what attracted him. Living near grizzlies became an instinctive "spiritual practice" that was immediate, inarticulate, and self-authenticating.[19]

For others, the wilds afford a deep solace in accepting the approach of death. Gerald May, in his last book, *The Wisdom of Wilderness*, spoke of camping alone in the Appalachian Mountains of western Maryland. He had been going there for years, finding healing in what he called "the Power of the Slowing." This was a spiritual practice that helped him face the cancer that eventually took his life. Wilderness taught him to welcome whatever each moment offered.

When a growling bear brushed the fabric of his tent in the middle of the night, he knew there was nothing he could do to protect himself. But he *could* choose in that instant to enter the "slowing," going into the quiet acceptance of his own terror. He could be present—"in a place beyond all coping"—to the immediacy of being alive, *within* the very fear that gripped him.[20]

What people commonly report as most unsettling about their experience in wilderness (and yet also most healing) is its defeat of the grasping ego. It makes them aware of their inability to control *anything*. Wilderness becomes an accomplice in the spiritual work of deconstructing the false self. "Survivors" of Outward Bound programs frequently talk of finding a new, integrated self that enhances their openness to wilderness and cooperation with each other. In being taken to their limits, they experience an increase in self-worth, mutual respect, and even transcendent awareness. Nature's "threat" dissolves into a wider awareness of community.

In October 1872, John Muir scrambled up a narrow avalanche gully on the slopes of Mt. Ritter in the High Sierras. Climbing in a place where hand- and footholds were slight, he reached a point where he could go no further. Arms outstretched, clinging to the rock wall, his strength left him. He began to shake, knowing he would fall at any moment. Then unexpectedly, in the loss of his skill and self-confidence, something happened: "Life blazed forth again with preternatural clearness, I seemed suddenly to become possessed of a new sense. The other self, bygone experiences, instinct, or Guardian Angel—call it what you will—came forward and assumed control."

This "other self," discovered beyond the paralysis of fear and self-blame, was a preconscious awareness interacting intuitively with the rock wall. Muir became sensitive to every crease and rift within it, "thinking with the stone" (and no longer against it). Writing later of the experience, he marveled that "we little know until tried how much of the uncontrollable there is in us."[21]

The lesson of wilderness is that in losing your self, you also find it. The mystics have always declared this. Once you've grappled with an angel through the long, dark night, says Rilke, you are no longer tempted by winning. "This is how [you] grow, by being defeated, decisively, by constantly greater beings."[22] The transformative power of wilderness is its ability to strip us of everything . . . while filling us also with wonder.

The Challenging Character of Wilderness Reading

My own experience of being stripped and healed by wild terrain goes hand in hand with the pattern of contemplative reading I've modeled in these pages. Practicing *lectio* alongside a spring-fed creek on the Ozark Trail, I give myself to a chosen text (protected from rain in a waterproof bag), to the saint behind the text (bringing another world crashing into mine), to the multifaceted, sensuous earth around me (full of unexpected things), and to the mystery of myself (made newly vulnerable on the trail). The joining of these disparate worlds charges my reading with unexpected energy.

When I read outside, as St. Augustine argued, I'm engaging two books at once. The "complementary texts" of Nature and Scripture reveal the mystery of God in alternative modes of discourse. Reading the one alongside the other allows for a wider play of the imagination in the work of interpretation.

The history of the "two-books" tradition began very early in Christianity. When someone asked Anthony of Egypt how he could live a devout life in the desert without any holy books, he responded, "My book is the nature of created things and any time I want to read the words of God the book is there before me." John Chrysostom argued that even the illiterate can read God's truth in the book of nature. They don't need any language skills; it's already translated for everyone.[23] Bonaventure spoke of a *duplex liber*, a double book containing the mystery of the Holy Trinity in Scripture and its "vestiges" discernible in the natural world. Cotton Mather declared nature a "publick library" available to everyone, even as Meister Eckhart, echoing Psalm 19, urged that all creatures—even caterpillars—are words clearly spoken by God.[24]

The tradition acknowledges that one's ability to read and interpret this "second book" is limited because of human sin. Catholics as well as Protestants caution that the book of nature has to be read in the light of Scripture, lest one exalt the beauty of the creature over the grandeur of the Creator. On the other hand, fifteenth-century Spanish theologian Raymond of Sabunde affirmed that "the book of the creature" provides a more reliable reading of God's truth than the Bible, being less susceptible to impious interpretation.[25] His idea was rejected by the Council of Trent as failing to honor the priority of Scripture and Tradition.

But the possibility of heresy has not prevented saints and scholars from extolling nature as an authentic "mirror," "school," or "theater" of God's grandeur and providential care. The enduring popularity of the "second book" in the Christian imagination is undeniable. From the hexameral literature in the early church (delineating the six days of creation) to the widely read medieval bestiaries (mixing animal stories with spiritual lessons)—from John Milton's *Paradise Lost* to Mary Oliver's "Wild Geese"—Christians have turned to nature's tome as an eloquent source of spiritual insight.

Reading a sacred text in a wilderness setting increases the sensory receptivity one brings to the work. Backcountry reading, as I've argued, has a kinship with the vocalized, sensuous reading of medieval monks. For them, the words on the page weren't merely "signs" scratched onto paper. They were "living things"—possessing a talismanic quality, holding the power of oracle and spell.[26] Seventh-century Celtic monks, in their monastery on Lindisfarne, the Holy Island, for example, looked on their recitation of the Psalms as actively influencing the rise and fall of the tidewater around them. The monks' manner of reading was deeply attuned to their environment, never far removed from the daily (and earthy) tasks of manual labor.

Out of their reading of the Gospels in the ninth century, for example, the monks on the island of Iona produced *The Book of Kells*, one of the most extraordinary books in the history of Christendom. This was a text wholly immersed in the wilderness from which it came. The calligraphers and illuminators who toiled on the manuscript in the monastery scriptorium gazed out onto the wild landscape of Scotland's western coast.

They joined the book and the earth in their labor, filling page after page with paintings of local animals and plants. These included images of birds, intertwined snakes taken from Pictish stone carvings, bunches of grapes from nearby vines, otters and fish seen along the shore, the cattle and red deer that roamed the island, even cats and mice that wandered the monastery's dark corridors.

The scriptorium was stocked with the vellum skins of calves (on which the monks wrote), crushed oak apples and sulfate of iron used in making the brownish iron/gall ink, and various materials gathered for creating pigments. To produce the vivid purple, green, blue, and red colors, they gathered lichens from local rocks, malachite from nearby peaks, dried indigo plants, even the bodies of insects. They utilized egg whites as a binding medium. Quills were cut from the tail feathers of wild geese. The entire process of reading, writing, and illustrating was deeply earthbound, connected in every possible way to the surrounding landscape. Viking raids on the Scottish coast eventually drove the monks to move their work to the monastery at Kells in Ireland, but the taste and smell of Iona remain on the pages of the text.[27]

One of the Celtic scribes made a habit of drawing a pair of lions at every point in the Gospels where the phrase "he said" appears (referring to the words of Jesus). The lions hold their paws to their mouths, as if cautioning the reader to be silent and listen. Would it be helpful today for us to imagine lions poised on the pages of the dangerous books that threaten to change our lives? This is the risk we run in our reading of hazardous texts in unpredictable places. We are ambushed by a world (and a God) that fills us with awe in breaking us open to love.

Notes

DEDICATION AND PROLOGUE

1. Terry Russell, *On the Loose* (San Francisco: Sierra Club Books, 1979), 81.
2. David Wagoner, *Traveling Light: Collected and New Poems* (Urbana: University of Illinois Press, 1999), 10.
3. Coleman Barks, trans. *Like This: Rumi* (Athens, GA: Maypop Books, 1990).
4. "The Manly Wisdom of Will Rogers," in *The Friars Club Bible of Jokes, Pokes, Roasts, and Toasts*, ed. Nina Colman (New York: Black Dog & Leventhal Publishers, 2001), 316. Ben Yagoda, author of *Will Rogers: A Biography* (Norman: University of Oklahoma Press, 2000), questions the authenticity of this quote. See his article, "You Should Look It Up," in the *Chronicle of Higher Education*, July 15, 2013.
5. See Cheryl Strayed, *Wild: From Lost to Found on the Pacific Crest Trail* (New York: A. A. Knopf, 2012); Anne LaBastille, *Woodswoman: Living Alone in the Adirondack Wilderness* (New York: Penguin Books, 1995); Gretel Ehrlich, *A Match to the Heart* (New York: Pantheon, 1994) and *This Cold Heaven: Seven Seasons in Greenland* (New York: Pantheon, 2001); Joan Halifax, *The Fruitful Darkness* (San Francisco: HarperSanFrancisco, 1993), 59–73.
6. Having said this, I acknowledge the irony of a book with so many endnotes. I add them not to make me look good as a scholar, but to guide the reader more deeply into the backcountry of his or her growth.
7. Robert Bly and Leonard Lewisohn, trans. *The Angels Knocking on the Tavern Door: Thirty Poems of Hafez* (New York: Harper Collins, 2008), 49.
8. C. S. Lewis, *The Last Battle* (New York: Scholastic, 1995), 181.
9. On pushing physical and spiritual edges, see Rob Schultheis, *Bone Games: Extreme Sports, Shamanism, Zen, and the Search for Transcendence* (New York: Breakaway Books, 1996), and the issue devoted to "Extreme Spirituality" in *Hungryhearts: A Quarterly Journal of Reformed Spirituality* 18:3 (Summer 2009).

CHAPTER 1

1. Jay Griffiths, *Wild: An Elemental Journey* (New York: Penguin, 2006), 84.

2. John Muir, *My First Summer in the Sierra* (New York: Penguin Books, 1987), 73.

3. David Abram, *Becoming Animal: An Earthly Cosmology* (New York: Pantheon Books, 2010), 110.

4. Bill Plotkin, *Soulcraft: Crossing into the Mysteries of Nature and Psyche* (Novato, CA: New World Library, 2003).

5. Keith Basso, *Wisdom Sits in Places: Landscape and Language Among the Western Apache* (Albuquerque: University of New Mexico Press, 1996).

6. See Chip Colwell-Chanthaphonh, *Massacre at Camp Grant: Forgetting and Remembering Apache History* (Tucson: University of Arizona Press, 2007), and Karl Jacoby, *Shadows at Dawn* (New York: Penguin, 2008).

7. G. K. Chesterton, *The Man Who Knew Too Much* (Mineola, NY: Dover Publications, 2007), 3.

8. Jay Griffiths, *Wild: An Elemental Journey*, 59.

9. John Burroughs, *Signs and Seasons* (Boston: Houghton, Mifflin, 1886), 5; John Muir, *Steep Trails* (San Francisco: Sierra Club Books, 1994), 19–20.

10. Gary Snyder, *Turtle Island* (New York: New Directions Books, 1974), 99.

11. Mihaly Csikszentmihalyi, *Flow: The Psychology of Optimal Experience* (New York: Harper and Row, 1990).

12. See Christopher McDougall, *Born to Run* (New York: A. A. Knopf, 2009).

13. Quoted in Robert Bly, *News of the Universe: Poems of Twofold Consciousness* (San Francisco: Sierra Club Books, 1980), 32.

14. David Abram, *The Spell of the Sensuous* (New York: Random House, 1997), 53–56.

15. Barry Lopez, *Arctic Dreams: Imagination and Desire in a Northern Landscape* (New York: Charles Scribner's Sons, 1986), 279.

16. Abraham Heschel, *Man Is Not Alone* (New York: Harper & Row, 1966), 127.

17. John of the Cross, *The Dark Night*, I.17.6 in *The Collected Works of John of the Cross*, trans. Kieran Kavanaugh and Otilio Rodriguez (Washington, DC: ICS Publications, 1991), 437; Sermon, *Expedit vobis*, in *Meister Eckhart: A Modern Translation*, ed. Raymond Blakney (New York: Harper & Row, 1941), 200f.; John Muir, as quoted in Richard Cartwright Austin, *Baptized into Wilderness: A Christian Perspective on John Muir* (Atlanta: John Knox Press, 1987), 77, 90.

18. Hildegard of Bingen, *The Book of Divine Works*, 1,2, in *Hildegard of Bingen: Mystical Writings*, ed. Fiona Bowie and Oliver Davies (New York: Crossroad, 1992), 91–92.

19. Mechthild of Magdeburg, *The Flowing Light of the Godhead*. See *Meditations from Mechthild of Magdeburg*, ed. Henry L. Carrigan (Brewster, MA: Paraclete Press, 1999), 42. I'm indebted to James Finley, author of *Merton's Palace of Nowhere*, for part of this translation.

20. See Sallie McFague, *The Body of God: An Ecological Theology* (Minneapolis: Augsburg Fortress, 1993) and Teilhard de Chardin, *The Divine Milieu* (New York:

Harper Perennial, 1960). For a discussion of Edwards' conception of God and nature, see Belden Lane's *Ravished by Beauty: The Surprising Legacy of Reformed Spirituality* (New York: Oxford University Press, 2011).

21. Quoted in Arthur Green's *Radical Judaism* (New Haven: Yale University Press, 2010), 77–78. Emphasis added.

22. In this book, I'm following Bernard McGinn's definition of mysticism as "a consciousness of the immediate or direct presence of God." *The Foundations of Mysticism* (New York: Crossroad, 1991), xvii. In affirming the wisdom of Reb Leib, I'd prefer to say that "Everything that exists is [*in*] God," clearly distinguishing a panentheist from a pantheist interpretation of God's relation to the world. Butterflies are *not God*, yet neither can they be said to exist without being *in God*.

23. See Peter Brown, *The Body and Society* (New York: Columbia University Press, 1988), 237, and John Climacus, *The Ladder of Divine Ascent* (New York: Paulist Press, 1982), 129, 186.

24. William of St-Thierry, *The Contemplation of God*, in *The Works of William of St. Thierry*, trans. Sister Penelope (Spencer, MA: Cistercian Publications, 1971), vol. 1, 115.

25. Chellis Glendinning, *My Name is Chellis and I'm in Recovery from Western Civilization* (Boston: Shambhala, 1994), 185–186.

26. Anne Lamott, *Help Thanks Wow: The Three Essential Prayers* (New York: Riverhead Books, 2012), 73.

27. Jack Kerouac, *Lonesome Traveler* (New York: Grove Press, 1989), 133.

CHAPTER 2

1. Henry David Thoreau, *The Writings of Henry David Thoreau*, vol. 1: *A Week on the Concord and Merrimack Rivers* (New York: AMS Press, 1968), 99.

2. David Tracy, *The Analogical Imagination* (New York: Crossroad, 1981), 102.

3. See Omer Englebert, *Saint Francis of Assisi: A Biography* (Chicago: Franciscan Herald Press, 1965), 306.

4. John Climacus, *Ladder of Divine Ascent*, 82, 216.

5. John Bunyan, *The Pilgrim's Progress* (New York: New American Library, 1964), 41.

6. John Climacus, 257.

7. John Climacus, 88, 120.

8. See James Hillman, "Peaks and Vales," in *Puer Papers* (Dallas, TX: Spring Publications, 1979), 114–135, and Thomas Moore, *Care of the Soul* (New York: Harper-Perennial, 1994).

9. These constitute steps or rungs 24, 20, and 21 respectively on the *Ladder of Divine Ascent*.

10. John Climacus, 196–200.

11. Jean-Pierre de Caussade, *Abandonment to Divine Providence* (New York: Doubleday, 1975), 24, 36–43, 57.

12. John Climacus, 75, 196.

13. De Caussaude, 27; John Climacus, 191–193.

14. He writes of being inflamed by his reading of the Psalms while on holiday out in the country. "I read on and on, all afire," he recalled. Augustine, *Confessions*, IX, 4, 8–11.

15. *Confessions*, VIII, 13–29.

16. *Confessions*, XIII, 17.

17. *Julian of Norwich: Showings*, trans. Edmund Colledge and James Walsh (New York: Paulist Press, 1977), 149–151.

18. Johann Baptist Metz, *Communicating a Dangerous Memory: Soundings in Political Theology* (Atlanta: Scholars Press, 1987), 47.

19. Julian of Norwich, 130–132.

20. As anyone must do in a wilderness setting, the monks had to identify real fears from those that were only imaginary. "Fear is danger tasted in advance," John reminded the brothers, "a quiver as the heart takes fright before unnamed calamity." *The Ladder of Divine Ascent*, 199.

CHAPTER 3

1. Barbara Kingsolver, *Small Wonder* (New York: HarperCollins, 2002), 40.

2. See Joseph Campbell, *The Hero with a Thousand Faces* (New York: Meridian Books, 1956); Bill Plotkin, *Nature and the Human Soul* (Novato, CA: New World Library, 2008); and Richard Rohr, *Falling Upward: A Spirituality for the Two Halves of Life* (San Francisco: Jossey-Bass, 2011).

3. John Burroughs, "The Natural Providence," in Thomas J. Lyon, ed. *This Incomperable Lande: A Book of American Nature Writing* (Boston: Houghton Mifflin, 1989), 235.

4. Oliver Davies and Fiona Bowie, eds. *Celtic Christian Spirituality* (New York: Continuum, 1995), 38.

5. John T. Koch, *Celtic Culture: A Historical Encyclopedia* (Santa Barbara, CA: ABC-Clio, 2006), 1744.

6. Freeman House, *Totem Salmon: Life Lessons from Another Species* (Boston: Beacon Press, 1999), 217.

7. Hāfez, "Tired of Speaking Sweetly," in *The Gift: Poems by Hafiz, the Great Sufi Master*, trans. Daniel Ladinsky (New York: Penguin/Arkana, 1999), 187.

8. Richard Rohr's books on men's spirituality include *Adam's Return: The Five Promises of Male Initiation* (New York: Crossroads, 2004).

9. See Adomnan's seventh-century *Life of Columba*, Book II, chapter 43, and the sixth-century *Voyage of Saint Brendan* in *Celtic Spirituality*, trans. Oliver Davies (New York: Paulist Press, 1999).

10. Peter Brown, *The Making of Late Antiquity* (Cambridge, MA: Harvard University Press, 1978), 86–87.

11. *The Sayings of the Desert Fathers* (The Alphabetical Collection), trans. Benedicta Ward (Kalamazoo, MI: Cistercian Publications, 1984), Theodore of Pherme: 16, p. 76.

12. Laura Swan, *The Forgotten Desert Mothers* (New York: Paulist Press, 2001), 35.

13. Quoted in David G. R. Keller, *Oasis of Wisdom: The Worlds of the Desert Fathers and Mothers* (Collegeville, MN: Liturgical Press, 2005), xv.

14. John Joseph Hogan, *On the Mission in Missouri, 1857–1868* (Kansas City, MO: John A. Heilmann Publishers, 1892). See also Rev. Dwight Frizzell's Irish Wilderness website, http://www.dwightfrizzell.com/IrishWilderness/History.html.

15. See A. O. Anderson and M. O. Anderson, trans. *Adomnan's Life of Columba* (Edinburgh: Thomas Nelson and Sons, 1991).

16. See Mary Low, *Celtic Christianity and Nature* (Edinburgh: Polygon, 1996), 74–75.

17. Esther De Waal, *The Celtic Way of Prayer* (New York: Doubleday, 1997), 156.

18. Oliver Davies, trans. *Celtic Spirituality* (New York: Paulist Press, 1999), 408.

19. F. Marian McNeill, ed. *An Iona Anthology* (Iona: The New Iona Press, 1990), 22.

20. De Waal, *Celtic Way of Prayer*, 96–97.

21. Ward Rutherford, *Celtic Mythology* (New York: Sterling Publishing, 1990), 34.

22. See Phyllis Rossiter, *A Living History of the Ozarks* (Gretna, LA: Pelican Publishing, 1992), 389f.; and Janice Tremeear, *Haunted Ozarks* (Charleston, SC: History Press, 2011), 32.

23. See Steven Chase, *Nature as Spiritual Practice* (Grand Rapids, MI: Eerdmans, 2011), 74, 110; and William Harmless, *Mystics* (New York: Oxford University Press, 2008), 99–103, 115–118.

24. John Scotus Eriugena, *Periphyseon: On the Division of Nature*, III.621a–622a.

25. Thomas Merton, *Thoughts in Solitude* (New York: Farrar, Straus & Cudahy, 1958), 18–19.

26. J. Philip Newell, *Christ of the Celts* (San Francisco: Jossey-Bass, 2008), 52. See also Newell's *Listening for the Heartbeat of God: A Celtic Spirituality* (New York: Paulist Press, 1997).

CHAPTER 4

1. Letter to his wife, June 24, 1907, in Rilke's *Letters on Cezanne*, trans. Joel Agee (New York: North Point Press, 2002), 4–6.

2. Franklin R. Rogers, ed. *The Works of Mark Twain*, vol. 2: *Roughing It* (Berkeley: University of California Press, 1972), 86.

3. *The Collected Poems of Wendell Berry* (New York: North Point Press, 1987), 140–141.

4. Rumi, "The Flute Weeps," in *Rumi: Fragments, Ecstasies*, trans. Daniel Liebert (Cedar Hill, MO: Source Books, 1981), 9.

5. Alice Miller, *The Drama of the Gifted Child* (New York: Basic Books, 1997), 34.

6. Letter to her sister Celine, October 20, 1888, in *Saint Thérèse of Lisieux, The Little Flower of Jesus: Her Autobiography and Letters*, trans. Thomas N. Taylor (New York: P. J. Kenedy & Sons, 1927), 334.

7. Bernard Bro, *The Little Way: The Spirituality of Thérèse of Lisieux* (London: Darton, Longman & Todd, 1979), 1.

8. *By Little and By Little: The Selected Writings of Dorothy Day*, ed. Robert Ellsberg (New York: A. A. Knopf, 1983), 105. See also Mary Frohlich, ed. *St. Therese of Lisieux: Essential Writings* (Maryknoll, NY: Orbis Books, 2003).

9. Dorothy Day, *Therese* (Springfield, IL: Templegate Publishers, 1979), 92.

10. *The Autobiography of St. Thérèse of Lisieux: The Story of a Soul*, trans. John Beevers (New York: Image Books, 2001), 9.

11. Quoted in Bill Plotkin, *Nature and the Human Soul*, 383.

12. Thérèse of Lisieux, *Autobiography*, 2.

13. Ibid., 118–119.

14. Brian Kolodiejchuk, ed. *Mother Teresa: Come Be My Light: The Private Writings of the Saint of Calcutta* (New York: Doubleday, 2007), 163, 186–194. See also James Martin, "A Saint's Dark Night," *The New York Times*, August 29, 2007.

15. Kolodiejchuk, *Mother Teresa: Come Be My Light*, 170.

16. Tony DeMello, *Sadhana: A Way to God* (St. Louis: Institute of Jesuit Sources, 1978), 113–114; and William Cowper, "The Waiting Soul," *Olney Hymns*, XXXIII, in *The Poetical Works of William Cowper* (Edinburgh: William P. Nimmo, 1868), 288.

17. C. S. Lewis, *Prince Caspian* (Hammondsworth, UK: Penguin Books, 1962), 184.

18. Coleman Barks, trans. *Feeling the Shoulder of the Lion: Poetry and Teaching Stories of Rumi* (Boston: Shambhala, 2000), 16.

CHAPTER 5

1. Marilynne Robinson, *Housekeeping* (New York: Farrar, Strauss and Giroux, 1980), 152.

2. Coleman Barks, trans. "Desire and the Importance of Failing," in *Feeling the Shoulder of the Lion*, 58. Rumi adds, "The gist is: whatever anyone seeks, *that* is seeking the seeker" (61).

3. Samuel Rutherford, quoted in *The Golden Treasury of Puritan Quotations*, ed. I. D. E. Thomas (Chicago: Moody Press, 1975), 17.

4. John Bradshaw, *Family Secrets* (New York: Bantam Books, 1995), 66.

5. Tim O'Brien, *The Things They Carried* (Boston: Houghton Mifflin, 1990).

6. *Sayings of the Desert Fathers*, trans. Ward, Poemen: 34, p. 172. This is also a central theme in Richard Rohr's work.

7. Basil of Ancyra, a fourth-century physician turned theologian, made this distinction. See Teresa M. Shaw, *The Burden of the Flesh: Fasting and Sexuality in Early Christianity* (Minneapolis: Fortress Press, 1998), 156.

8. Teilhard de Chardin, *The Heart of Matter* (New York: Harcourt, Brace, Jovanovich, 1979), 35.

9. Thomas Traherne, *Centuries of Meditation,* in *Centuries, Poems, and Thanksgivings,* ed. H. M. Margoliouth (Oxford: Clarendon Press, 1958), 2 vols. His major works were never published in his lifetime, and some have only recently been discovered. See Denise Inge, *Wanting Like a God: Desire and Freedom in Thomas Traherne* (London: SCM Press, 2009).

10. *Bernard of Clairvaux: Selected Works,* trans. G. R. Evans (New York: Paulist Press, 1987), 191.

11. *Centuries,* I:25–38, 13–19.

12. *Centuries,* I:44, 22.

13. *Centuries,* II:20, 66; Brian Swimme, *The Universe is a Green Dragon: A Cosmic Creation Story* (Santa Fe, NM: Bear & Company, 1984), 48–50.

14. Ursula Goodenough, *The Sacred Depths of Nature* (New York: Oxford University Press, 1998), 132–133.

15. *Centuries,* I:51, 25.

16. Inge, *Wanting Like a God,* 40.

17. Gerald May wrestles with this paradox in his excellent book, *The Awakened Heart* (San Francisco: Harper, 1991).

18. *Centuries,* II:19–21, 64–67.

19. *Centuries,* I:58, 30.

20. *Centuries,* I:33, 17.

21. *Centuries,* I:90, 49.

22. *Centuries,* IV:9, 174.

23. Coleman Barks, trans., *Feeling the Shoulder of the Lion,* 62.

24. *Centuries,* I:18, 9.

25. Traherne, "Desire," in *Centuries,* II:177. *Catherine of Siena: The Dialogue,* trans. Suzanne Noffke (New York: Paulist Press, 1980), 92, p. 170.

CHAPTER 6

1. Richard J. Foster, *Celebration of Discipline: The Path to Spiritual Growth* (San Francisco: Harper & Row, 1988).

2. William Feather, *The Business of Life* (New York: Simon & Schuster, 1949).

3. Alfred North Whitehead, *Religion in the Making* (Cambridge: Cambridge University Press, 1926), 6.

4. Jack Kerouac, *Lonesome Traveler* (New York: Grove Press, 1989), 128.

5. Quoted from the 7,000 pages of his *Journals* in Charles E. Moore, ed. *Provocations: Spiritual Writings of Kierkegaard* (Maryknoll, NY: Orbis Books, 2002), 240.

6. Søren Kierkegaard, *Concluding Unscientific Postscript,* trans. David F. Swenson and Walter Lowrie (Princeton, NJ: Princeton University Press, 1968), 182.

7. *The Journals of Kierkegaard*, ed. Alexander Dru (New York: Harper & Row, 1959).

8. See Kierkegaard's *Attack Upon "Christendom,"* trans. Walter Lowrie (Boston: Beacon Press, 1963), 181; and his *Journals*, 173–174.

9. Quoted in Moore, *Provocations*, 242, 371. See also *Concluding Unscientific Postscript*, 110.

10. *The Life and Sayings of Catherine of Genoa*, trans. Paul Garvin (New York: Alba House, 1964), 81.

11. See *Teresa of Avila: Interior Castle*, trans. Kieran Kavanaugh (New York: Paulist Press, 1979); Augustine's *Confessions*, III.6.11; Eckhart's German Sermon #12 in *Meister Eckhart: Teacher and Preacher*, ed. Bernard McGinn (New York: Paulist Press, 1986), 268; and *Life and Sayings of Catherine of Genoa*, 81. For al-Bistami, see Muhammad Hisham Kabbani, ed. *The Naqshbandi Sufi Way: History and Guidebook of the Saints of the Golden Way* (Chicago: KAZI Publications, 1995), 97–104.

12. See Calvin's *Institutes of the Christian Religion*, I.1.i.

13. See Matthew Fox, *Meditations with Meister Eckhart* (Santa Fe, NM: Bear & Company, 1982), 29; and Eckhart's German Sermon #68.

14. *Attack Upon "Christendom,"* 200.

15. *Attack Upon "Christendom,"* 81.

16. See Søren Kierkegaard, *Papers and Journals: A Selection* (New York: Penguin Books, 1996), 117; and Joakim Garff, *Søren Kierkegaard: A Biography* (Princeton, NJ: Princeton University Press, 2007), 132ff.

17. *Attack Upon "Christendom,"* 166.

18. *Journals of Kierkegaard*, ed. Dru, 142.

19. *Journals of Kierkegaard*, ed. Dru, 98, 57.

20. *Journals of Kierkegaard*, ed. Dru, 248; *Attack Upon "Christendom,"* 163.

21. *Journals of Kierkegaard*, ed. Dru, 150; *Provocations*, 251.

22. *Journals of Kierkegaard*, ed. Dru, 240. Kierkegaard wrote his most important book, *Concluding Unscientific Postscript* (1846), under the pseudonym of the desert monk. It is a masterful defense of the passionate individual who throws himself into what may seem absurd, renouncing the "professor" with all of his needs for objective proof.

23. Quoted in Anselm Gruen, *Heaven Begins within You: Wisdom from the Desert Fathers* (New York: Crossroads, 1999), 30.

24. *Sayings of the Desert Fathers*, trans. Ward, Syncletica: 6, p. 231; Anthony: 10, p. 3; and Henri Nouwen, *Out of Solitude* (Notre Dame, IN: Ave Maria Press, 1974), 22.

25. Robert Kull, *Solitude: Seeking Wisdom in Extremes* (Novato, CA: New World Library, 2008), 96–97.

26. Jerome's Letter to Rufinus of Aquilea, quoted in *The Lives of the Desert Fathers: The Historia Monachorum in Aegypto*, trans. Norman Russell (Kalamazoo, MI: Cistercian Publications, 1980), 3.

27. Gordon Hempton, *One Square Inch of Silence* (New York: Free Press, 2009), 2.

28. Catherine Doherty, *Poustinia: Encountering God in Silence, Solitude, and Prayer* (Washington, DC: Madonna House, 2000), 91.

29. Edward Abbey, *Serpents of Paradise: A Reader* (New York: Henry Holt & Co., 1995), 305; and Henry David Thoreau, *Walden*, ed. J. Lyndon Shanley (Princeton, NJ: Princeton University Press, 1971), 137.

30. Mark Jenkins, "Destination Nowhere," *Backpacker* 36:7 (September 2008), 60–63.

31. Alexis de Tocqueville, "Two Weeks in the Wilderness," in *Democracy in America*, trans. Gerald E. Bevan (New York: Penguin Classics, 2003), 907.

32. Holmes Rolston, *Philosophy Gone Wild* (Buffalo, NY: Prometheus Books, 1989), 228–229.

33. D. H. Lawrence, "Escape," in his *Complete Poems* (New York: Penguin Classics, 1994).

CHAPTER 7

1. Antoine de Saint-Exupéry, *Wind, Sand, and Stars* (New York: Reynal & Hitchcock, 1940), 175.

2. Dag Hammarskjöld, *Markings* (New York: Alfred A. Knopf, 1966), 89.

3. Thoreau, *Walden*, 14.

4. *Backpacker*: The Survival Issue, 36:8 (October 2008), 40.

5. Lawrence Buell, *The Environmental Imagination* (Cambridge, MA: Belknap Press of Harvard University, 1995), 144ff.

6. *Markings*, 91.

7. Henry P. Van Dusen, *Dag Hammarskjöld: The Statesman and His Faith* (New York: Harper & Row, 1967), 4.

8. *Markings*, 14.

9. *Sayings of the Desert Fathers*, trans. Ward, Euprepius: 3, p. 62; Macarius: 18, p. 131.

10. *Sayings of the Desert Fathers*, trans. Ward, John the Dwarf: 2, p. 86.

11. Echoing the desert monks, Thomas Merton said the same thing to Jim Finley, one of his novices. Finley was absorbed at the time in a self-analysis of his spiritual progress, trying to decide whether he was in the fourth or fifth mansion of Teresa of Avila's *Interior Castle*. Merton simply laughed, saying it was none of his damned business where he was on a scale of spiritual achievements. See Finley's talks at the conference on "Following the Mystics: Through the Narrow Gate," Center for Action and Contemplation, Albuquerque, NM, January 22–24, 2010.

12. *Markings*, 159.

13. *Markings*, 195.

14. *Markings*, 70, 83.

15. Ken Carey, *Flat Rock Journal: A Day in the Ozark Mountains* (San Francisco: HarperSanFrancisco, 1994), 36.

16. *Markings*, 174.

17. Robert Kull, *Solitude*, 78, 96, 276.
18. Nathan Thornburgh, "Change We Can (Almost) Believe In," *Time*, March 7, 2011, 56–61.
19. *Moody Bible Institute Monthly* 22:7 (March 1922), 919.
20. Vance Randolph made a career of tracking down exotic Ozark tales. See, for example, his *Ozark Magic and Folklore* (New York: Dover Publications, 1964).
21. *Markings*, 91.

CHAPTER 8

1. Quoted in Thich Nhat Hanh, *Living Buddha, Living Christ* (New York: Riverhead Books, 1995), 14.
2. Thich Nhat Hanh, *Taming the Tiger Within* (New York: Riverhead Books, 2004), 187.
3. Simone Weil, "Reflections on the Right Use of School Studies with a View to the Love of God," in *Waiting for God* (New York: G. P. Putnam, 1951), 57–65.
4. Quoted in Pema Chödrön, *The Places That Scare You* (Boston: Shambhala, 2001), 119.
5. Thich Nhat Hanh, *The Miracle of Mindfulness* (Boston: Beacon Press, 1976), 12. The word for mindfulness in the Pali language of the Buddhist sutras is *sati*, meaning "bare attention."
6. Quoted in Simon Tugwell, *Ways of Imperfection* (Springfield, IL: Templegate Publishers, 1985), 16; *The Wisdom of the Desert Fathers* (The Anonymous Sayings), trans. Benedicta Ward (Fairacres, Oxford: SLG Press, 1975), 1; *Miracle of Mindfulness*, 30.
7. See Thich Nhat Hanh, *Walking Meditation* (Louisville, CO: Sounds True, 2006).
8. See Susan Clayton and Susan Opotow, eds. *Identity and the Natural Environment: The Psychological Significance of Nature* (Cambridge, MA: MIT Press, 2003), 29.
9. See Shierry Weber Nicholsen, *The Love of Nature and the End of the World: The Unspoken Dimensions of Environmental Concern* (Cambridge, MA: MIT Press, 2003), 95.
10. Father Thomas Keating's emphasis on the "welcoming prayer," drawn in part from Jean-Pierre de Caussade's *Abandonment to Divine Providence*, is an application of this principle in the practice of contemplative prayer.
11. I'm indebted to Jim Finley's superb analysis of this practice in his conference with Richard Rohr on "Jesus and Buddha: Paths to Awakening," in Albuquerque, New Mexico, January 25–27, 2008.
12. *Miracle of Mindfulness*, 3–4. For nature exercises in practicing mindfulness, see Mark Coleman, *Awake in the Wild: Mindfulness in Nature as a Path to Self-Discovery* (Makawao, HI: Inner Ocean Publishing, 2006).
13. *Miracle of Mindfulness*, 24, 29.

14. Taken from Thich Nhat Hanh's *Present Moment, Wonderful Moment: Mindfulness Verses for Daily Living* (Berkeley, CA: Parallax Press, 2006).

15. Dan Gerber, "Walking in Tierra del Fuego," in *Sacred Trusts: Essays on Stewardship and Responsibiity*, ed. Michael Katakis (San Francisco: Mercury House, 1993), 66–73.

16. *Miracle of Mindfulness*, 12.

17. *The World of the Desert Fathers* (Stories from the Anonymous Series), trans. Columba Stewart (Oxford: SLG Press, 1986), 2.

18. *Miracle of Mindfulness*, 38–40.

19. *Miracle of Mindfulness*, 15–16. See also Thich Naht Hanh, *Stepping into Freedom: An Introduction to Buddhist Monastic Training* (Berkeley, CA: Parallax Press, 1997).

20. Thich Nhat Hanh, *Being Peace* (Berkeley, CA: Parallax Press, 1996), 7.

21. Annabel Laity, ed. *Thich Nhat Hanh: Essential Writings* (Maryknoll, NY: Orbis Books, 2001), 25–26, 108–110.

22. Thich Nhat Hanh, *Peace Is Every Step: The Path of Mindfulness in Everyday Life* (New York: Bantam Books, 1992), 28. See William James, *The Will to Believe* (Cambridge, MA: Harvard University Press, 1979).

23. Jon Kabat-Zinn, *Wherever You Go, There You Are: Mindfulness Meditation in Everyday Life* (New York: Hyperion, 1994), 16; see also his *Arriving at Your Own Door: 108 Lessons in Mindfulness* (New York: Hyperion, 2007), 9.

CHAPTER 9

1. Wendell Berry, *The Wilderness Unforeseen* (Emeryville, CA: Shoemaker Hoard, 2006), 42–43.

2. Hāfez, "Your Mother and My Mother," *The Gift: Poems by Hafiz, the Great Sufi Master*, trans. Daniel Ladinsky, 39.

3. Golden Webb, "Exploring the Flint Trail," in *Utah Outdoors* internet magazine, November 1999, at www.utahoutdoors.com/pages/flinttrail.htm.

4. David Day, *Canyonlands National Park: Favorite Jeep Roads and Hiking Trails* (Orem, UT: Rincon Publishing Company, 2004); and "America's Ten Most Dangerous Hikes," *Backpacker* 36:8 (October 2008), 2–3.

5. Sophocles, *Acrisius*, in Hugh Lloyd-Jones, trans. *Sophocles: Fragments*, Loeb Classical Library, no. 483 (Cambridge, MA: Harvard University Press, 1996), 29.

6. Frank Herbert, *Dune* (New York: Berkley Books, 1965), 230.

7. *Backpacker* 36:8 (October 2008), 34–37. The realistic (if relatively rare) dangers posed by creatures in the wild are detailed, often in grisly detail, by Gordon Grice, in his book *Deadly Kingdom* (New York: Dial Press, 2010).

8. Mark Jenkins' article on backcountry "Panic" in *Backpacker* 35:9 (December 2007), 114.

9. Journals of Kierkegaard, ed. Dru, 79.

10. Rudolf Otto, *The Idea of the Holy*, trans. John W. Harvey (London: Oxford University Press, 1928), 12–24.

11. Ibid., 71.

12. See Gerald Brenan, *St. John of the Cross: His Life and Poetry* (Cambridge: Cambridge University Press, 1973), 30.

13. *The Dark Night*, 1.5, in *Collected Works of St. John of the Cross*, trans. Kavanaugh and Rodriguez, 372.

14. *The Ascent of Mount Carmel, John's Diagram of the Ascent*, in *Collected Works*, 111; *and The Spiritual Canticle*, 1.7, in *Collected Works*, 480.

15. *Spiritual Canticle*, 14.1, in Collected *Works*, 525. In describing preferred places for prayer, John spoke of "solitary and austere locations," like desert terrain and barren mountains, as being ideal, relatively free of the "impediment or detainment caused by visible things." *Ascent of Mount Carmel*, III.39.2, in *Collected Works*, 340.

16. *Spiritual Canticle*, 5.3, in *Collected Works*, 496; and *Ascent of Mount Carmel*, I.4.3; III.20.1, in *Collected Works*, 124, 301.

17. John describes this "night of the senses" and the subsequent "night of the spirit" in *Dark Night*, I.8–14 and II.1–13, in *Collected Works*, 375–394 and 395–428.

18. *Spiritual Canticle*, stanzas 6–7, in *Collected Works*, 472.

19. *Spiritual Canticle*, 4.1–7 and 14–15.25, in *Collected Works*, 494–495, 536.

20. *Spiritual Canticle*, 11.5–7, in *Collected Works*, 512. Emphasis added.

21. *Spiritual Canticle*, 13.9, in *Collected Works*, 523.

22. Golden Webb, "Exploring the Flint Trail."

23. The Enneagram is a typology of interconnected personality types used increasingly in spiritual as well as business contexts. Rooted in the work of Oscar Ichazo, its teachers include Helen Palmer, Don Riso, Russ Hudson, and Richard Rohr. See Don Riso and Russ Hudson, *The Wisdom of the Enneagram* (New York: Bantam, 1999).

24. Teresa of Avila, *The Book of Her Life*, in *The Collected Works of St. Teresa of Avila*, Kieran Kavanaugh and Otilio Rodriguez, trans. (Washington, DC: ICS Publications, 1987), vol. I, 223.

25. Ibid., 248.

26. For a reflection on the Jewish pattern of lament prayer, see Belden C. Lane, "*Hutzpa K'lapei Shamaya*: A Christian Response to the Jewish Tradition of Arguing with God," *Journal of Ecumenical Studies* 23 (1986), 567–586.

27. *Spiritual Canticle*, 1.4 and 1.12, in *Collected Works*, 479, 482.

28. *Dark Night*, I.3.3, in *Collected Works*, 399.

29. Gerald May, *The Dark Night of the Soul* (San Francisco: Harper, 2004), 72.

30. Jon Kabat-Zinn says this so well in his *Arriving at Your Own Door*, reflection #12.

31. C. G. Jung, *The Development of Personality*, trans. R. F. C. Hall (New York: Pantheon Books, 1954).

32. Mary Oliver, "The Wild Geese," in *Dream Work* (Boston: Atlantic Monthly Press, 1986), 14.

33. *Sayings of Light and Love*, #60, in *Collected Works*, 90.

CHAPTER 10

1. Tito Colliander, *The Way of the Ascetics* (San Francisco: Harper & Row, 1982), 54.

2. James Joyce, *Ulysses: A Critical and Synoptic Edition*, ed. Hans Walter Gabler (New York: Garland Publishing, 1984), vol. I, 406.

3. Gary Snyder, *The Practice of the Wild* (San Francisco: North Point Press, 1990), 23.

4. The Zeigarnik Effect in psychology, identified by Russian psychologist Bluma Zeigarnik, underscores the lingering power of unfinished work in one's life. People remember uncompleted or interrupted tasks better than completed ones. See Annie Van Bergen, *Task Interruption* (Amsterdam: North-Holland Publishing, 1968).

5. Thomas Merton, *The Other Side of the Mountain: The End of the Journey*, ed. Patrick Hart, in *The Journals of Thomas Merton*, vol. 7: 1967–1968 (New York: HarperCollins, 1998), 284.

6. Paul Tillich, *The Courage to Be* (New Haven: Yale University Press, 1952), 155–178.

7. Martin Luther, *Tabletalk*, trans. Theodore Tappert, in *Luther's Works*, vol. 54 (Philadelphia: Fortress Press, 1967), 19–20.

8. Richard Rohr is similarly critical of a religion that is ego-driven, regulating behavior through belonging systems that offer approval by labeling and ranking people as "in" or "out." "Early-stage religion," he says, "is more about belonging and believing than about transformation." *On the Threshold for Transformation* (Chicago: Loyola Press, 2010), 276.

9. From a letter of 1516, quoted in Marc Lienhard, "Luther and the Beginnings of the Reformation," in Jill Raitt, ed. *Christian Spirituality: High Middle Ages and Reformation* (New York: Crossroad, 1987), 270–271.

10. Julian of Norwich, *Showings*, trans. Edmund Colledge and James Walsh (Mahwah, NJ: Paulist Press, 1978), 245.

11. Martin Luther, *Tabletalk*, 158–159.

12. See Roland Bainton, *Here I Stand: A Life of Martin Luther* (New York: Abingdon-Cokesbury Press, 1950), 298.

13. *Tabletalk*, 142–143.

14. Simon Tugwell, *Ways of Imperfection* (Springfield, IL: Templegate, 1985), 15, 2.

15. *Sayings of the Desert Fathers*, trans. Ward, Gelasius: 1, p. 46. Translation adapted.

16. *Sayings of the Desert Fathers*, trans. Ward, Ammonas: 10, p. 28.

17. John Climacus, *Ladder of Divine Ascent*, 156–157.

18. See Janet Terner and W. L. Pew, *The Courage to Be Imperfect: The Life and Work of Rudolf Dreikurs* (New York: Hawthorne Books, 1978).

19. *Sayings of the Desert Fathers*, trans. Ward, Poemen: 92, pp. 179–180. Translation adapted.

20. Robert Bolt, *A Man for All Seasons* (New York: Vintage Books, 1990), 40.

21. See Pauline Clance and Suzanne Imes, "The Imposter Phenomenon Among High Achieving Women," *Psychotherapy Theory, Research and Practice* 15:3 (1978), 241–247.

22. See, for example, Luther's appropriation of Paul's theology of justification by faith in his *Lectures on Galatians*, in *Luther's Works,* vol. 26, ed. Jaroslav Pelikan (St. Louis: Concordia Publishing House, 1963), 11–13.

23. Richard Rohr, *Falling Upward: A Spirituality for the Two Halves of Life*, xxii. Illuman is an international organization that incorporates the traditions of Western spirituality, biblical theology, and ritual experiences of transformation in its work with men. It sponsors the work of MALES, which was founded by Richard Rohr, OFM, of the Center for Action and Contemplation in Albuquerque. It invites men to a new accountability in their lives, encouraging a contemplative practice, a renewal of the spirit through access to wilderness, small group work, and a commitment to social justice. See www. Illuman.org.

24. Behavioral psychologist Paul Watzlawick spells out this principle in his books: *Change: Principles of Problem Formation and Problem Resolution* (New York: W. W. Norton, 1974) and *The Language of Change: Elements of Therapeutic Communication* (New York: W. W. Norton, 1993).

25. Herb Gardner, *A Thousand Clowns* (New York: Random House, 1962), 10.

26. *John of the Mountains: The Unpublished Journals of John Muir*, ed. Linnie Marsh Wolfe (Madison: University of Wisconsin Press, 1979), 186–187.

CHAPTER 11

1. Daniel Ladinsky, *Love Poems from God* (New York: Penguin Compass, 2002), 7.

2. Terry Tempest Williams, *Red: Passion and Patience in the Desert* (New York: Pantheon Books, 2001), 254–255; and Michael Austin, ed. *A Voice in the Wilderness: Conversations with Terry Tempest Williams* (Logan: Utah State University Press, 2006), 56.

3. See Philip L. Fradkin, *Everett Ruess: His Short Life, Mysterious Death, and Astonishing Afterlife* (Berkeley: University of California Press, 2011), 2.

4. Everett Ruess, Letter to his brother Waldo, July 12, 1932, from Chinle, Arizona, printed in W. L. Rusho, *Everett Ruess: A Vagabond for Beauty* (Layton, UT: Gibbs Smith, 1973), 78.

5. Letter to Edward Gardner, May 1934, in *Vagabond for Beauty*, 147.

6. Mary Austin, "Lost Others" (unpublished essay), quoted in John P. O'Grady, *Pilgrims to the Wild* (Salt Lake City: University of Utah Press, 1993), 128; Mary Austin, *Earth Horizon* (Boston: Houghton Mifflin, 1932), 187.

7. See Francis Thompson, *The Hound of Heaven and Other Poems* (Wellesley, MA: Branden Publishing, 2011). Thompson (1859–1907) was an English poet and drug addict whose famous poem gives an account of his religious conversion.

8. Richard Rohr, *Adam's Return* (New York: Crossroad, 2004), 92–107; Rainer Maria Rilke, *Rilke's Book of Hours: Love Poems to God*, trans. Anita Barrows and Joanna Macy (New York: Riverhead Books, 1996), 319.

9. See Henri Nouwen, *The Way of the Heart* (New York: Ballantine Books, 1991), 15.

10. Eckhart Tolle, *The Power of Now* (Novato, CA: New World Library, 1999), 38.

11. See Michael Sells, *Early Islamic Mysticism* (New York: Paulist Press, 1996), 251–265; and Diana Eck, *Encountering God: A Spiritual Journey from Bozeman to Benaras* (Boston: Beacon Press, 1993), 69–72, 97–98, 136–142.

12. Quotation adapted from *Sayings of the Desert Fathers*, trans. Ward, Poemen, 164.

13. Bill Plotkin, *Soulcraft*, 105.

14. Mary Oliver, "Prince Buzzard," in *Evidence* (Boston: Beacon Press, 2009), 5–6.

15. See *The Cloud of Unknowing*, ed. James Walsh (New York: Paulist Press, 1981), chapter VI, 130; and Aelred Squire, ed. *Hugh of Saint-Victor: Selected Spiritual Writings* (New York: Harper & Row, 1962).

16. *Cloud of Unknowing*, VIII, 136.

17. "A Letter of Private Direction," in *The Pursuit of Wisdom and Other Works by the Author of The Cloud of Unknowing*, ed. James A. Walsh (New York: Paulist Press, 1988), 222.

18. *Cloud of Unknowing*, XXXIV, 186.

19. *Cloud of Unknowing*, LXXV, 265.

20. *Cloud of Unknowing*, V, 128.

21. Ibid.

22. *Cloud of Unknowing*, XXXIV, 185. See also Richard Rohr, *Everything Belongs: The Gift of Contemplative Prayer* (New York: Crossroad, 2003), 29.

23. Thomas Merton, *New Seeds of Contemplation* (New York: New Directions, 1972), 283.

24. Thomas Merton, "The Inner Experience," in *Thomas Merton: Spiritual Master*, ed. Lawrence Cunningham (New York: Paulist Press, 1992), 351.

25. *Cloud of Unknowing*, VII, 134, and XLVI, 209. Father Thomas Keating, a Trappist monk from Snowmass, Colorado, offers a fine introduction to this pattern of prayer in his book *Open Mind, Open Heart* (New York: HarperCollins, 1988). The World Community for Christian Meditation in London continues the work of John Main, the Benedictine teacher of prayer.

26. Letter of May 1934, in *Vagabond for Beauty*, 151.

CHAPTER 12

1. Campbell, *Hero with a Thousand Faces*, 193.

2. Rose Mary Dougherty, *Group Spiritual Direction* (New York: Paulist Press, 1995), 31.

3. Hāfez, *The Gift: Poems by Hafiz, the Great Sufi Master*, 160.

4. See the newspaper article, "Rediscovered Falls of Wild Cat Mountain Recalls Indian Legends," in *The Southeast Missourian*, Cape Girardeau, Missouri, July 19, 1935, 5.

5. Sue Hubbell, *A Country Year* (New York: Random House, 1986), 63.

6. "I look out at everything growing so wild and faithfully beneath the sky and wonder why we are the one terrible part of creation privileged to refuse our flowering," says David Whyte in his book, *The House of Belonging* (Langley, WA: Many Rivers Press, 1997), 90.

7. For the best introduction to Rumi and his work, see Franklin D. Lewis, *Rumi Past and Present, East and West: The Life, Teaching and Poetry of Jalal al-Din Rumi* (Oxford: Oneworld Publications, 2000).

8. Jesuit theologian William Harmless reflects on the popularity of Coleman Barks' "translations" of Rumi's poetry, for example. He observes that Barks, "who does not read Persian, has faced criticism both from native speakers and from scholars. He has been chided for excising or downplaying the Qur'anic echoes and Islamic themes that pervade Rumi's poetry and for giving him a vague, 'new age' feel. Even so," he adds, "Barks deserves credit for catapulting Rumi into the contemporary limelight." See William Harmless, *Mystics* (New York: Oxford University Press, 2008), 173.

9. *The Mathnawi of Jalalu'ddin Rumi*, ed. Reynold Nicholson (London: Luzac, 1925–1940), I.1–18. See also Coleman Barks, trans. *The Essential Rumi* (San Francisco: HarperSanFrancisco, 1995), 17–19.

10. Jalal al-din Rumi, *Kulliyat-e Shams*, ed. Badi al-Zaman Foruzanfar (Teheran: Amir Kabir Press, 1966), 10 vols., #171. This work comprises the *Collected Poetry (the Divani) of Shams*, written by Rumi but attributed to his master. An English translation of selected poems can also be found in A. J. Arberry, trans. *Mystical Poems of Rumi* (Chicago: University of Chicago Press, 1968, 1979). This translation is from Barks, *Essential Rumi*, 36.

11. Quoted in Annemarie Schimmel, *I Am Wind, You Are Fire: The Life and Work of Rumi* (Boston: Shambhala, 1992), 189.

12. *Mathnawi*, II.1720–96. Adapted from *Rumi: The Book of Love*, trans. Coleman Barks (New York: HarperCollins, 2003), 166–169.

13. *Mathnawi*, III.4260–68, 4197–4208. Cf. *Essential Rumi*, 132–133.

14. *Mathnawi*, I.3056–3063. Adapted from Schimmel, 112.

15. Rumi, *Kulliyat-e Shams*, #1077. See Schimmel, 122. "I became Him," Rumi explained, "Then he threw my self out of me." Quoted in James Fadiman and Robert Frager, *Essential Sufism* (New York, HarperOne, 1999), 250.

16. *Mathnawi*, I.1704. See Schimmel, 88. Cf. *Mathnawi*, III.189–211 and *Essential Rumi*, 155.

17. Sura 2:257.

18. In one of the hadiths (or sayings) of the Prophet Muhammad, Allah proclaims, "I was a hidden treasure and I wanted to be known, so I created the world." Quoted in Schimmel, 74; Rumi, *Kulliyat-e Shams*, #531, lines 5664–5665. See John Renard, "In the Mirror of Creation: A Muslim Mystic's View of the Individual in the Cosmos," *Horizons* 12:2 (Fall 1985), 311–327.

19. Quoted in Schimmel, 71. This ninth-century Persian teacher was one of the first to speak of the annihilation of the self in God. He was accused of being a heretic for having proclaimed, "Glory be to me! How great is my majesty!"

20. Ignatius Loyola, "Contemplation to Attain the Love of God," in *The Spiritual Exercises*, section 235–236, and Rumi, *Kulliyat-e Shams*, #648.

21. See Annemarie Schimmel, *The Triumphal Sun: A Study of the Works of Jalaloddin Rumi* (Albany: State University of New York Press, 1993), 289–290.

22. Rumi, *Kulliyat-e Shams*, #171. Cf. *Essential Rumi*, 36.

23. Shams al-Din, *Maqalat-i Shamsi Tabriz* (Sham's conversations with Rumi), 18. Quoted in Lewis, *Rumi Past and Present, East and West*, 136.

24. Lori Branch, "The Desert in the Desert: Faith and the Aporias of Law and Knowledge in Derrida and *The Sayings of the Desert Fathers*," *Journal of the American Academy of Religion* 71:4 (December 2003), 814–816.

25. *The Sayings of the Desert Fathers*, in *Western Asceticism*, ed. Owen Chadwick (Philadelphia: Westminster Press, 1958). Anthony: 1, p. 37; 11, p. 39.

26. Ignatius speaks of discernment in sections 23, 175–177, 184–188, and 316–327 of his *Spiritual Exercises*. He goes on to suggest putting yourself in the place of another (asking what advice you might give to someone who came to you with the same dilemma), maintaining a holy indifference as to the outcome of your decision, and avoiding making any significant choices during a time of desolation. See David L. Fleming, trans. *The Spiritual Exercises of Saint Ignatius* (St. Louis: Institute of Jesuit Sources, 1978), 22, 106–118, 206–213.

27. Joanna Macy and Chris Johnstone, *Active Hope* (Novato, CA: New World Library, 2012), 13–33.

28. Ken Carey, *Flat Rock Journal*, 227; and Lama Anagarika Govinda, *The Way of the White Cloud* (London: Hutchinson & Co., 1966), 77–81.

29. Reynold A. Nicholson, *Selected Poems from the Divani Shamsi Tabriz* (Cambridge: Cambridge University Press, 1898), 125.

30. See Sam Hamill, trans., *Endless River: Li Po and Tu Fu: A Friendship in Poetry* (New York: Weatherhill Publishing, 1993).

CHAPTER 13

1. John Muir, *My First Summer in the Sierra* (San Francisco: Sierra Club Books, 1990), 157.

2. Thomas Berry, *The Dream of the Earth* (San Francisco: Sierra Club Books, 1988), 8.

3. *The Journals of Thomas Merton*, January 12, 1950. Vol. 2: *Entering the Silence: Becoming a Monk and a Writer*, ed. Jonathan Montaldo (New York: HarperCollins, 2009), 398.

4. See Michael Battle, *Reconciliation: The Ubuntu Theology of Desmond Tutu* (Cleveland, OH: Pilgrim Press, 1997), 4–7. Tutu likes to quote the Xhosa saying that

"A person is a person through other persons." See Shirley Du Boulay, *Tutu: Voice of the Voiceless* (Grand Rapids: Eerdmans, 1988), 114.

5. Paul Gruchow, *The Necessity of Empty Places* (Minneapolis: Milkweed Editions, 1999), 181.

6. Ibid., 172.

7. See Joanna Macy and Molly Young Brown, *Coming Back to Life: Practices to Reconnect Our Lives, Our World* (Gabriola Island, BC: New Society Publishers, 1998); James Grier Miller, *Living Systems* (New York: McGraw-Hill, 1978); Ervin László, *The Systems View of the World: A Holistic Vision for Our Time* (New York: Hampton Press, 1996); and Ken Wilbur, *Sex, Ecology, Spirituality: The Spirit of Evolution* (Boston: Shambhala, 2000), 40–85.

8. Quoted in Matthew Fox, *Passion for Creation: The Earth-Honoring Spirituality of Meister Eckhart* (Rochester, VT: Inner Traditions, 2000), 198.

9. Pierre Teilhard de Chardin, *The Divine Milieu* (New York: Harper & Row, 1960), 89; *The Heart of Matter* (New York: Harcourt Brace Jovanovich, 1978), 71. See also Ursula King, *Spirit of Fire: The Life and Vision of Teilhard de Chardin* (Maryknoll, NY: Orbis Books, 1996), 38.

10. Teilhard de Chardin, "Reflections on Happiness," quoted in King, *Spirit of Fire*, 180.

11. Teilhard de Chardin, *Heart of Matter*, 71.

12. *Divine Milieu*, 89; Letter to Victor Fontoynont, March 15, 1916, quoted in Henri de Lubac, *Le Pensée religieuse du père Pierre Teilhard de Chardin* (Paris: Les Éditions du Cerf, 2002) 350; Augustine, *Confessions*, I, 3.

13. *Divine Milieu*, 112, 35.

14. Teilhard de Chardin, *The Phenomenon of Man* (New York: Fontana Books, 1965), 58–72.

15. Ibid., 291–292. See also Teilhard's "The Eternal Feminine," quoted in King, *Spirit of Fire*, 72.

16. An international body of neuroscientists met in the UK on July 7, 2012, to issue the Cambridge Declaration of Consciousness in Non-Human Animals. They affirmed that mammals, birds, and even octopuses have an ability to employ tools, experience emotive states, and exercise a degree of consciousness. See Katherine Harmon, "Octopuses Gain Consciousness (According to Scientists' Declaration)," *Scientific American*, August 21, 2012.

17. See Belden Lane, *Solace of Fierce Landscapes*, 155–159.

18. Teilhard de Chardin, *Forma Christi* (1918), quoted in Henri de Lubac, *Teilhard de Chardin: The Man and His Meaning* (New York: New American Library, 1965), 37–38; *Divine Milieu*, 30.

19. Teilhard de Chardin, *Mon Universe*, 1924, quoted in de Lubac, *Teilhard de Chardin*, 62; Teilhard de Chardin, *Hymn of the Universe* (New York: Harper & Row, 1961), 19, 14.

20. Teilhard de Chardin, "The Cosmic Life," quoted in Ursula King, *Christ in All Things* (Maryknoll, NY: Orbis Books, 1997), 154–155. See also de Lubac, *Teilhard de Chardin*, 27–32.

21. *Heart of Matter*, 35. In 1950, Teilhard wrote an article on "Zest for Life," published in a collection of his essays, *Activation of Energy: Enlightening Reflections on Spiritual Energy* (New York: Mariner Books, 2002), 229–244.

22. See his *Letters from a Traveler* (Whitefish, MT: Kessinger Publishing, 2007).

23. *The Letters of Teilhard de Chardin and Lucile Swan*, ed. Thomas M. King and Mary Wood Gilbert (Scranton, PA: University of Scranton Press, 2005).

24. Teilhard de Chardin, *Letters to Léontine Zanta* (London: Collins, 1969), 34f.

25. Letter to the Jesuit superior general, Father Janssens, October 12, 1951, in *Letters from a Traveler*, 41–44.

26. See Hubbell, *Broadsides from the Other Orders: A Book of Bugs* (New York: Mariner Books, 1998), 111; Barbara Perry Lawton, *Seasonal Guide to the Natural Year* (Golden, CO: Fulcrum Publishing, 1994), 122.

27. Stephen Jay Gould, "Unenchanted Evening," *Natural History* (September 1991), 14.

28. *Phenomenon of Man*, 291.

CHAPTER 14

1. Edward Abbey, *A Voice Crying in the Wilderness* (New York: St. Martin's Press, 1989), 40.

2. Wendell Berry, *The Art of the Commonplace: The Agrarian Essays* (Washington, DC: Counterpoint Press, 2002), 304.

3. Wendell Berry, "How to Be a Poet," in *Poetry* 177:3 (January 2001), 269–270.

4. From the film poster for "Alice Walker: Beauty in Truth," 2011.

5. Gustavo Gutierrez, *On Job: God-talk and the Suffering of the Innocent* (Maryville, NY: Orbis Books, 1987), 42; and Lenardo Boff, *Cry of the Earth, Cry of the Poor* (Maryknoll, NY: Orbis Books, 1997).

6. Sue Hubbell, *Country Year*, 181.

7. See Linda Garmon, "Dioxin in Missouri: Troubled Times," *Science News* 123:4 (January 22, 1983), 61–63; Marie-Monique Robin, *The World According to Monsanto* (New York: New Press, 2010), 9–47; and William Powell, "Remember Times Beach: The Dioxin Disaster, 30 Years Later," *St. Louis Magazine* 18:12 (December 2012), 116–124.

8. Linda Garmon, "Dioxin Digest," *Science News* 124:10 (September 3, 1983), 156–157. See also K. Napier, "Re-evaluating Dioxin: the Implications for Science Policy," *Priorities* (Winter 1992), 35–37.

9. John Muir, *The Yosemite* (New York: Century, 1912), 260–262.

10. See Rex Weyler, *Greenpeace: How A Group of Journalists, Ecologists and Visionaries Changed the World* (Emmaus, PA: Rodale, 2004).

11. See Gomercindo Rodrigues, *Walking the Forest with Chico Mendes: Struggle for Justice in the Amazon*, trans. Linda Rabben (Austen: University of Texas Press, 2007); and Roseanne Murphy, *Martyr of the Amazon: The Life of Sister Dorothy Stang* (Maryknoll, NY: Orbis Books, 2007).

12. Edward Abbey, *The Monkey Wrench Gang* (New York: Avon Books, 1975), 163.

13. Dave Foreman, "Violence and Earth First!" in *Earth First!* 9:1 (1988), 2. See Bron Taylor, *Dark Green Religion: Nature Spirituality and the Planetary Future* (Berkeley: University of California Press, 2010), 71–102.

14. See Julia Butterfly Hill, *The Legacy of Luna: The Story of a Tree, a Woman, and the Struggle to Save the Redwoods* (New York: HarperCollins, 2000).

15. Louis Fischer, ed. *The Essential Gandhi: An Anthology* (New York: Vintage Books, 1962), 317. "It is good to cultivate the habit of sleeping in the open under the stars," he declared in a speech on August 13, 1942.

16. *Essential Gandhi*, 160. See Erik H. Erikson, *Gandhi's Truth* (New York: W. W. Norton, 1969), 162; and Mohandas K. Gandhi, *An Autobiography: The Story of My Experiments with Truth*, trans. Mahadev Desai (Boston: Beacon Press, 1972), 504.

17. Gandhi, *Autobiography*, 349. See Gandhi, "Ahimsa, or the Way of Nonviolence," in *A Peace Reader*, ed. Joseph J. Fahey and Richard Armstrong (New York: Paulist Press, 1992), 171–174.

18. Julia Hill, *Legacy of Luna*, 24.

19. This quote is attributed to Gandhi, but there is no evidence that he ever actually said it. My adding the word "both" brings it closer to his thinking. For examples of the success of nonviolent direct action efforts since Gandhi, see Gene Sharp, *Waging Nonviolent Struggle* (Boston: Extending Horizons Books, 2005).

20. Quoted in Louis Fischer, *Gandhi: His Life and Message for the World* (New York: New American Library, 1954), 48.

21. See Peter Storey, "A Different Kind of Justice: Truth and Reconciliation in South Africa," *Christian Century* 114:25 (September 10–17, 1997), 788–793.

22. Yevgeny Yevtushenko, *A Precocious Autobiography*, trans. Andrew R. MacAndrew (New York: E. P. Dutton, 1963), 90.

23. See Dorothee Sölle, *The Silent Cry: Mysticism and Resistance* (Minneapolis: Fortress Press, 2001).

24. *The Lives of the Desert Fathers: The Historia Monachorum in Aegypto*, trans. Norman Russell (Kalamazoo, MI: Cistercian Publications, 1980), 102, 35.

25. Thich Nhat Hanh, *Call Me by My True Names: The Collected Poems of Thich Nhat Hanh* (Berkeley, CA: Parallax Press, 1999), 72–73.

26. This is another quote often attributed to Gandhi and synchronous with his thinking, but not found (to my knowledge) in his work.

CHAPTER 15

1. G. K. Chesterton, *Orthodoxy* (London: John Lane Company, 1908), 223.

2. Thomas Merton, "Day of a Stranger," in *Thomas Merton: Spiritual Master*, 217.

3. David Whyte, "Santiago," from his book *Pilgrim* (Langley, WA: Many Rivers Press, 2012), 20.

4. See Cheryl Strayed, *Wild: From Lost to Found on the Pacific Crest Trail*.

5. Chesterton, *Orthodoxy*, 224. See Enid Welsford, *The Fool: His Social and Literary History* (Gloucester, MA: Peter Smith, 1966); John Saward, *Perfect Fools: Folly for Christ's Sake in Catholic and Orthodox Spirituality* (New York: Oxford University Press, 1980); and Belden C. Lane, "The Spirituality and Politics of Holy Folly," *Christian Century* 99:40 (December 15, 1982), 1281–1286.

6. Desiderius Erasmus, *The Praise of Folly*, trans. Clarence H. Miller (New Haven: Yale University Press, 2003), 13–14.

7. See C. S. Lewis, *The Screwtape Letters* (New York: Macmillan, 1943), Letter XIV.

8. *Sayings of the Desert Fathers*, trans. Ward, Arsenius, 38, p. 18; Macarius, 1, p. 125; John the Dwarf, 1, p. 85; Zeno, 1, p. 65.

9. See Thomas Merton, *The Seven Storey Mountain* (New York: Harcourt, Brace, 1948), and Edward Rice, *The Man in the Sycamore Tree: The Good Times and Hard Life of Thomas Merton* (Garden City, NY: Doubleday, 1970).

10. Merton, "Is the World a Problem?" *Commonweal* 84:11 (June 3, 1966), 305.

11. Michael Mott, *The Seven Mountains of Thomas Merton* (Boston: Houghton Mifflin Co., 1984), 381.

12. Merton, "Day of a Stranger," in *Thomas Merton: Spiritual Master*, 217.

13. Monica Furlong, *Merton: A Biography* (San Francisco: Harper & Row, 1980), 219.

14. Thomas Merton, "Rain and the Rhinoceros," in *Thomas Merton: Spiritual Master*, 392.

15. Merton, *Zen and the Birds of Appetite* (New York: New Directions, 1968), 44.

16. Merton, "Learning to Live," in *Thomas Merton: Spiritual Master*, 366–367.

17. Kathleen Deignan, ed. *When the Trees Say Nothing: Thomas Merton's Writings on Nature* (Notre Dame, IN: Sorin Books, 2003), 173–174; Merton, "The Inner Experience," in *Thomas Merton: Spiritual Master*, 354; and Merton, *New Seeds of Contemplation* (New York: New Directions, 1961), 21.

18. Merton, "The Inner Experience," in *Thomas Merton: Spiritual Master*, 302, 353–354. He observes how early Desert Fathers like Evagrius had contrasted these two forms of contemplative practice as *physike* and *theologia*, natural contemplation (of creation) and pure contemplation (or mystical theology).

19. Merton, quoted in David Steindl-Rast, "Man of Prayer," in *Thomas Merton, Monk*, ed. Patrick Hart (Garden City, NY: Doubleday, 1976), 82.

20. Merton, *Thoughts in Solitude* (New York: Farrar, Straus & Cudahy, 1958), 70.

21. Richard Rohr, *Immortal Diamond: The Search for Our True Self* (San Francisco: Jossey-Bass, 2013), 5.

22. Rainer Maria Rilke, *Duino Elegies: A Bilingual Edition*, ed. Edward A. Snow (New York: Farrar, Straus and Giroux, 2001), Second Elegy, line 1.

23. O. E. Rölvaag, *Giants in the Earth: A Saga of the Prairie* (New York: Harper & Brothers, 1927), 33.

24. See Belden C. Lane, "The Breath of God: A Primer in Pacific/Asian Theology," *Christian Century* 107:26 (September 19–26, 1990), 833–838.

25. The Desert Fathers spoke of a mystery they called *theosis* or deification, the soul's innermost participation in the divine nature. They longed to be set afire by the grandeur of God, known (to their amazement) in the deepest intimacy of their own being. They wanted to be "so united with him that whatever we breathe, whatever we understand, whatever we speak, may be God." Boniface Ramsey, trans. *John Cassian: The Conferences* (New York: Paulist Press, 1997), 375.

26. Catherine of Genoa, quoted in Richard Rohr, *Immortal Diamond: The Search for Our True Self*, 5; Chandogya Upanishad, 6.8.7.

27. Martin Buber, *Tales of the Hasidim: The Later Masters* (New York: Shocken Books, 1975), 245–246.

EPILOGUE

1. Terry Russell, *On the Loose* (San Francisco: Sierra Club Books, 1979), 7–8, 45.

2. Aldo Leopold, quoted in Curt Meine, *Aldo Leopold: His Life and Work* (Madison: University of Wisconsin Press, 2010), 435.

3. David Abram, *The Spell of the Sensuous* (New York: Random House, 1997), 131–132.

4. Abram, *Becoming Animal*, 206.

5. Recounted in Nikos Kazantzakis, *Report to Greco* (New York: Bantam Books, 1971), 2.

6. Daniel Coleman, *In Bed with the Word: Reading, Spirituality, and Cultural Politics* (Edmonton: University of Alberta Press, 2005), 13.

7. Abram, *Becoming Animal*, 206, 232.

8. Jay Griffiths, *Wild: An Elemental Journey*, 15.

9. Guido II, *The Ladder of Monks: A Letter on the Contemplative Life and Twelve Meditations*, trans. Edmund Colledge and James Walsh (Garden City, NY: Image Books, 1978). See also Raymond Studzinski, *Reading to Live: The Evolving Practice of Lectio Divina* (Collegeville, MN: Cistercian Publications, 2009), and Thelma Hall, *Too Deep for Words: Rediscovering Lectio Divina* (New York: Paulist Press, 1988), 36–56.

10. Ivan Illich observes that the monks were known as "mumblers and munchers" because of their practice of oral reading. See his book *In the Vineyard of the Text* (Chicago: University of Chicago Press, 1993), 54.

11. David Abram, *Becoming Animal*, 171.

12. Much of my information is drawn from American Forests, the oldest nonprofit conservation organization in the United States, founded in 1875, with offices in Washington, DC. The Whitebark Pine Ecosystem Foundation, headquartered in Missoula, Montana, sponsors education, research, and advocacy for these endangered trees.

13. See Joanna Macy, "Dependent Co-arising: The Distinctiveness of Buddhist Ethics," *Journal of Religious Ethics* 7:1 (Spring 1979), 38–52.

14. I'm indebted to Bob Sabath of the Rolling Ridge Study and Retreat Center near Harper's Ferry, West Virginia, for his insights on the difficulties of contemplative prayer.

15. David Abram, *Becoming Animal*, 224.

16. Buddhist teachers since twelfth-century China have portrayed the necessary steps toward enlightenment in the Ten Ox-Herding Pictures. These depict the seeker's search in the wilderness for the elusive Ox of enlightened awareness, his capturing and taming the creature, the subsequent *disappearance* of both of them (in the stillness of meditation), and his return home.

17. Quoted in George Steiner, *Language and Silence* (New York: Atheneum, 1970), 67.

18. Craig Childs, *The Way Out: A True Story of Ruin and Survival* (New York: Little, Brown, & Co., 2004), 99, 1.

19. Johann Baptist Metz, in Fred Lawrence, ed. *Communicating a Dangerous Memory: Soundings in Political Theology* (Atlanta: Scholars Press, 1987), 38–39.

20. John Muir, *The Mountains of California* (London: T. Fisher Unwin, 1894), 79.

21. David Abram, *Becoming Animal*, 80.

22. See the poems of John of the Cross, "Stanzas Given a Spiritual Meaning" and "The Living Flame of Love," in *Twenty Poems by St. John of the Cross* (Radford, VA: Wilder Publications, 2008), 21–22, 15.

23. Stegner used this engineering term as the title and organizing principle of his Pulitzer Prize–winning novel, *Angle of Repose* (New York: Penguin, 1971).

24. Samuel H. Dresner, ed. *I Asked for Wonder: A Spiritual Anthology: Abraham Joshua Heschel* (New York: Crossroad, 1992), 2–3.

APPENDIX

1. Aron Ralston, *Between a Rock and a Hard Place* (New York: Atria Books, 2004).

2. The Wilderness Act of 1964, Public Law 88–577, 88th Cong., 2nd sess. (September 3, 1964) § 2.

3. Roderick Nash argues that Christians have generally viewed raw nature as "the earthly realm of the powers of evil that the church had to overcome.... Their Bibles contained all they needed to know in order to hate wilderness." See his *Wilderness and the American Mind* (New Haven, CT: Yale University Press, 1982), 17, 34–37.

4. Susan Power Bratton says this wilderness tradition prompted an enduring respect for the land, celebrating wilderness as "the primary visionary landscape . . . expansive enough to allow angels to walk by, springs to appear, wrestling matches to take place, and, most importantly Yahweh to appear in glory." See her *Christianity, Wilderness, and Wildlife* (Scranton, PA: University of Scranton Press, 1993), 247.

5. See George H. Williams, *Wilderness and Paradise in Christian Thought* (New York: Harper, 1962), 50f.

6. See Aldo Leopold, *A Sand County Almanac* (New York: Oxford University Press, 1949), and Loren Eiseley, *The Immense Journey* (New York: Random House, 1957).

7. Edward Abbey, *Desert Solitaire* (New York: Ballantine Books, 1968), 41, 208, 200.

8. Bill McKibben, *The End of Nature* (New York: Anchor Books, 1999), xv.

9. We lose one million square kilometers of rainforest every 5 to 10 years, according to Stuart Pimm and Peter Raven. "Biodiversity: Extinction by Numbers," *Nature* 43 (February 24, 2000), 843–845. The United Nations' Millennium Ecosystem Assessment reports that over the last fifty years, 20% of the world's coral reefs have been lost and 35% of its mangrove ecosystems destroyed. Joseph Alcamo, et al., *Ecosystems and Human Well-Being: Synthesis* (Washington, DC: Island Press, 2003), 1–3.

10. Irwin Altman and Joachim F. Wohlwill, eds. *Behavior and the Natural Environment* (New York: Plenum Press, 1983), 10. See also Michael Pollan, *Second Nature* (New York: Atlantic Monthly Press, 1991).

11. Edward Abbey, *A Voice Crying in the Wilderness (Vox Clamatis in Deserto): Notes from a Secret Journal* (New York: St. Martin's Press, 1989), 84.

12. Thomas Traherne observed that "the angels in heaven continually cry 'Holy, Holy, Holy,' not because they wish to emphasize God's purity or aloofness but because they are stunned again and again by the excess and violence of his love." Quoted in Denise Inge, *Wanting Like a God: Desire and Freedom in Thomas Traherne*, 76.

13. Christopher Southgate, *The Groaning of Creation: God, Evolution, and the Problem of Evil* (Louisville, KY: Westminster John Knox Press, 2008), 16.

14. See Elenore Stump, *Wandering in Darkness: Narrative and the Problem of Suffering* (New York: Oxford University Press, 2012), 177–226.

15. Abraham Joshua Heschel, *Between God and Man* (New York: Free Press, 1997), 41.

16. See R. Driver, R. Nash, and G. Haas, "Wilderness Benefits: A State of Knowledge Review," *Proceedings: National Wilderness Research Conference*, R. C. Lucas, compiler (Ogden, UT: U.S. Department of Agriculture, Forest Service, Intermountain Research Station, 1987), 294–319.

17. Laurence Gonzales, *Deep Survival* (New York: W. W. Norton, 2003), 170–171.

18. Richard Louv, *Last Child in the Woods* (Chapel Hill, NC: Algonquin Books, 2005).

19. Doug Peacock, *Grizzly Years: In Search of the American Wilderness* (New York: Henry Holt & Co., 1990).

20. Gerald G. May, *The Wisdom of Wilderness: Experiencing the Healing Power of Nature* (New York: HarperCollins, 2006), 31–32.

21. John Muir, *The Mountains of California* (1894) (San Francisco: Sierra Club Books, 1988), 50–52.

22. Rainer Maria Rilke, "The Man Watching," from *Selected Poems of Rainer Maria Rilke*, trans. Robert Bly (New York: Harper & Row, 1981), 105–107.

23. Anthony of Egypt, quoted in Thomas Merton, *Wisdom of the Desert: Sayings from the Desert Fathers* (New York: New Directions, 1960), 62; John Chrysostom, *Homilies on the Statues*, IX, 5–9.

24. Bonaventure, *Breviloquium*, II.xi.2, in *Works of St. Bonaventure*, trans. Dominic Monti (Saint Bonaventure, NY: Franciscan Institute Publications, 2005); Cotton Mather, *The Christian Philosopher*, ed. Winton Solberg (Chicago: University of Illinois Press, 1994), 18; Meister Eckhart, *German Works*, I: 156, quoted in Matthew Fox, *Meditations with Meister Eckhart* (Santa Fe, NM: Bear & Co., 1983), 14.

25. On the tradition of the two books, see Clarence Glacken, *Traces on the Rhodian Shore: Nature and Culture in Western Thought* (Berkeley: University of California Press, 1967), 203–205, 239.

26. Douglas Burton-Christie, *The Word in the Desert* (New York: Oxford University Press, 1993), 61–62, 107–129. See Paul J. Griffiths, *Religious Reading: The Place of Reading in the Practice of Religion* (New York: Oxford University Press, 1999).

27. See Bernard Meehan, *The Book of Kells* (New York: Thames and Hudson, 1994).

Index